11/10

ILLINOIS CENTRAL COLLEGE

W9-BWI-086

I.C.C. LIBRARY
Withdrawn

DEMCO

More praise for *Twitterville*

"Shel Israel tells compelling stories of like minds making things happen. It shows Twitter as **a small town with the reach and speed of the Internet.**"

> —Liz Strauss, Web Strategist and author of Successful-Blog.com (@lizstrauss)

"Shel Israel explains how **a simple idea has unleashed a social phenomenon** that is reverberating across the business world."

> —J. D. Lasica, author of *Darknet: Hollywood's War Against the Digital Generation* (@jdlasica)

"I may insist that *Twitterville* be **required reading** for all prospective clients and employees. A delightful read."

> —K. D. Paine, CEO of KDPaine & Partners (@kdpaine)

"Shel Israel goes well beyond the uses of Twitter to how companies have **joined the community and prospered as a result.**"

> —Kami Watson Huyse, social media consultant

Twitterville

Also by Shel Israel

Naked Conversations: How Blogs are Changing the Way Businesses Talk with Customers

Twitterville

How Businesses Can Thrive in
the New Global Neighborhoods

SHEL ISRAEL

Portfolio

I.C.C. LIBRARY

WITHDRAWN

PORTFOLIO

Published by the Penguin Group

Penguin Group (USA) Inc., 375 Hudson Street, New York, New York 10014, U.S.A.

Penguin Group (Canada), 90 Eglinton Avenue East, Suite 700, Toronto, Ontario, Canada M4P 2Y3
(a division of Pearson Penguin Canada Inc.)

Penguin Books Ltd, 80 Strand, London WC2R 0RL, England

Penguin Ireland, 25 St. Stephen's Green, Dublin 2, Ireland (a division of Penguin Books Ltd)

Penguin Books Australia Ltd, 250 Camberwell Road, Camberwell, Victoria 3124, Australia
(a division of Pearson Australia Group Pty Ltd)

Penguin Books India Pvt Ltd, 11 Community Centre, Panchsheel Park, New Delhi – 110 017, India

Penguin Group (NZ), 67 Apollo Drive, Rosedale, North Shore 0632, New Zealand
(a division of Pearson New Zealand Ltd)

Penguin Books (South Africa) (Pty) Ltd, 24 Sturdee Avenue, Rosebank, Johannesburg 2196,
South Africa

Penguin Books Ltd, Registered Offices: 80 Strand, London WC2R 0RL, England

First published in 2009 by Portfolio, a member of Penguin Group (USA) Inc.

10 9 8 7 6 5 4 3 2

Copyright © Shel Israel, 2009
All rights reserved

LIBRARY OF CONGRESS CATALOGING IN PUBLICATION DATA

Israel, Shel, 1944–

   Twitterville : how businesses can thrive in the new global neighborhoods / Shel Israel.
      p.   cm.
   Includes index.
   ISBN 978-1-59184-279-8
   1. Twitter (Firm)   2. Internet industry—United States—History.   3. Online social networks—
Economic aspects.   I. Title.
   HD9696.8.U64T955 2009
   658.8'72—dc22   2009023415

Printed in the United States of America

While the author has made every effort to provide accurate telephone numbers and Internet addresses at
the time of publication, neither the publisher nor the author assumes any responsibility for errors, or for
changes that occur after publication. Further, publisher does not have any control over and does not
assume any responsibility for author or third-party Web sites or their content.

Without limiting the rights under copyright reserved above, no part of this publication may be
reproduced, stored in or introduced into a retrieval system, or transmitted, in any form or by any means
(electronic, mechanical, photocopying, recording or otherwise), without the prior written permission of
both the copyright owner and the above publisher of this book.

The scanning, uploading, and distribution of this book via the Internet or via any other means without
the permission of the publisher is illegal and punishable by law.   Please purchase only authorized
electronic editions and do not participate in or encourage electronic piracy of copyrightable materials.
Your support of the author's rights is appreciated.

10/10 B&T 23.95

To Charlie O'Brien.

You should have been here.

Foreword

Twitter was made for my mom.

That's because she's always infinitely interested in what I am doing and thinking, no matter how mundane—or inane. You know what it's like—the minute your mom reaches you, she wants to know where you are and what you are doing. The ability to peek into my world goes to the heart of being a mom, as she wants to share in the joys, tribulations, and excitement of my daily life.

But not everyone is my mom, which goes to the core of why there is sometimes such skepticism of Twitter. For example, she couldn't care less what I had for lunch today—unless I was having it with someone that she knew!

For me, Twitter is less about what you are doing and more about what you are paying attention to and willing to share. Tim Berners-Lee envisioned the Web to be "a universal medium for sharing information" and Twitter makes it easy to do. But there is judgment in writing tweets, as most people do not run a full commentary of their lives. They are circumspect, casting aside the debris of daily life to pull out the nuggets that they deem worthy of sharing with the world.

It is this exercise in judgment—expressed in 140 characters at a time—that so intrigues me and should intrigue you. Millions of people sharing the things that capture their attention—and some of those things might be your company, products, and services. These vignettes come together into a dialog, a conversation. These conversations are sometimes coherent discourses, sometimes not. But when they are, you had better be paying attention.

That's because, as *The Cluetrain Manifesto* put it so succinctly, "markets are conversations." When *Cluetrain* was written in 1999, the authors didn't know what a blog was. YouTube had yet to be invented. And Twitter's birth was still almost a decade into the future. But what they wrote about—that markets aren't inanimate objects, but instead, are made up of people eager to engage in the discourse of commerce—applies even more today with the advent of these technologies.

Just like a parent, you should care deeply about what your customers and prospects are thinking and sharing. Aren't you curious about what people are saying about you? Of course you are! If people are sharing that they love your product, you'd want to thank them. If they are having a problem, you'd want to reach out and see if you can help them. And if they are really unhappy with your service, you'd like to know how you can improve and hopefully win back their trust.

Twitter is not a technology. It's a conversation. And it's happening with or without you. It's up to you to decide if, when, and how you will listen and join in. Won't you come and take a walk around Twitterville?

—Charlene Li
Founder, Altimeter Group
coauthor, *Groundswell*

Contents

Part 3: How and Why

Twitterville

James Buck Gets Out of Jail and Inspires This Book

James Buck's tweet was but a single word: "Arrested."

That tweet would get him out of jail, and inspire me to write *Twitterville*. But neither of us knew that at 9:33 AM on April 10, 2008, when Buck was in the backseat of a police car and being taken to a holding cell in the Nile Delta city of Mahalla, Egypt.

Buck was a graduate student at the University of California, Berkeley, majoring in photojournalism. He had come to Mahalla to photograph the food strikes in this manufacturing-agricultural city of four hundred thousand.

Days earlier, the streets had turned violent. Fires were started, and people got hurt. Police clubbed and arrested several protesters.

On April 10, Buck took a cautious approach. He stayed back from the crowds, using a telephoto lens to capture his story.

He got busted anyway.

I knew something about Egyptian police. In 2007 I had interviewed Wael Abbas (@WaelAbbas), as part of my Social Media Global Reports blog post series. Abbas is an Egyptian citizen journalist who kept posting videos on YouTube of uncharged "suspects" being tortured in Egyptian police stations similar to the one where Buck was heading.*

---

* On April 10, 2009, precisely one year after the James Buck incident, a police officer broke down the door to Abbas's home and beat up both Abbas and his

It was when I saw the word "arrested" on Twitter that I realized how much bigger this new social media communications tool had become—more than I had previously thought possible.

I didn't know James Buck. I didn't follow him on Twitter until that one-word post. I didn't even know that I connected with him.

When a "tweeter," as someone who posts on Twitter is called, reads something posted by another tweeter and thinks that it's worth repeating, he or she adds the letters RT and posts it again. Someone else may then read it, and repeat the process. This is called retweeting and it is the essential process that makes word often travel so far and fast on Twitter.

Retweeting is an important part of Twitter's magic: you may follow—or be followed by—just a small handful of people. Yet even if only one person follows you, through just a few degrees of separation you are connected to the growing millions of people who tweet all over the world.

James Buck was a new tweeter. He only had a few followers; as I already mentioned, I wasn't one of them. But a friend of his retweeted the "arrested" post and added a brief explanation. A friend of mine saw that and retweeted it. I was four steps removed from Buck. I saw the post about thirty minutes after he had posted from the police car.

A few weeks earlier, while saying good-byes to friends in Berkeley, one had turned Buck on to Twitter. The friend thought it might be good to have on his BlackBerry in case some emergency popped up.

While Buck sat in the cell, the one-word message he sent to

---

mother. Abbas went to a police station and insisted that they arrest the attacking policeman. Instead they arrested Abbas. They put him into a holding cell, where he tweeted about what had happened, and word quickly spread around the world. He too got out in a day, but I do fear for my friend's safety.

Berkeley friends via Twitter kept moving. For some reason, the Egyptian police let him keep his BlackBerry and he kept tweeting. His small personal network kept retweeting. Word spread on Twitter. Someone contacted the U.S. State Department, which swung into uncharacteristically quick action.

Within twenty-four hours, Buck's government had intervened. He was released from jail and was about to be driven to the airport where he would receive a free trip home.

Before he stepped into the car, he stopped to type in another single-word message, or tweet as they are universally called.

The message said "Free."

This changed my personal view of Twitter. Until then it was something fun to use, occasionally useful for business purposes. Tweeting had landed me some paid speaking engagements. I had friends who lived in other countries and it was a faster, easier way to keep in touch.

But the James Buck incident took my breath away. I realized that this Twitter phenomenon had bigger implications than I had understood. I started paying closer attention and taking notes.

Dramatic Moments

I began to notice that now and then Twitter has very dramatic moments. In the coming months, this would include a Dutch student in a bookstore in South China who would report the first deadly rumble of the Szechuan earthquake. A team of surgeons in Detroit tweeting real-time progress to medical professionals at a Las Vegas conference as a robotic device removed a tumor from a patient. A young entrepreneur on a ferry on the Hudson River, witnessing a passenger jet skid to a halt nearby, then start to sink.

And it would be easy to have written a book just about those moments of life and death. There are enough of them that unfolded, and there will undoubtedly be many more.

But drama is not the entire story.

Much of the time, Twitter is just about everyday people discussing everyday things. Increasingly, it has become a highly effective tool of business communication. This book chiefly focuses on telling you how people use Twitter to get closer to customers and constituents.

Twitter is also about stumbling into old acquaintances. On the day that Buck typed in "arrested," I was sitting comfortably at home, having crossed paths with an old friend on Twitter. We were sending little spoonfuls of conversation to each other, details of jobs and travel, pets and grandchildren, catching up on the past thirty years since we'd lost each other.

Equally, Twitter is about meeting new people who are relevant to you, in business or whatever else interests you. You can find them easily, start a simple conversation and watch how quickly and deeply it can often develop.

Ultimately, this is a book about what Twitter can do for you. I'm going to tell you what others have done and are doing and my hope is that it will give you a few interesting or useful ideas.

Telephone Metaphor

As Chris Brogan (@ChrisBrogan), one of Twitterville's most respected pioneer-champions, likes to say, "It's very much like a telephone." He's right, and the telephone is a good starting point, but it seems to me that Twitter is more than that.

Brogan maintains that Twitter, like the phone, is a personal communications tool. And you can use it to conduct any conversation you choose to discuss.

Those conversations, however, are usually private on the phone.

You can talk privately in Twitter through a feature called direct message, or DM. Yet in most cases, Twitter works best when it is public and anyone can see what you are saying, so that anyone can respond to what you say or retweet it.

Twitter is also superior to a telephone for meeting new people. When a stranger calls you on the telephone, it is usually to try to sell you something you don't want. The practice got so out of hand on the telephone that laws have been created to constrain telephone peddlers.

But on Twitter, meeting strangers can be both enjoyable and valuable. If you meet someone you'd prefer to avoid, there are filters and functions that work relatively well at keeping that person away from you. It is almost always an easier experience than receiving a cold call.

People use Twitter for personal or business reasons. Many of us find we cannot help but mix the two together, just like many folks do on the phone or face-to-face.

I've been asked why any employer in her right mind would allow workers to tweet on company time. The answer is simple, and again it's like using a telephone at work or, for that matter, e-mail or a fax: you use Twitter to communicate. The topic is up to you.

The Blog Metaphor

Twitter is as much like a blog as it is like a telephone, except that you need to picture a very small blog post. In fact, Twitter is the leading software in a category called microblogging. You publish what you have to say, and people respond if they wish. You publish to one person or to the whole world, and people respond in the same manner.

Space is limited to just 140 characters; therefore, messages must cut to the chase. Shorthand necessarily becomes part of tweeted language; it's more egalitarian than full-size blogs because people respond in equal length and equal placement on Twitter pages or "tweetstreams." The constraints of size lead to speedy conversation. Twitter moves faster than any blog.

There are several books that will tell you how to use Twitter and why you should. This book does a little of both, but neither is my central focus. I share with you the stories of people using Twitter in the home office and in the global enterprise. People tweet to raise money for causes; to make government more responsive; to find and distribute news; to build personal or business networks; or to just kill a little time with people you enjoy.

I believe that many of us learn best from other people's stories. If I tell you about someone who has used Twitter to improve his personal brand or to get more customers into a coffee house or to shop in one market over another, my hope is you will read one of these stories and adapt Twitter to whatever it is you do.

Twitter is a pretty simple tool. Most people can pick up the mechanics just by fiddling with Twitter for a few minutes. Once you start talking with people, they tend to be pretty generous in helping newcomers find their way around. Before you know it, you'll be helping others who have followed you into Twitterville.

A Tool for All Seasons

I am beginning this book in the toughest economic climate since the 1930s. I hope that we will have entered better times before you start reading it.

I could argue that Twitter is ideally suited for tough times. At a time when economic constraints are causing most businesses to make painful cuts, they still must interface with customers; Twitter is the most efficient and effective way to do it this side of a face-to-face meeting.

It's not just customers, it's your entire business ecosystem—your prospects, partners, employees, investors, analysts, and media. You'll probably find many of them are already in Twitterville when you arrive, already having conversations relevant to your business. The sooner you join the conversations, the faster you may get out from under the business pressures you are facing.

But when you think about it, Twitter is not just a tool for tough times, but for all times. There is no economic situation in which businesses do not need to interact with constituents. There are very few instances when the most economic way of doing it is not the wisest course to take.

Good-bye, Broadcast. Hello, Conversation

We live in an era when what used to be considered best practices are not so good as they used to be. Methods that have been in place for years, refined and optimized over time, just aren't getting the results they used to. Among them are customer support, traditional marketing, and product research.

My previous book, *Naked Conversations*, coauthored with Robert Scoble (@scobleizer), assailed the excesses of marketing. In 2006 that seemed a revolutionary idea to some. Now it seems pretty obvious. Marketing programs are too expensive, and they produce diminishing results.

Twitterville examines the inefficiency of traditional marketing. It argues the case for using social media instead of ads. It argues that from a business perspective, Twitter is the most effective tool yet delivered into the growing arsenal of social media tools.

But Twitter alone is limited. It is too shallow in its constrained space. It is not visual. It is limited in its ability to conduct safe transactions or hear someone's voice.

A carpenter building a home would have to use a hammer—but

not *just* a hammer. This book shares numerous stories of how Twitter works best with other social media tools, particularly blogs. When considering Twitter, this book advises you to consider an entire toolset, which in fact can lead to an entirely new way to conduct your business.

In *Naked Conversations*, Scoble and I predicted the death of a so-called Broadcast Era, and the birth of a new Conversational Era. *Twitterville* looks upon the three years between books as a transformational time. This transformation has accelerated during this recession because businesses now understand that they need to explore new avenues. Those avenues seem to converge on Twitterville's Main Street.

The Generosity of Crowds

I have often written about social media being built on a "cult of generosity." Tweeters have been more than a little generous with me in the process of writing this book.

As I started each chapter, I posted on Twitter what I was covering, and requested people tell me good stories on the various topics explored in each chapter. My cup overflowed with results.

I received several hundred suggestions. Tweeters generated about three-fourths of the stories reported in *Twitterville*. The process I used is called crowd sourcing, which I find to be better for research than anything else, including Google.

In Google you enter a keyword, and a "spider" crawls all over the Internet's data to give you results. That's a pretty remarkable process. But by crowd sourcing in Twitterville, I got people I know and trust to give me information, insights, and specific examples, which this book shares with you.

The way in which I wrote this book confirmed to me my very best thoughts about Twitter. Twitterville has its darker streets, as I will discuss, but it is dominated and culturally shaped by a cult of generosity. The people who are most generous in Twitterville are among its most influential members.

Why Call It "Twitterville"?

I am not sure whether or not I was the first to coin the term "Twitterville." I came up with it after Laura Fitton (@Pistachio) described her "Twitter Village" in a very thoughtful blog post in January 2008. I had not previously heard the term, and I've been using it ever since.

Twitterville connotes a certain homey, small-town feel, a place where you meet people you know as you stroll down familiar streets. These are people with whom you share common friends, interests, and ethics. When you meet a stranger here, chances are you have mutual friends or interests.

While Twitterville has millions of people in it, and is growing faster than the world's largest megalopolises, it still feels cozy to most of its residents and visitors. It still feels safe for the most part.

This is due, in my opinion, to Twitterville's most important characteristic, something I have named global neighborhoods. The concept came to me several years ago, while I was having coffee with Charlene Li, who wrote the foreword to this book.

She told me geography is becoming irrelevant because of social media.

For Charlene it seemed to be a throwaway thought. But for me, it was a very large idea. It gave me the sense of global neighborhoods, which became the name of my blog and has been my central focus since completing *Naked Conversations*.

Through social media, society is being rearranged very fundamentally and at a faster rate than many people realize. Until the Conversational Era came along, people were constrained by geography. We really could not get to know people we did not encounter face-to-face.

When you think about that, you realize that each of us has been denied access to billions of people, many of whom share similar passions and interests, some of whom can help us, some of whom we can help.

By no means have the barriers disappeared. Everybody simply cannot know everybody else on the planet. But the barriers between people have been lowered through social media. Doors have been opened. Restrictions are being reduced as people start discovering there are others like themselves all over the world. It has the potential to reverse the combination of suspicion and ignorance that people of one culture feel about people of another.

We no longer need airplanes to meet new people who are physically far away from us. We can now go online and visit a virtual place to do this. That place may not be tangible or even real. But the people you meet there are real, and so are the relationships you form there—and *Twitterville* will hopefully show you their value.

In her foreword, Charlene Li writes that Twitter is "a conversation," a reference to *The Cluetrain Manifesto*, the fountainhead book of the social media revolution. She is right, of course. Markets are conversations, *Cluetrain* taught us. Twitterville is a marketplace, and the conversations are meaningful to a growing number of businesses.

So I fully agree, but I see something even more promising.

Twitter lets us behave online more closely to how we do in the tangible world than anything that has ever preceded it. And we find neighborhoods that suit us. If we love to talk about politics, we can find many neighborhoods where everyone cares about just that. The same with hummingbirds, cooking, sports, or needlepoint. You can find a neighborhood where you can hang out to learn and share and chat about the topic.

You can join as many or as few as you like. These are global neighborhoods, yet they are small and personal and cozy at the same time that they make your world far bigger.

I hope you enjoy reading *Twitterville* as much as I have enjoyed writing it.

—Shel Israel
January 21, 2009

PART 1

How It Started

CHAPTER 1

A Pinot Kills Odeo

The road to success often has detours. Twitter's was no exception. In fact, Twitter began as a detour for another company called Odeo.

Founded at the end of 2004, Odeo was going to do for online audio what Google does for online text. It would let you do a keyword search for digital and video content on the Web. It was provingmore difficult and less interesting than its small team had expected.

The story really starts with Ev Williams (@Ev), cofounder of Odeo. He was the known player, the reason why Odeo had such a high profile, and why Silicon Valley start-up observers had such great expectations.

In his early thirties, Williams was already on his third start-up with Odeo. His first one was a company he'd founded in Nebraska. That didn't go that far, but his second one did.

After he moved to the San Francisco Bay Area, Williams cofounded Pyra in 1999. The company began as a project-management software developer, but that also didn't work out so well. So the cofounders took a component of the software and developed the first software to make it easy for end users to create what was then called weblogs.

To name the new internet software, Williams invented a word: "blogger." Users went to Blogger.com to sign up for the free service. Thus Williams popularized the abbreviation tech insiders were using for weblogs.

The word may have caught on more than the company. While Blogger.com adoption went well enough, the service was free, and there was no clear business model.

At one point, after working for a stint without pay, most of the staff including its cofounder walked out. Williams then was resourceful enough to approach Dan Bricklin (@DanB), father of VisiCalc, the first PC spreadsheet, who invested in the company.

With pay restored, most members of the company returned. And after all these potholes and detours along Pyra's road, it arrived.

> @ev: AdWords in my Gmail: "Start your OWN Twitter—
> PHP Micro-Blogging Script less than $35—Tons of
> Features—Ajax." Damn, wish I'd known. (Ev Williams,
> cofounder of Twitter)

In February 2003, Google acquired Pyra for an undisclosed sum (as it was too small to impact Google's bottom line). Williams did very well personally. He and four other Pyra team members joined Google, where he headed the Blogger.com work group.

In October 2004, shortly after meeting his earn-out requirements from the acquisition, Williams left Google. Eight weeks later he cofounded Odeo, his third start-up.

While speaking in 2009 at the Churchill Club, a Silicon Valley business and technology forum, Williams said he had learned two important lessons during his Google tenure:

1. Get the product right and make users happy before you worry about making money. Google had done that, and for that matter, so had Pyra.
2. Focus is everything. Every company has to choose between what it *can* do and what it *should* do. The marketplace can be noisy and distracting. Don't let that push you off course.

Those two lessons seem to have guided Williams along the way. From 2004 until well into 2009, even after Twitter was experiencing a prolonged ascent that seemingly had no end in sight, the issues of product reliability and focus would keep coming back, and Williams and his small team consistently stayed focused, and continuously put product reliability in front of other considerations.

From Xanga to Odeo

Biz Stone (@Biz) was raised in the affluent Boston suburb of Wellesley, Massachusetts. But he wasn't a rich kid. His mother, who died when Stone was a child, had worked as an administrator in Wellesley's public school system. He was raised by his father, an immigrant auto mechanic. He worked summers mowing lawns, and in his spare time, he hung out at prestigious Wellesley College, where he would eventually teach for a year. But he attended Northeastern University, the same working-class college that I attended years before.

People who knew Stone back then and now still agree that he is generally pretty easygoing, yet incredibly smart.

He eventually found his way to New York City, where he cofounded Xanga.com in 1999. Xanga started as a photo and booksharing site but, as you may have guessed, took a detour. When Pyra developed a ProBlogger version, Xanga licensed the technology and started serving as one of the first blog-authoring sites.

That led to a long-distance business relationship between Stone and Ev Williams. Over time, the two became tight. The friendship continued when Williams went over to Google.

In early 2004, after Stone had published a couple of early and modestly well-received books on blogging, he accepted Williams's invitation to join Google's blogger group.

The two had started out with a standard business relationship, but over time they found that they shared an interest—actually a passion—for social media. First they became business associates, and then they became friends. Eventually Biz would come to work for Williams.

There is really nothing very remarkable about that sort of thing. It happens all the time, all over the place. People start as business associates and become friends, or vice versa.

I point this out because this is also the sort of thing that happens on Twitter all the time. People start chatting about something, and it develops into a friendship or a business relationship—just as Williams and Stone did in real life.

> @jack: One could change the world with one hundred and forty characters. [Jack Dorsey, cofounder and principal creator of Twitter]

Good-bye, Dot-com. Hello, Web 2.0

A few months after Stone arrived at Google, Williams left to start Odeo. A few months later, Stone followed and became his partner.

Odeo was representative of what was being called Silicon Valley's Next Big Thing. In 2004 the final remnants of the dot-com bubble had been swept away, but investors still had bitter memories and lighter wallets. They viewed Silicon Valley's seemingly endless parades of Next Big Things with an increasingly skeptical eye.

But in fact, a significant handful of enduring companies had emerged from the dot-com era, including eBay, Amazon.com, and of course, Google.

Something else would endure as well, and Blogger was a part of it. It would involve new ways of having conversations in public on the Internet, and would be defined as social media by Chris Shipley (@cshipley), cofounder of Guidewire Group, an emerging IT research firm.

But let's get back to Odeo, and the detour that became Twitter.

What Were They Doing?

By 2006, the Odeo guys knew they had problems.

It wasn't as Biz Stone described it—"that the resolution of one technology problem seemed to immediately lead to another"—it was that passion seemed to have seeped out of the project.

And there was something else. It seemed less important, but still, it was annoying. Stone and Williams just couldn't find anyone when they needed to. It was hard calling a meeting.

If you work in a traditional business, this may seem surprising. But in Silicon Valley and the other technology start-up clusters it would make sense.

Early phase start-up cultures are dominated by software developers. These guys work long hours, and hard. They are highly motivated, yet few of their managers have ever successfully gotten developers to conform to nine-to-five schedules. They work where and when they want: at home, in Wi-Fi-enabled coffee shops, at night or predawn, on weekends and holidays—whatever works for them.

So when an issue popped up and Stone and Williams needed to call a few team members together, it was difficult. It was also hard to figure out if the meeting was more important than the work that would be interrupted. Someone was always asking a tech team member, "What are you doing?"

In early 2006, Williams and Stone decided to take the team offsite for some collective naval gazing. At one point, they broke off into smaller groups to drill into specific issues.

Stone and Jack Dorsey (@Jack), Odeo's software architect, were part of the group that was to examine the problem of team members finding one another. Dorsey said he thought he might be able to fix that by dusting off an old idea, one that had traveled a few detours of its own since it started to form more than fifteen years earlier.

When Dorsey was a fourteen-year-old kid growing up in St. Louis, he grew fascinated with dispatch routing issues—the technology that pointed police, firefighters, ambulance drivers, and taxi drivers to where they were most needed. The part that interested him most was figuring out how to pinpoint fleets of vehicles that are mostly in motion, and then redirect them as priorities change. For vehicles like taxis and delivery trucks, real-time dispatch could be the difference between profit and loss, or happy and unhappy customers. For emergency vehicles—ambulances, patrol cars, and fire engines—real-time dispatch could save lives.

Lives did not depend on real-time dispatch at Odeo. But whether or not the company would succeed just might depend on locating developers in motion and redirecting them by priority.

Dorsey had left St. Louis, went east to get an engineering degree from NYU, and then moved to the Bay Area. His thoughts on mobile dispatch stayed with him. In 2000, while living in a converted Oakland biscuit factory, he started a Web-based municipal dispatch service. The business got some attention as an innovative dot-com start-up, but it struggled financially and a year later, when the bubble imploded, Dorsey's start-up succumbed.

But during that effort, his idea for Web-based personal status updates got refined. In 2006, he posted his original handwritten sketch that would become Twitter on Flickr.com, the photo sharing site. He commented,"I thought about this concept and tried repeatedly to introduce it into my various projects.

"It slipped into my dispatch work. It slipped into my networks of medical devices. It slipped into an idea for a frictionless service market. It was everywhere I looked: a wonderful abstraction, which was easy to implement and understand."

As new technologies evolved in the early 2000s, he refined his ideas further. He was influenced by LiveJournal.com, a new, simple, and fast blog-authoring platform.

There was also SMS, the most popular mobile-messaging technology. If you are among the 2.4 billion cell-phone users who have sent or received a text message, you already know how it works. SMS is short and personal. Messages are limited to 160 characters, which leads to some creative and occasionally mystifying abbreviations.

But none of that mattered, because no one wanted to support Dorsey's desire to take this idea and make a product out of it.

That was until Dorsey told Stone he could dust off his old idea.

Birth of TWTTR

With Stone's assistance, Dorsey made some enhancements to SMS. He shortened the length by twenty characters, so that messages could identify the author's name. The screen was bone-dead simple. You just answer a single question, one that the Odeo team members kept hearing: "What are you doing?"

Dorsey's little tweaks made some big differences, perhaps more than even Stone and Dorsey realized during the two weeks it took them to build the small piece of software.

First, while phone text messaging was private or "one-to-one," Dorsey's new tool had a public option, which was intended to share information among members of a small, mobile work group. An Odeo employee could post once, and all other team members would see that she was at lunch or on the way in to the office or working at home that day.

To do this, coworkers had to select a "follow" option, which was quite easy to do. Later, another fundamental option allowed users to block out people they wished to avoid in conversation. When someone posted, you could reply instantly, thus starting a conversation that could go back and forth. Others could join in.

It was designed as a message system, but the LiveJournal influence had slipped in. It was actually a very small blog—or "microblog."

In one important way Dorsey's innovation was more egalitarian than a full-size blog, in which one person picked the subject, wrote a main piece, and then others added comments or moved the conversation to another location. With this new microblog, the conversation moved from person to person with ease and speed. The conversation flowed like a river and was soon called a tweetstream (or just stream).

Dorsey originally named his baby Stat.us, but the domain had already been taken. He opted for TWTTR. Many people thought this was in keeping with the vowel-deprivation trend started by the astronomically popular Flickr. It's more likely that he was simply using an SMS abbreviation.

Technically speaking, there was nothing earth-shattering about TWTTR. Some of the functionality was already contained in Dodgeball, another company using SMS messaging that Google had acquired.

Dorsey finished TWTTR on March 13, 2006. It had taken—with some help from Stone—about two weeks to build.

What had happened was a case of instant love and organic sharing. When Dorsey and Stone brought it to their team, members started steadily posting tidbits of personal information about where they were and what they were doing. Sometimes it was milestone announcements of a string of software being coded, or sometimes one developer was asking for some help. At other times, someone would post where they were having lunch.

Do I Care What You Had for Lunch?

There's a book titled *No One Cares What You Had for Lunch*. I would concede that is sometimes the case—but not always. One tweeter would post that she was in a restaurant; another would see it and recommend a menu item to eat or avoid. They'd give each other tips on where the quiet seats were, or which waiter or waitress to request. Sharing information became an early part of TWTTR culture, and that aspect would remain embedded even as the growth hit the exponential end of the hockey stick.

"Twitter brought us closer to each other in ways that surprised us," Stone told me. As Twitter grew, he recollected, "You'd start discovering that an old friend who you had not connected with in many years was talking about what he had for lunch somewhere, and that meant a great deal, to reconnect in such a casual way."

Odeo team members fell in love with TWTTR. In a short time, it had solved the immediate problem of finding one another when necessary. But it didn't stop there. Every day, someone found another reason to use it, and others would tweet about the new use. Pretty soon, more people were talking about TWTTR than about Odeo, even inside Odeo.

There was another thing, something I call Jurassic Park syndrome. Life has a way of busting through the fences. At the end of Day One a product designed for the internal use of a twelve-member team had twenty users. The Odeo folks just couldn't resist sharing it with friends, who in turn could not resist sharing it with friends.

Three years and two months after its public launch, there would be an estimated 32 million users.

To achieve this, the company had invested zero dollars in traditional marketing, PR, or advertising.

> @rbonini: @shelisrael Which is why one shouldn't jump into Twitter conversations without the low down, first.

Try My Secret Sauce

Traditional companies probably would have treated something like TWTTR as a highly guarded "secret sauce," to be used behind a secure firewall. If employees started sharing it with friends, they would have been sacked at a minimum, sued at a maximum.

But the Odeo founders did not come from traditional companies. They were entrepreneurs. They began their careers as part of the open-source movement, which was restructuring how technology is built, shared, used, and distributed.

"Open source" is a self-defining term. Instead of making software's source code proprietary, it made it open. Anyone is free to use, copy, or redistribute open-source software. Of perhaps equal importance is that the software moved from people's desktop computers onto the Internet, where content could be protected if you chose, or shared with others. For example, Google Docs is free word-processing software that makes it easy for several people to collaborate on a project together. A developer could take open-source code from multiple places and create something entirely new with it. Developers can create open APIs, which lets other people connect to the software you have created to enhance it in some way.

TWTTR was open-source software, and over time more than three hundred developers would add all sorts of enhancements through those open APIs.

The other thing that was open was the Odeo culture. It would never have even dawned on Stone, Williams, or Dorsey to stop employees from sharing TWTTR with outsiders.

There was yet another concept to open source, or Web 2.0 as the software that is created is categorized, that is relevant to the Twitter story: Web 2.0 software is also free. While others would debate the issue of Twitter monetization for years to come, this never appeared to concern those at the helm of the company, including investors.

But back in March 2006, what was most relevant was that Dorsey had solved the immediate problem. Odeo team members could now find one another.

But there would be unexpected consequences. The team really loved TWTTR. They talked more about it than they did Odeo. They cared more about it than they did Odeo, and now that they could keep track of one another, they talked about TWTTR when they met, not Odeo.

"We realized we were going to change something," Stone told me.

A Defining Moment

The defining moment would come one hot August day in 2006, when Stone and his wife, Livia, unwisely chose to tear up carpet in their Berkeley, California, apartment. It was dirty, difficult work. By late afternoon, the couple was exhausted. They took a break.

Feeding what had become an addict's habit, Stone immediately flopped into a chair. Hot and uncomfortable, he whipped out his cell phone to check his TWTTR account. There was a message from Williams, who had taken his wife to Napa Wine Country to kick back for the weekend. Williams had posted a link on TWTTR to share with all Odeo team members.

Stone clicked and landed on Williams's Flickr site. There, smiling serenely over the rim of an appealing glass of Pinot, was a cool and relaxed Williams.

"I just cracked up. There I was, wiping sweat off my forehead, and there he was, kicking back and gloating," Stone recalled. Other team members had been working on the product that weekend, and shared Stone's response to Williams and his Pinot.

"That became the defining moment. We knew we needed to make a change."

Williams and Stone called the team together, probably using TWTTR. It took a short time to reach a unanimous decision, one that was almost unprecedented in venture-backed start-up history. They gave the Odeo investors their money back, and started a new company.

For a short while, the new company was called Obvious Corp., but that soon changed. They elevated Dorsey to partner status, and added two vowels to the new company and product name. Both would be called Twitter.

Twitter, Inc. formed in October 2006. It was comprised of the same team that had been Odeo. They still occupied the same South Park offices in the SOMA section of San Francisco. The only structural change was that Dorsey was made a cofounder and CEO. A couple of years later, he and Williams would juxtapose titles: Williams took over as CEO, and Dorsey replaced Williams as chairman.

Twitter was still designed for small, mobile work groups that would use it to keep in touch in simple ways. The founders thought each user might have ten followers or so, and post maybe three times daily. In fact, that estimate turned out to be generally true for most users, even after the company had millions of users all over the world speaking to one another in at least 18 languages in over 120 countries.

But there were also new media stars, well-known people, and some real-life celebrities who would start being followed by tens of thousands of people, sometimes over a million. Over time, the ways that people put Twitter to use would vary as much as the way people use phones or e-mail.

But I'm getting ahead of myself. Most of this book is dedicated to telling you about that.

Migration of the Fail Whale

Howard Rheingold, author of *Smart Mobs*, a book that revealed the power of mobile SMS,* invited Stone to guest-lecture at UC Berkeley one night in 2009. That night, Stone revealed that for a short time, some people had wanted to name the new company Jitter rather than Twitter.

Stone had wisely nixed the idea. During the period in which Twitter was on the most winding part of its road to success, the ridicule might have been overwhelming.

For a period of at least eight months, the company's single and overwhelming challenge was to prevent the dramatic increases in usage and adoption from crashing Twitter either into oblivion or by frustrating users so badly that they would turn to one of several new microblogging competitors.

Sometimes Twitter users found they could not even get onto the social media platform for stretches as long as three days. When users were finally able to get on, they posted mostly about how gummed-up Twitter was.

During these prolonged and painful downtimes, the Twitter guys would post a cute cartoon of a whale being airlifted, apparently to a medical aid station, by a flock of bluebirds. The "fail whale," as it became universally called, soon became a pop-art icon, finding its way onto T-shirts and jewelry, even inspiring a Fail Whale Fan Club

---

* In *Smart Mobs*, Rheingold showed a vision for Twitter's potential that predated the actual technology by over five years. He recounted how mobile text messaging played an essential role in overthrowing the dictatorial regime of President Joseph Estrada in 2001. Rheingold wrote: "Tens of thousands of Filipinos converged on Epifanio de los Santas Avenue, known as 'Edsa,' within an hour of the first text message volleys: 'Go 2EDSA, Wear blck.' Over four days, more than a million citizens showed up, mostly dressed in black. Estrada fell. The legend of 'Generation Txt' was born."

(failwhale.com). It launched the career of Yi Yung Lu, the young illustrator who had created it.

But while many people became fans of the artist, the collective feeling toward the platform provider emerged as one of frustration and anger. Had the company called itself Jitter, it might have been as unfortunate as a deer with a target birthmark on its chest.

For a while it looked like the company's inability to keep the platform from jittering and collapsing could cause its user base one day to collectively just pick up and leave, particularly when competing microblogging platforms such as Jaiku and Pownce were being delivered to market apparently with the intention of accommodating fed-up Twitter users.

In the end, almost everyone stayed in Twitterville. First off, whenever one of these challengers started amassing followers, it too would crash just as Twitter had. Second, and more important, most people resolved to stay where their friends hung out, and the value of those friendships exceeded the frustrations of the technology. Better to stick with the flawed community you know, than join a flawed community you don't.

The other cause was the rise of the Twitterati, luminaries who amassed thousands of followers, such as Robert Scoble who at the time was Twitter's fifth most popular user.

Stars like Scoble were a factor in the young company's scaling problems and Stone complained in an interview that while he personally only posted a few times a day, people like Scoble "just clogged the streams."

Stone expanded in a blog that pointed out every time Scoble posted, which was often more than a hundred times daily, Twitter was obliged to relay that to all thirty-eight thousand of his followers. Worse, a few thousand of his followers were located overseas, where Twitter—just like any international user—had to pay a premium to cellular carriers for delivering Scoble's tweets to followers for free.

Eliminate Scoble and the others who were being hugely followed, and the technology framework would carry a much lower burden and could be built up and refined at an easier pace. The downside to that thinking, as the Twitter guys also wisely realized, was that ditching your most passionate and popular customers was not usually a wise business strategy.

They realized that they needed to build Twitter to suit how people wished to use it, rather than try to get people to use Twitter as they had originally intended it to work.

In the end the technology problem would get solved the old-fashioned way—with money. The company raised another round of venture capital and added some wise veterans to its board of directors, including Jeff Bezos, founder-CEO of Amazon.com, the world's largest retailer.

The new board and the founders agreed on a strategy. They would focus on solving the underlying technology issues first, and worry about making money later.

By autumn 2008, the fail whale was becoming an endangered species, although it would make occasional and unwelcome brief reappearances as late as June 2009.

The infusion of financial and technical resources had apparently solved the problem, for the most part. The jokes and complaints all but disappeared. Twitter jittered no more, and what some had viewed as significant competitive threats from other microblogging competitors faded into the background. By the middle of 2009, Twitter was the leader and the other players had just about disappeared from the landscape.

Speaking at year's end in San Francisco, Williams declared he "saw no end in sight" to Twitter's continuing exponential growth. Company insiders were whispering bullishly about having fifty million users by the end of 2009. Forrester analyst Jeremiah Owyang (@jowyang) said in April 2009 that Twitter was growing faster than any social media program so far. In fact, I can think of no other technology product enjoying such exponential growth for such a prolonged period of time.

But in the beginning no one—not the company, the users, the analysts, or the media—were quite so sure that Twitter would make it around so many hairpin curves on their road to success.

In fact, some weren't quite so sure they would make it through the low-cost and humble official launch.

CHAPTER 2

Showtime

Twitter's coming-out party started in March 2007, just before its first birthday. It lasted five days. Nearly the entire company had come to Austin, Texas, for South by Southwest (SXSW), the world's most popular interactive festival.

Some SXSW regulars were not all that happy about how the conference had grown year after year. When it started as a music festival in 1986, only seven hundred had attended. Then, as in 2007, nightlife was a significant part of SXSW. Attendees mingled with locals in the numerous nightclubs in Austin's downtown.

By 1994, when the producers added film and interactive media tracks to the festival, there were several thousand people attending; the clubs were closed to everyone but conference goers. Still, a culture of intimacy endured. Most folks knew lots of others who were present, and nearly all shared an interest in interactive media.

But as Twitter was to learn, growth changes the feel of a community. Eventually SXSW had to move into the cavernous, 900,000-square-foot Austin Convention Center, not exactly a place for up-close-and-personal conversations. The show produced three separate tracks; each attendee could participate in one, two, or all of them.

But the tracks were not physically separated, and people tripped and scurried from one end of the Convention Center to the other trying to see their choices from a score of panel talks that were taking place simultaneously. You might walk a half mile to your top pick, only to discover an overflow crowd. Then you'd have to scurry to your second choice, and you'd have to move fast before that one filled up as well.

By 2007, five thousand people were attending SXSW. Finding friends in hallways or in coffee bars or lunch haunts or anywhere had become a frustrating, often futile exercise.

In 2006 Dodgeball, the Twitter competitor that Google had acquired, began to solve this problem by serving as a peer-to-peer communications tool. Dodgeball had been selected as Best Product of SXSW in 2006. Now, with Google's backing, the company had returned as the incumbent champion and planned to repeat its championship ranking.

Choosing SXSW 2007 as its launch venue was therefore a bold play for Twitter. It was a thrive-or-die move. Going face-to-face against a better-known foe with a bigger budget was a little like butting heads with an elephant.

Twitter's travel costs pretty much ate up the launch budget. What they had left over they invested on two large HDTV screens, which they arranged to position at two high-traffic points in the Convention Center hallways. When people posted tweets, the screens would display them.

That was it. There was no PR agency, no advertising campaign, no leaflets under hotel-room doors. The company employed no communications professional as it prepared to face off against Google's forces behind Dodgeball.

But Twitter had one additional asset, or so they hoped. In the year since they started with twenty users, they had grown to a user base of about twenty thousand. These were mostly Web 2.0 community members, many of whom were at SXSW. Those who could not make it to the show would watch it on Twitter and participate in the conversations streaming out of the Convention Center. Several in attendance were popular and respected bloggers; over the five days of the festival, they would post news and their perceptions as well.

So with about ten team members, a few blogger friends, and a couple of HDTV screens, Twitter would launch. They had worked hard to refine the product, so that old users would have something new to say about the product.

Williams, Dorsey, and Stone had a clear goal, and they had been transparent in expressing it. They wanted to displace Dodgeball and have Twitter named Best Product of SXSW.

Mystery did not prevail on the outcome.

Twitter took SXSW 2007 by storm. Attendees turned to Twitter to find one another and to share recommendations of which day and night events to attend. Much of the intimacy the SXSW veterans had bemoaned losing in Austin was rediscovered in the virtual space of Twitterville.

While people tweeted about the show, there was a larger topic, and that was Twitter itself.

"Twitter is ruling SXSW," declared Michael Calore in his first-day Wired.com story about the conference—and in so doing, told his online readers to tap into Twitter if they wanted to stay in the loop. Greg Reinacker, cofounder of Newsgator (newsgator.com), a pioneer in RSS subscription services, observed in a blog post, "Wow, it seems like everyone is using Twitter here. I am too."

Reinacker was one of the first to "live tweet" what was being said on the SXSW dais as well as in the hallways. A few years back, conferences began to change when a small group of blog enthusiasts, many of them professional writers, began to "live blog" conferences. This undermined traditional tech writers who, attending the same events, had to file stories to editors who then published the stories several hours or days later. I knew a good deal about this; I had been a cofounder of *Conferenza Premium Reports,* a subscription newsletter covering tech conferences.

One day in 2006, while sitting at a conference, I realized that I was surrounded by bloggers, most of whom were authors and former professional journalists. *Conferenza* provided more in-depth coverage than any one of these bloggers. But the problem was twofold for me: first, these bloggers were giving away for free what my partner and I were publishing in a paid newsletter. Second, while it took us about a week to edit, polish, and refine a newsletter, these guys were publishing in pretty close to real time. Third, and most lethal, was that instead of competing with one another like traditional media reporters did at such events, these guys collaborated. When one of them wrote something new, the others would send their readers over to check it out.

For *Conferenza,* this final point was tantamount to having the *New York Times, Wall Street Journal,* and *BusinessWeek* all collaborating against our little newsletter. We simply could not compete. Shortly before I moved on, *Conferenza* turned itself into a blog, where it continues to be available (conferenzablog.typepad.com).

Now Reinacker was taking live blogging a step further into something new: live tweeting. He was one of several social media writers posting tweets that were being read around the world even as the person on stage was still speaking. While a handful of bloggers had participated before, now scores of people joined Reinacker, and the power of the information network increased exponentially.

> @tstitt: @shelisrael Why fight with TypePad editor? Ecto can't make you happy? http://illuminex.com/ecto/ iBlogger & Evernote make it even easier.

Tipping the Tuna

Ross Mayfield (@ross), a social media thinker-pioneer who had founded Socialtext (socialtext.com), the first business wiki provider, was a well-known live blogger. He also started live tweeting during the SXSW panel sessions, then taking it a step further by blogging longer, deeper expansions at night. On the second night, Mayfield declared, "On Wednesday, Twitter tipped the tuna. By that I mean it started peaking. Adoption among the people I know seemed to double immediately, an apparent tipping point."

The live bloggers became the first live tweeters. No one planned it out, but this would generate the largest and longest experiment in collaborative journalism, one that continues today, one that would give some skeptical observers an understanding that Twitter's potential went well beyond reports on what your friend had for lunch.

This also became evidence to refute the conventional but misguided perception that Twitter was just another example of gabby kids' stuff. Adult professionals addressing a business problem had started Twitter. Its early adopters and proponents may have been young, but they were business professionals. This was an early—and important—differentiation from Facebook and MySpace, whose respective user bases were college and high school students.

Twitter's early adopters were still young enough to party, judging by the nightlife at SXSW in 2007.

Twitter After Dark

Austin has long had a reputation as a party town. The SXSW founders said they had selected Austin in 1987 because it had so many desirable nightspots in those few blocks on Fourth through Sixth streets, between the Congress Street Bridge and the Convention Center.

Twitter demonstrated its real power at SXSW 2007 after sunset, when the social interaction ramped up. Let's also not get the wrong idea. These parties were not of the wild and crazy kind so much as they were business and social networking with drinks and occasional live music. The question "What do you do?" is asked many more times than "What's your sign?"

The after-hours events mattered, not just to attendees, but to big companies who sponsored these events as well.

In 2007 the tech economy was flourishing. Big brands still had discretionary dollars for producing posh parties. These events were good investments for companies seeking to market goods and services for interactive start-ups, even for those looking to acquire start-ups or cherry-pick the best and brightest talent.

Companies like Google, Microsoft, Dell, AMD, Intel, Seagate, and Cisco held elaborate gatherings to attract attendees. They showered them with free food, drinks, and entertainment. And size mattered. The bigger the party and the more industry luminaries and prominent bloggers in the room, the more word of mouth would be generated.

That year, as in years previous, party promotion was often outsourced to the pros. Corporate marketing teams and contracted promoters used all the usual resources to entice people to attend events: flyers, e-mail, and online invitation sites that encouraged sign-ups.

No one had anticipated the herding power of Twitter, however. Forrester analyst Owyang was among the first to blog that he was using Twitter to check out what was happening at parties. He would post when he heard about a party, and then when he was at an event, he'd post about the crowd, music, and refreshments. Other tweeters started sharing the same information, and when they did, it usurped traditional party promotion efforts because tweeters moved traffic from one party to another with greater speed and less effort.

During daytime, live tweeters had turned tech reporting upside down. Now, at party time, they did the same to the best practices of party marketing. Twitter-generated word of mouth would determine the success or failure of social get-togethers. The partiers would henceforth determine the success of a party more than the promoters.

> @davidyack: @shelisrael wasn't this your month to pay for Madoff's penthouse apartment, since the rest of us are kicking in $5 for Ford, GM, and Chrysler?

The Choreography of "Sux"

The partier-in-control phenomenon was best illustrated on the third night of SXSW 2007. A young woman walked down a crowded street en route to a much-touted party when she saw a succinct tweet on her handheld device from a friend who had already arrived.

"Sux," it said.

She slowed in her tracks, considering what to do. Additional tweets were confirming the bad news. A few moments later, another tweet landed on her mobile screen from someone at a competing event, reporting ample room, live music, blog industry notables, and best of all: free drinks.

As she reversed direction, something strange happened on the street. As if on a choreographer's cue, nearly all the conference attendees who had been walking in the direction of the first party executed a simultaneous about-face.

Twitter had just undermined some well-laid marketing plans and demonstrated the power of users in control.

This may not be a particularly dramatic example of how Twitter can affect communications. In the coming months, as personal dramas and natural disasters unfolded; as elective candidates mobilized their troops; as terrorists assaulted venerable Mumbai facilities; as rumors threatened some corporate images and salvaged others; as individual reputations were trashed and rescued; and as Israel and Gaza engaged in hostilities, the dynamics of partygoers in Austin would demonstrate their application to a great many larger situations.

Twitter, not surprisingly, was named Best Product of SXSW 2007. But so much more had happened because of this show at this time, and in this place. The small team returned to San Francisco. It now had sixty thousand users, triple the number it had just five days earlier.

But even more than that had occurred. Seeds were planted in a few business minds, which would germinate into some very useful— and diverse—commercial endeavors.

CHAPTER 3

Dell's Parallel Avenues

Ricardo Guerrero, an online marketer for Austin-headquartered Dell Computer, attended the SXSW 2007 conference, and was among the first business people to take a look at Twitter.

His first glimpse was on one of those two flat-panel screens in the Convention Center's corridors. As he stood in the hallway for a few minutes, he watched terse, rapid bursts of disconnected commentary steadily stream down the screen.

There was no order to what he watched. One comment was about a lunch meeting, another about a presentation being held elsewhere in the Convention Center. Then a third talked about the weather.

A friend explained to Guerrero that attendees were sending messages by phone, or sometimes by laptop, from all over the conference. He saw the messages on the monitor at the same time other people all over the world.

Neat trick, Guerrero thought, but he "totally didn't get what was really going on." He was also clueless on how anyone could possibly use Twitter for business, as were so many other professionals attending the event and seeing Twitter for the first time. Some dismissed it as a new toy, yet another "shiny object" for the digitally obsessed.

But Guerrero was among several serious business people in those hallways who thought that there may be something useful to business in there somewhere.

The next day he created a personal Twitter account (@ggroovin) and figured he'd "use it to chat with friends" to understand how it worked.

The problem was that he could only find two of his friends among the twenty thousand early Twitter adopters, and "they weren't using it much either." He went home and, after a couple of weeks, wrote Twitter off.

About a month later, a *New York Times* article about Twitter appeared, and that rekindled his interest in it as a potential business tool. "The point I got from the article was that Twitter can give you a social 'sixth sense' about what's going on in the lives of the people you follow," Guerrero said. "While some of it could be mundane, if you wanted to get to know people more intimately, then Twitter could be a really useful tool. The article made me wonder if Twitter could be used for marketing."

He decided to give Twitter another try.

> @oeolson14: the inconvenient truth is it's -7 degrees in MN. If CA wants to be proactive against Global Warming tell 'em to send it here.

Thirty Clueless Days

I relate to Guerrero's story. When a friend talked me into trying Twitter in August 2007, I found myself reluctant. I was busy. I had enough communications tools. I had never much cared for online chatting. I already had all the contacts I thought I needed, and had plenty of interaction with people through traditional and social media.

But in the conversations I was having at conferences, blogger dinners, on my blog, and meetings with people in technology and business, Twitter had pervaded the conversation.

Like Guerrero, I was curious and started an account. My first post was in August 2007. "Well here I am," I wrote. "What happens now?"

I ignored Twitter for several days, and when I returned I discovered that forty-five people were following me. Half of them were people I did not know and had never heard of.

What did these people want? Why were they following me when I wasn't going anywhere?

My misgivings turned out to be far from uncommon. "Almost everyone is absolutely baffled when they first get to Twitter," Ev Williams conceded in a December 2008 talk. "We really need to fix that," he said.*

It took me a couple of weeks to start following other people, but at first I was shy about joining conversations. It took me two weeks or so before I posted a reply to someone else's comment, and a few days more before I tweeted to start a conversation.

I often got lost in Twitterville, because the mechanics of what to do with favorites, who to follow, how to make a comment private or public were not intuitive to me.

It was like moving into a new, unfamiliar neighborhood. I found myself depending upon a few "Twitter buddies," who had been around the neighborhood before I got there.

---

* Some progress has indeed been made. In the winter of 2009, new users could find people on contact lists who were already on Twitter. It does help when you can talk with a few friends. However, most Twitter newcomers tell me that it still takes a while to get a sense for how the place works.

After a while, I started putting up posts about my work, and absolute strangers would send me encouraging words in doses of 140 characters or less.

But still Twitter was no more than a diversion to me at first, an interesting and fun thing to do on breaks from serious work.

In early September things started happening. Someone who I did not know asked about visiting Maui. I posted a link to an old blog post I had written about a Maui-based lavender farm. Three weeks later I was startled to get a message saying, "Thanks. Loved the lavender farm. It was special."

It felt good helping someone else. It usually does. But still nothing had happened on Twitter that was particularly helpful to me.

Then I got to have dinner with a good friend when we were both over three thousand miles from home. I was wrapping up a New Hampshire vacation. My wife, Paula, and I were in the Marriott Cambridge, catching a flight out in the morning. I tweeted that information for no special reason, and to nobody in particular.

It turned out that my friend Jeremiah Owyang (@jowyang), who lives about three miles from me in California, was also in town. He saw my tweet, responded, and the three of us enjoyed a memorable time in Boston's North End. It was mostly a social dinner, but over chianti and tender veal, I picked up a couple of informational tidbits that proved useful to me professionally. Owyang also gave me a few useful pointers on how to use Twitter better.

Since then, Twitter has continued to get more useful to me. I keep meeting people in Twitterville who share my interests; we exchange information and build relationships that get stronger over time.

At the start, however, it took me about forty-five days to traverse the standard Twitterville newbie's disorientation. I was clue-less at first, then I joined some conversations and started having fun. Next I helped a stranger, and felt good about sharing my experience to her benefit. Finally, a random tweet had caused a real-world experience to take place, and it was one that was both fun and useful.

From that point on, Twitter became an increasingly important tool for me. I can't call it either just a personal tool or a business tool. What it is for most people is a communications tool. And as this book will tell you, people keep finding new ways to use it. Some of them, like James Buck, achieved jaw-dropping moments with a single tweet. Sometimes you just stumble on an old friend.

I share all this with you to make one key point. It takes a lit-tle while to get the feel for Twitterville. Use it for a while, and chances are pretty good that you will find enough value there that it will evolve into being one of your preferred communica-tions tools.

Let's get back to Ricardo Guerrero at Dell.

A Frontier Shop

Back in April 2007, when Guerrero was first toying around with it, Twitterville had a global user base of perhaps seventy thousand. For an online social network, a population that small was no more than a frontier village.

Instead of cowpokes and homesteaders, however, Twitterville's early settlers were overwhelmingly technical people. While Dell is a company built on technology, its customers are business and home users.

And while Guerrero is technically adept, he's primarily interested in sales. His role at Dell has changed, but at the time he was involved in selling closeout and refurbished computers, most often computers that had been leased and returned after a period of use.

Any retailer will tell you that markdowns are a headache. By definition they are offered at reduced cost, which means you'll want to reduce the advertising and marketing costs of selling them. Second, because companies very often decide at the last minute whether or not they wish to purchase, extend, or return computers at the end of the lease, there was no way to predict inventory coming in. Third, there was pressure to get rid of closeouts fast to make room for new offerings.

Dell sold most of its refurbished products at Dell.com, the company's humongous e-commerce site, where refurbished computers had to compete for limited space with other Dell products. The other course was to market them in costly paper catalogs that were mailed to millions of customers.

Guerrero figured that Twitterville might give Dell the opportunity to open up a new low-cost channel. The financial barriers were nonexistent. All you needed was to open an account, and you had an instant virtual store.

There was one issue, however, that could not be overlooked: there was no way to conduct a transaction on Twitter at that time.*

In June 2007 Guerrero opened up Dell Outlet (@DellOutlet), the first Twitterville retail shop. It was an experiment that opened quietly and without fanfare. This was intentional. If it failed to move goods, it would close in the same manner.

He addressed the transaction problem with an old retail tactic, one that had worked previously for many online merchants, including Dell—coupons. Each contained a discount code that customers could redeem at Dell.com or other Dell online sites.

---

* While there are now a few PayPal-type services that can be used for small transactions, none had really caught on by April 2009. None were useful for a transaction covering a computer price.

Whenever a new offer becomes available, Dell Outlet store manager Stefanie Nelson (@StefanieatDell) posts a link containing a coupon code good for a discount—very often 20 percent—at another Dell online property. Sometimes she makes it a special promotion with a code good for the next ten people who click through and type it in. Sometimes she creates a custom code for an exclusive deal offered to just one customer, whom she notifies through the private direct message (DM) feature.

The advantage to Dell is that the overhead model is dramatically reduced. There is no brick and mortar. No one at Dell Outlet touches or ships a product. Yet customers feel like they are getting close, personal service; they tell their friends that they got a good deal easily, and were treated well.

According to Guerrero, surveys indicated that after the first few months, between twenty-five and thirty Dell Outlet customers were unaware that Dell *had* an online outlet operation until they found it in Twitterville. As any retail merchant will confirm that is a huge bump in customer acquisition.

The question was if that sort of early-stage growth could be maintained. Eighteen months later there were 2,500 followers of Twitter's Dell store. The company liked the result well enough to open up two Twitterville specialty stores, Dell Home Offers (@DellHomeOffers) and Dell Small Business (@DellSmallBusiness), which operated on a similar model. There are also Twitter sites for UK and Australian customers. The company is reportedly planning to open additional Twitterville stores, including one for students.

In June 2009, the company issued a press release announcing that Dell Outlet had sold $2 million dollars on Twitter primarily through Dell Outlet. Additionally, it said, people who started at Dell Outlet purchased over $1 million in new Dell Computers.

Now, you may think that $3 million in just over two years is an insignificant amount for a company like Dell, which reported sales of $16 billion in the prior year. Perhaps so, but it reiterates Malcolm

Gladwell's *Tipping Point* theme. Dell's little shops are looking like they may make a big difference as Twitter grows.

> @jweinberger: I'm thinking HuffPo is closer to Op-Ed than investigative/reporting. Mostly. Still mostly agree it's a glimpse of the future

Growing Pie Slices

Not that long ago, traditional retailers smirked at online retail's meager piece of the retail pie.

One prominent retail merchant quipped that he was losing more to shoplifters than he was to online competitors. In 1994 an executive at Barnes & Noble, then the leading U.S. bookstore, told a booksellers' conference, "Amazon.com hasn't yet grossed what we sell at clearance."

In April 2009 Amazon became the world's largest retailer in all categories. Consider that retail is among the largest segments of the global economy, where trillions of dollars' worth of goods are bought and sold.

My point is that sometimes you should take little slivers seriously. Twitter, as it has emerged since Dell Outlet formed, has not grown meteorically in retail sales. But it keeps getting more important in every aspect of conversations with customers.

This was also true at Dell. While Guerrero and Nelson were exploring this new avenue, other folks at Dell had started in the same place, and pursued an entirely different direction in Twitterville.

Learning to Listen

Lionel Menchaca also attended SXSW 2007. He too watched the stream of tweets scroll down the flat-panel TV screens. He too was clueless as to how the thing could be used for business, and decided to explore it further.

Unlike Guerrero, whose job is selling product, Menchaca is one of Dell's top social media honchos. He is principal author of direct2dell. com (D2D), the flagship blog of the much-praised Dell social media program. His title is Chief Blogger. When Dell first started blogging, it faced a firestorm of angry customers for its first thirty days.

I watched D2D as it started and thought the effort would simply be shouted down, but that is not what happened. Menchaca kept listening and showing he cared. He was apologetic where it seemed appropriate, but never defensive. At some point, you could almost hear a collective sigh as the shouters ran out of steam. Customers seemed to feel better after a good prolonged rant. It eased frustration, and that Dell guy had clearly listened and talked to them.

That guy was Menchaca, and he had proved a point some people had argued: customers get more polite and collaborative when they see someone at a big company is listening.

The D2D conversation steadily became more congenial and constructive. Menchaca and the blog became a favorite case study of how an enterprise could turn around customer sentiment with social media.

Of course, Dell has other problems that neither a blog nor a Twitter account can resolve. It's a big company, and changing its direction and strategy is like trying to turn around a fully laden supertanker moving at full throttle on open seas: it takes a lot of time and distance.

But Dell's social media team has contributed to a long turnaround, which is starting to show promise. Customer hostility has changed to customer conversations, and those conversations have created a more congenial relationship for Dell with its user base.

When I interviewed founder-CEO Michael Dell in February 2008, he made it clear that social media was an integral part of the company's strategy—not just a little skunk works project.

"When you look at the world and see that the number of people online will double from one to two billion in a few years, it makes a compelling case for understanding where this growth is occurring and what it means," he said. "Our goal is to join the conversation and speak directly and candidly with our customers. The more we engage, the more we learn and the better we can do for our customers."

It was pretty clear to Menchaca, as he stared at the flat-panel screen, that if this new Twitter thing had some usefulness to Dell Computer, his boss expected him and his team to figure it out and use it. But just like others who gazed with him in the hallway, he thought the thing was a real head-scratcher from a corporate perspective.

Right after the show, he went back to his office and became the first person at Dell to open a Twitter account. He probably didn't give it much thought, but he made his Twitter name, or handle, @LionelatDell. This style would become a corporate thumbprint in time.

Menchaca's first attempt to use Twitter involved the same thinking that other enterprise, media, and luminaries would use to get started. He decided that Twitterville could serve as a new way to distribute Dell content, or more specifically, to get people on Twitter to come read his blog.

Whenever he posted something new on D2D, a robotic (bot) software tool would automatically post a link on Twitter. This resulted in a little bump in D2D's visitor traffic: nice, but not particularly monumental.

But then Menchaca noticed something interesting. When he posted on Twitter, people would link to the D2D blog in minutes, sometimes seconds. If someone on Twitter had something to say, their comments were posted faster than others. But the comments were tweeted, not posted on D2D.

In short, tweeters moved the conversation and accelerated the dialogue.

He started realizing the earliest conversations that were relevant to his blog posts were taking place not on his blog, but in Twitterville. Tweeters also started encouraging him to be more conversational in Twitter. Just using it to broadcast feeds to his blog was pretty much like driving only in one direction on a two-way street.

So Menchaca started talking with his friend and fellow senior member of the social media team, Richard Binhammer (@Richard atDell). The two started poking around more in Twitterville. The closer they looked, the more interesting it got.

> @kencamp: That would require a clue. Some people wouldn't know a clue if it crawled up in their lap and peed. ;-)

Listening as a Strategy

Binhammer had little interest in what Guerrero was doing. He was a communications guy, and sales were not part of his mission. He had once been press secretary to the Canadian prime minister. He became a PR agency executive in New York City, and eventually a U.S. citizen. He joined Dell's communications team and had settled in well to Texas life. He takes long photo explorations into the desert, and recently acquired a cowboy hat. He has learned to ride horses "pretty well," he told me.

He and Menchaca had become the two social media lightning rods at Dell Computer. Partly because of this shared passion, the two have become pretty close.

While Binhammer wasn't that interested in Dell Outlet, he was entirely interested in what Menchaca was discovering. The two started exploring together. "Once we learned that Twitter's real power was as a listening tool more than a broadcasting tool, it became amazingly valuable," he said. "A huge part of what we do on social media is inbound. What we write on our blogs is important. But equally important is that we listen to what people have to say about us, and respond accordingly and fast. This is called blog monitoring, and we consider it to be the social media team's top priority."

Most large organizations now collect information on company blogs using monitoring and analysis tools such as Radian6 (@radian6). While such tools helped the company understand how and where they were being mentioned, they were limited in abilities to give conversational feedback.

Binhammer explained that Dell wasn't just counting mentions. Team members pored over social media conversations looking for fixable situations, in which they could repair a situation by joining a conversation.

They understood—as do pollsters and politicians—that at any given time, 20 percent of the people watching your candidate or organization will flat-out dislike you, no matter what you do.

If someone posts that they just plain out hate Dell Computer, Binhammer figures it's not worth spending time trying to change that person's opinion. As Ben McConnell at Church of the Customer (churchofthecustomer.com/blog) has often said, "Don't waste your time trying to convert atheists. Work on the agnostics in the room."

Where Binhammer and Menchaca invest time is looking for Dell agnostics who express themselves in social media—doubters who might be turned into believers through conversation. Binhammer explained, "If someone referred to a specific company gaffe—that a product didn't work right, or a customer had to wait too long on a support line—then our blog-monitoring team members leap into outreach mode. That means we try to correct a bad situation and we move as fast as we possibly can.

"It's not a tactic. It's connected to reputation. So for our team, listening is a strategy. We are actually more interested in joining blog conversations than we are in posting stuff that boasts about how great we are. Ultimately it is a bottom-line issue, and blogs taught us that we could reduce the cost of listening and turn unhappy customers into happy ones faster and at lower cost than by other possible means. The closer we looked, the more we realized that Twitter worked just like a blog, except it was smaller and thus faster.

"Twitter's smallness allowed more posts to go up more frequently. Likewise, it was faster and easier for people to respond, and thus the conversation moved faster and very often went further on Twitter than it did on standard blogs."

Lurking and Poking

Dell's social media team started by "lurking" in Twitterville. This practice is not nearly so clandestine as it sounds. A social media lurker is simply someone who watches without participating. Statistics confirm there are far more people lurking on blogs, in Facebook, and on Twitter than there are conversationalists.

It seems to me that lurking is a smart way to get started. It allows people to listen and watch; to get a sense of the mechanics and rhythm on a conversational platform.

The Dell team lurked and poked without participating for a while. Binhammer and Menchaca started using the Twitter Search feature which looks and works a lot like Google. People with Twitter accounts have search bars on the home pages.

Like Google, Twitter Search gives you fast results. If someone tweeted about Dell—or a relevant keyword—the social media team could see it very fast, often in less than a minute. It gives new results much faster than a Google Blog Alert, which sometimes lags in posting new results by more than a day.

As future chapters will demonstrate, a day in a Twitter-based crisis can be a long and damaging epoch.

For the Dell team to find what was being said in Twitterville, they just needed to type in the company name, product, or a topical keyword to see what was being said.

Dell's blog-monitoring team was often called the most responsive in the Global 100 project, which ranks the enterprises on sustainability issues. Team members considered themselves worthy of that claim. But when Twitter came into their universe, they were surprised to discover they were late to the conversation.

"There were all sorts of discussions going on about Dell when we got there," Binhammer recalled. "But we weren't in them. None of us had been listening."

Yet the team learned there was more value to Twitter than tracking what people said about you, or "ego feeding" as it is sometimes called.

They soon realized that Twitter is a great discovery tool. It pointed them to timely and useful Internet content they might have missed for days, weeks, or perhaps entirely. Tweeters were constantly posting links to blogs, articles, statistical reports, videos, even photos of interest—and content was continuously being updated.

In that light it became an early warning system for the company.

"There was an immediacy to Twitter," Binhammer told me. "It was not as thorough and perhaps not always as accurate as, say, Google Reader, Google Blog Alert, Technorati, or other search tools, but we learned to watch Twitter for early reports on a great number of subjects."

During this lurking phase, Binhammer was also taken in by the candor of Twitter users: "Folks will tell you when you suck and when you are wonderful with equal bluntness."

Nonstop Feedback Loop

Twitter's economic advantages became clear early on. As the Dell team started evolving from lurker status to participation, the company realized that Twitter could actually play a role in bringing better products and services to market, partly because of all that bluntness. For one thing, Binhammer soon realized, the company no longer needed to invest in focus groups. Twitter provided real-time feedback from real customers who were passionate and well informed. "A focus group is sort of a spot check," he said. "Twitter is a nonstop feedback loop."

Menchaca started using Twitter as a research lab. "I call it 'Twitter answers.' When I want to know what the market thinks, I hop on Twitter and ask a question. I get instant results and it's free." This is another example of crowd sourcing. As I mentioned, I used crowd sourcing to research *Twitterville*. The results were phenomenal. But more about that later.

Twitter also gave Dell something of an omniscient presence. "If a conversation occurred in a Minneapolis—or Beijing—Starbucks concerning our new Dell Mini, I simply could not know about it while sitting in my Round Rock, Texas, cubicle," Menchaca told me. "But if one of the participants tweets about it, not only can I listen and learn, I can join the conversation."

During my chat with Binhammer, he called Twitter "the most intimate social media platform. It's almost as natural a way to interact as is this telephone conversation."

The Dell team also made a point to make clear who was speaking from a Twitter account. It started with @LionelatDell, then @RichardatDell, and over the coming months the @NameatDell would be a company thumbprint. There are currently over 150 @NameatDell tweeters. While some companies would elect to tweet under a brand name, using unidentified authors, Dell set a standard for transparency that has been followed by a great many other companies. Personally, I think it is the wisest course.

> @scobleizer: Shhh @fanclerks I have to talk in a low voice so the bots can't hear me. I'll tell you in the next tweet.

No Shills Allowed

Each Dell tweeter also posts an authentic photo of his or herself. "We are trying to humanize Dell," Menchaca said. "We think people would rather talk to us than to a brand logo."

Binhammer says that company tweeters are encouraged to post on company time and to talk about their jobs, but not *just* their jobs. "We talk about whatever interests us. Our jobs interest us, most of the time, but hopefully more things in life than that cross our minds," Binhammer said.

No Dell team member just pushes out pro-Dell information. "It is important that no one serve as a company shill on Twitter," said Binhammer.

Sometimes the no-shills policy can be a challenge. Both traditional and social media journalists closely follow Binhammer and Menchaca. They get pitched by their own PR people to help with announcements, but consistently decline if it isn't something they are known to care about.

Even when discussing their work, Dell employees hang out in some very diverse global neighborhoods. For example, Matt Domsch (@mdomsch), a recognized open-source technology guru, tweets prolifically about Linux. Domsch's job requires that he watch all social media for open-source software discussion. When a customer suggested on the Dell IdeaStorm blog (ideastorm.com) that the company produce a Linux-based computer, it was Domsch who jumped all over the idea, serving as a catalyst to convert the idea into a product that has enhanced Dell's stature in the developer community.

You're unlikely to find Binhammer tweeting about Linux. He has no passion for programming languages and operating systems. But he is enthusiastic about the environment, small business, and social media. He posts about a dozen tweets daily covering those topics. Only about a quarter of them mention Dell at all.

While Binhammer insists that he has no interest in sales, every now and then his Twitter account reels one in. Erin Kotecki Vest (@queenofspain), a popular "mommy blogger" and writer for the Huffington Post, wrote this account of how she bought a new PC:

"I asked my friends via Twitter what I should get. Within a few hours I was speaking directly with Richard from Dell.

"He never pressured a sale, just asked me what I was looking for and made a few recommendations. He and his colleagues took the time to get to know me. And guess what? We had all been talking about other things like politics and conferences and parenting well before I needed a computer. They were already part of my community. People support their friends, their communities, be they actual or virtual. When I finally opened my wallet, you bet your ass I bought a Dell."

Another tweeter, Sean Alexander (@SeanAlex), used the platform instead of traditional Dell support when he had a problem. "I tweeted it and they've been bending over backwards to fix it ever since."

"Part of who we are"

In his video interview with Owyang, Bob Pearson, who at the time was the highest-ranking member of Dell's social media team, stressed that for Dell, which has had more bad financial quarters in recent years than good ones, social media becomes even more important during tough financial times "because it is not that expensive, and it gets you closer to your customer." It has also evolved from a novelty to a normal, at-work communications tool. "It has become a part of who we are," Pearson said.*

Guerrero and Menchaca had started in the same place at the same time. They figured out how to make Twitterville valuable for their employer. In so doing they demonstrated the diverse appeal that Twitter would have for business-minded people.

---

* Pearson left Dell in May 2009 to assume an executive position with the Blog Council, an association of Global 1000 companies dedicated to sharing social media insights, experiences, and strategies.

CHAPTER 4

Why Comcast Cares

Customer support can make an enterprise schizophrenic. On one hand, it's obvious that a well-supported customer is a happy customer, and a happy customer will recommend you to friends.

On the other hand, supporting customers is expensive. It eats margin and profit. Some customers act like codependents. They just want to stay on the phone. Still others are chronically cranky and just won't be happy, no matter what you do for them. Ben McConnell at Church of the Customer calls them "support atheists."

Companies are caught in a real quandary. If you cut support too far, as Dell found out, you lose sales and trust. People who could have been company champions become company haters.

In this case, Twitter has become a quandary-buster. It lets companies support their customers at lower cost while yielding higher rates of success.

> @ssloansjca: Why do people say "just friends" as if being friends is not something that is in itself way cool?

A Caring Comcast

Comcast, the largest cable company in the United States, is Twitter's poster child for reversing a bad service reputation.

For years, Comcast had ranked consistently at or near the bottom of customer satisfaction surveys. When the Internet came along, it amplified Comcast's reputation problem by giving customers new venues to express complaints to each other faster and more creatively. One such example was ComcastMustDie.com, a site whose purpose is obvious.

You may consider such online rants a bit excessive, and maybe not even that damaging to a company, but consider the home owner who thought that the Comcast repair guy she let into her home was fixing her problem, only to find him asleep on her leather couch.

Instead of waking him, she video recorded a few minutes of his slumber making sure the audio picked up his rhythmic snoring. Then she uploaded it to YouTube, where it had been viewed about 1.4 million times by May 2009.* The speed that the clip passed around was significantly accelerated by people on Facebook, blogs, and Twitter pointing people to it.

There is probably no tool yet for measuring a company's precise online unpopularity, but I'm among a growing number of people who use the Google "sucks" test. It's quite simple. Go to Google Search and type in the name of a company, product, or person. Then add the word "sucks" to your search query. The higher the number of results you get, the more unhappy customers probably are.

In April 2009 "comcast sucks" drew 269,000 returns. This is far

---

* The soundtrack has been muted, apparently because Comcast lawyers argued it was an unauthorized recording of their employee.

from the worst I've seen, but it is unlikely to encourage you to use this company's services if you have a choice.

What gets interesting is if you then search for "comcast cares twitter."* You get over 625,000 results. More than that, the results, if you check, are generally newer than the "sucks" entries, indicating Comcast is a company who has turned around a bad reputation—or is at least in the process of doing so.

In 2009, Comcast's bottom of barrel ranking in customer service measurably reversed itself. According to the American Customer Satisfaction Index, Comcast's customer satisfaction rating rose over 9 percent in the first quarter of 2009, the largest gain among cable and satellite providers. The survey attributed the improvement exclusively to Comcast's Twitter participation.

That particpation started in April 2008, when Frank Eliason, a midlevel Comcast customer support employee, opened up an account: @ComcastCares. It was the first large enterprise Twitter account dedicated exclusively to customer support. Eliason would later say he chose Twitter over other social media platforms because that's where the Comcast customers were.

It started just when the YouTube clip of the sleeping repair guy was reaching an apex of popularity, but Eliason wisely ignored all that. He wasn't there to defend what had happened. Nor was he there to talk about how great Comcast really was or hoped to be.

Instead, Eliason made it clear he was on Twitter to solve customer problems. He addressed tweeting Comcast customers the same way a call center service person does it—one at a time. He never made grandiose claims. He eschewed marketing rhetoric. He just asked what the problem was and tried to fix it.

---

* If you don't add the word "Twitter," you pull 7.5 million, but that is because the company also has a heavily promoted Comcast Cares Day that is not relevant to the comparison.

Twitterville greeted this with suspicion at first. They generally tend to be bristly about big company representatives who come in talking. Second, Twitter seemed to be overflowing with people who had stories about bad Comcast experiences; Eliason's presence gave them more reason to vent. Third, one of the first customers Eliason helped just happened to be Michael Arrington, publisher of TechCrunch, a high-profile tech industry blog.

When Arrington wrote in glowing terms about the great service he received, many wondered whether @ComcastCares was a real support service or a high-visibility concierge for famous people like Arrington. Some charged that the account was a publicity stunt.

When I talked to Eliason in December 2008, he bristled at the accusation. "We treat all our customers the same way," he sniffed. "We don't care who they are. We care about fixing the problem."

As months went by, Eliason's deeds backed up his words. Customer after customer extolled Eliason's efforts. He seemed to be on Twitter around the clock. To dig into details, he'd call up customers and help them without the intrusion—or company expense—of a house visit. When a repairperson was needed, Eliason was vigilant in getting him or her to show up on time and to already understand what the problem was.

After one year Eliason had helped over two thousand customers. Most are not luminaries like Arrington, and nearly all who have tweeted about the experience express satisfaction with Eliason's efforts.

The general consensus is that Frank Eliason really cares. He has passion for helping customers, and he uses an engaging personal approach.

One customer, Francine Hardaway (@Hardaway) of Half Moon Bay, California, explained how Eliason worked with her via Twitter to solve a tricky weak signal problem for nearly a week. Eventually, Eliason figured it out and solved it, but something else happened in the process: "Frank became a friend," she told me.

The Comcast Twitter team had expanded to ten members by April 2009. Thousands of customer problems are being resolved on Twitter with apparently more success and customer satisfaction than can be achieved in call centers.

Each Comcast representative can cover about the same number of customers by tweeting that can be accomplished in a phone center, but with Twitter there are several advantages, the biggest being that service is being performed in public. So when a customer gets help from one of the ten-member team, thousands of people are able to see it.

There are other advantages. On the phone, a customer has to wait while a technician runs diagnostics on the cable line. On Twitter, you live your life while they do the checking.

The Comcast online team is now active on several social media platforms in addition to Twitter, and they seem to be listening for any relevant mention.

When blogger Mike McDuff posted a link to a photo of a banner declaring "ComcaStink" (*sic*), which an irate homeowner had posted on his lawn in Philadelphia, Comcast's home base, Eliason posted a comment saying he'd look into it. Less than a day later, he put up a second comment telling McDuff—and his readers—that the matter had been resolved. The irate customer became a happy customer, and the sign was removed.

Early cynics have been turned around. "I had been prepared to settle in for a weeks-long fight with the cable company," wrote Techdirt blogger Tom Lee. "Instead, Frank's quick intervention left me feeling oddly positive about a company that I had long considered to be more or less the embodiment of malevolent, slothful incompetence."

The team has also gone beyond resolving technical issues. When Ken Yeung (@TheKenYeung) tweeted that he was receiving unsolicited Comcast sales calls even though he was already a customer, he received an apologetic reply from @ComcastGeorge, a new team member. A day later he received a telephone apology. The calls stopped.

Eliason is not part of Comcast's PR team, but it's likely the PR team has to scramble to keep up with him in terms of media coverage. He has been covered in numerous traditional publications such as the *New York Times*, as well as on CBS and ABC. He is a frequent speaker at business conferences.

In addition to improving perceptions and realities of customer services while lowering support costs, Twitter suggestions are improving company efficiency.

For example, by taking a tweeter's suggestion, the company has decentralized the overnight parking locations of its national fleet of vans. Now each van is parked closer to the neighborhood it serves. In the morning each driver gets to her or his first customer sooner. The company owns a great many vans, and each one now puts on fewer miles, burns less gas, and creates less pollution.

Comcast has not yet solved the riddle of how to provide twenty-four million U.S. households with this level of support. It will be a long time before all customers will turn to Twitterville. But a door has been opened, and the increased activity over one year—Eliason has sixteen thousand followers, and there are nine other Comcast tweeters with him now—shows a strongly positive trend.

> @ruchitgarg: @shelisrael my fav "Some people have a master plan. I have a monster plan!" frm @sheridanzig she runs a monster ranch.

Flying over Twitterville

I'm not sure why, but any company described as a carrier tends to have reputation problems with customers. Cable, cell-phone, aircraft, and insurance carriers all seem to fall into this pit.

Comcast faces a daunting task. It is a large incumbent, and it took many years to damage the reputation it is now repairing. For complex reasons it may have time to do so.

In the airline industry, building a reputation through social media, particularly Twitter, is taking a different form.

Upstart airlines are using Twitter to make customers happier and to pull some customers away from older incumbents who continue, for the most part, to ignore social media conversations about them.

There are other issues here. Old airlines, if you'll pardon the pun, have lots of baggage that seems to weigh them down during times of high fuel costs and lower passenger counts.

But while entrenched airlines continue tactics that make talking with them when you have a problem frustrating, new ones such as JetBlue, Southwest Airlines, and Virgin America are finding opportunities and moving with gusto into Twitterville.

These three airlines joined Twitter early. They are taking slightly different approaches from one another, but each is clearly listening to conversations and joining them aggressively.

Let's look at a few examples of what's happened so far:

In March 2008 all airlines were short of passengers. But the SXSW conference caused a bubble in demand from the San Francisco Bay Area to Austin. All direct flights got booked up, and people in Twitterville started complaining about it.

In the Bay Area, two airlines—American and JetBlue—had most of the direct routes to Austin. JetBlue was the first airline to join Twitter. American Airlines had still not joined as of June 2009.

American did not see the demand surge, thus JetBlue was the only airline to seize the opportunity. They added extra flights to Austin. Making clear whom they were trying to attract as new customers, JetBlue announced the new flights only on Twitter.

They sold out in a few hours.

Sometimes @JetBlue has seemed eerily omnipresent. Joel Postman (@JPostman), a social media author, mentioned @JetBlue in a tweet. A few minutes later, he discovered that @JetBlue had started to follow him. He blogged about the experience, calling what happened "spooky." He also wondered if the company was using an automated software bot to follow people who mentioned it.

A few minutes later, he received a comment from Morgan Johnston, a corporate communications officer at JetBlue, insisting that no bots were used. "It's merely me and my team keeping our ears to the ground and listening to our customers talk in open forums so we can improve our service," he said. "It's not marketing. We're trying to engage on a level other than mass broadcast, something I personally believe more companies should do."

Johnston's uncanny speed of response has jarred others as well. When author Jonathan Fields (@JonathanFields) was waiting for a JetBlue flight out of Burbank, California, he tweeted that actor William Shatner was sitting across from him in the waiting area.

@JetBlue immediately started following him. Fields asked @JetBlue if he had been found through some sort of mysterious Wi-Fi monitoring system. Nope, it turned out, just Johnston again.

Southwest Airlines (@SouthwestAir) has also used Twitter to respond quickly to customer discontent. Paul Colligan (@Colligan), a social media webinar instructor in Portland, Oregon, complained when a Southwest flight was canceled and he was rebooked on a later flight. When he reached his destination, he discovered a tweet from @SouthwestAir offering to make things right with a free future flight.

In less than 140 characters, the company saved a customer relationship. Of course, Colligan just had to tell his 2,500 followers about the experience, which didn't hurt Southwest's reputation either.

Virgin America (@VirginAmerica), yet another of the new fleet of upstart airlines, is also on Twitter, and has also surprised its customers by jumping into conversations. Tony Haile (@ArcticTony) was impressed after he posted a Twitter complaint about the entertainment options while his plane was taxiing for takeoff.

"Within four minutes," he told me, "I received an e-mail from someone on the Virgin America staff who had seen my tweet, checked with the head of in-flight entertainment, matched my Twitter to the plane I was on, found my e-mail address, and sent me an e-mail explaining what the current entertainment rotation schedule was and what they were doing to improve on it. Naturally, my next tweet was astonished praise of Virgin America. I've loved them ever since."

Skidding Out of the Conversation

Now let's look at what happens when airlines don't bother to join the conversation.

There are many examples of lost opportunities suffered by companies ignoring public conversation in which they are being discussed unfavorably. As Dell's Lionel Menchaca noticed, people get more polite when they know you're listening.

When a Continental Airlines flight skidded off a Denver runway during an aborted takeoff on December 20, 2008, passenger Mike Wilson (@2DrinksBehind) tweeted by-the-minute accounts of what had happened, and many of the two hundred people who followed him relayed the information to thousands of others across Twitterville.

Wilson also posted a photo on what was then a new tool called TwitPic, which lets tweeters view user-generated digital photos without leaving Twitter. Wilson's tweeted account and his photo had circulated around the world and wended their way into traditional media reporting before the airline had the chance to muster up an announcement that an incident had occurred.

Continental was accustomed to having their official version of the story be the only version. They found themselves being asked questions they had not anticipated, because they were clueless about what had happened in Twitterville. Subsequent traditional media reports incorporated the unauthorized photo, as well as Wilson's less-flattering account of what happened rather than the story airline officials wanted told.

@dickc: In honor of Cheney's speech on the Iraq War, I'd like to request that all federal institutions fly their flags at Half-Assed.

Passengers Take the Controls

December 20, 2008, was a bad day for airline passengers all over the country. At a time of peak holiday season travel, the weather was awful throughout much of the United States. Many passengers got stuck in airports, or worse.

While Mike Wilson was skidding off a Denver tarmac on a Continental flight, author Jean Ann Van Krevelen (@JeanAnnVK) was sitting on an American Airlines flight at Portland International Airport in Oregon with her partner and two small children.

Passengers were told that heavier-than-expected snows were delaying the takeoff, but everyone needed to sit tight because the flight would take off as soon as they got a little break in the weather.

As they sat there, Van Krevelen killed a little time by tweeting. Her posts were lighthearted at first, but people following noticed her sense of humor was tapering and the storm was not. Passengers sat there and were periodically advised that the flight would take off in just a few minutes. There was no food on the flight. Passengers were doled out a single dentist-size cup of water.

After two and a half hours, American finally allowed passengers to step off the plane but to stay near the gate in case a storm break came. Ten minutes after deplaning, passengers were directed to reboard. The break in the weather had come.

People quickly got back on the plane. Very few had managed to obtain or scoff down any food during the short break. The doors closed. Passengers belted up, and there they would sit for another two and a half hours, without food or drink.

Now Van Krevelen's tweets took on a more urgent tone. Some

passengers needed medications that they had packed into their luggage for what was supposed to have been a short flight. Everyone was hungry. Many had become downright cranky, and still the plane sat.

Nearly seven hundred miles south of Portland, in Silicon Valley, California, Cathy Browne (@cathybrowne) was sitting at her computer. It was a gray and rainy day, but at least it wasn't snowing. She was following her Twitter friend @JeanAnnVK's posts and was concerned about the deteriorating situation.

She was retweeting the reports issuing from inside the plane. Word was spreading in Twitterville. Browne is a PR practitioner. "I know how to make noise," she told me. "I'm a pro at it."

To help her Twitter friend, Browne contacted the Portland TV stations, which had not heard anything about the airport being immobilized and passengers being virtually imprisoned. They dashed off to the airport and started raising the kind of media ruckus the airport and airlines had probably hoped to avoid.

They wanted to know why the passengers were still on the plane; no one had an answer, but apparently someone with authority figured out that it would be a good idea to once again allow the passengers off the plane. Not counting the ten-minute break, they had been cooped up for five hours.

When Van Krevelen stepped off the plane, she was identified as the person who had tweeted the passengers to freedom. KATU-TV, a local station, put a camera and lights on her. They wanted her to explain how this Twitter thing worked.

Two hours later, passengers once again reboarded the plane, this time to actually take off—a full seven hours late. Van Krevelen and her family were not among them. They'd had enough. They cut their losses and went home, where they would spend their holiday.

This story had special impact for me, although I did not connect the dots until I met Browne nearly a month after it occurred. But I had seen her retweets on December 20 through someone twice removed from Van Krevelen. My wife, Paula, her eighty-seven-year-old mother, and I were scheduled to fly up to Portland for a family Christmas.

We had been checking official Internet reports that advised us to expect delays into Portland, but none said anything about seven hours on a tarmac without food.

However, I got more reliable information from retweets that Cathy Browne was relaying from the front line. I was fortunate in deciding to trust Twitterville more than official information sites.

Portland International Airport would be opened and closed several times over the next few days. Quite a few people found themselves stranded for the holidays. It was a nightmare worth missing.

In the coming months there were more incidents involving TwitPic and airplanes. Traditional and social media started realizing and respecting each other's mutual value.

> @micah: another rule of thumb: when stealing concepts, at least be funny. Funny can always be forgiven. Anything else is pedantic at best.

A Tree Falls on U-Haul

If your business depends at all on public perceptions, this is one of those don't-let-this-happen-to-you true stories.

It started while David Alston (@DavidAlston) and his family were preparing for a move in August 2008. His wife called a New Brunswick U-Haul rental shop to arrange for a family move. She didn't like the way the company representative dealt with her, and she told her husband.

Alston, a marketing executive for Radian6, tweeted, "My wife just went through a totally rude customer service experience with our local U-Haul rep. Downright rude. Do they want the business?"

Now, if a complaint like that were posted about Dell or Comcast, JetBlue or Southwest, it's a good bet that someone would have jumped on it in minutes.

Not so with U-Haul. No one from the company watched Twitter. They didn't know that a potential customer was telling hundreds of people why he was about to not be a customer. Soon thousands would know about the Alston incident as word spread through the social media community.

Kaitlyn Wilkins, an Ogilvy PR operative, posted: "So, for those of you who are playing along at home—in less than two hours, dozens of people responded to a single tweet regarding U-Haul and effectively told 3,763 other people that they disliked the brand. And the conversation is still going." She added, "For a company that is not listening to social media—this tree just fell in the forest, and nobody heard it."

The Alston tweet had been a touchstone to a prolonged wave of conversations about poor U-Haul service experienced by more people than was generally realized. People in Twitterville who wanted to share their shoddy U-Haul experiences quickly formed a global neighborhood.

U-Haul became a Trending Topic, meaning that Twitter identified it as among the most discussed issues in the entire community. Tweeters who had never rented from the company joined in, vowing not only to never use U-Haul but to warn their friends away as well.

And still, no one from U-Haul knew about it.

Alston is a mild-mannered guy. It was clear when I talked with him that he was not out to cause U-Haul any lasting damage. It would have stopped right after Alston's first tweet if someone from the company had been there, but no one was, and it just kept getting worse.

Old scars reopened. Alston was directed to a February 2008 report on *Inside Edition* that reviewed earlier customer complaints of U-Haul's safety negligence. CEO Joe Shoen told an interviewer that the buck stopped with him. He was the guy who would make it better.

"People can't get this organization to behave," he declared. "But I can." Shoen told viewers to call him on his cell phone, and gave out his number on the air: 602-390-6525.

Using the number, Alston sent Shoen a text message. Recalled Alston, "[Shoen] called and left me a voice mail later that day and said he would call again later." But Shoen did not call back. Alston text-messaged again, and another time, but Shoen did not respond.

That was U-Haul's second chance to make it right. Alston told me he would have loved to use his social media tools to say how the U-Haul CEO had personally stepped up to the plate and made it right, but nothing happened.

There would be one more chance. I blogged many of my *Twitterville* interview notes. My interview with Alston was posted on December 18, 2008. On January 14, Marla Palmisano, an executive assistant to U-Haul's president, posted a comment saying she would like to have Alston contact her to set up a time for a telephone conversation. I told Alston, and they spoke a couple of days later. He later related to me details of the conversation and the final conclusion of the incident.

Palmisano apologized, conceding that her CEO and several employees could have performed better. She told Alston that the first she had learned of the incident was when someone from U-Haul's "Internet department" came across my post.

To make things better, she offered Alston $40 in U-Haul coupons for his next move. Noting that he was hopeful he would not be moving again anytime soon, he suggested that she give the coupons to the local Boys & Girls Club, a favorite charity.

"At least I got to talk to someone who listened," he told me after the call. He would hear from her one more time via e-mail that $40 in coupons had been sent to the Boys & Girls Club. In a congenial note, she concluded, "I know we can do better."

Ironically, one way U-Haul might do better is to use the tool that Alston markets: Radian6 provides the leading social media monitoring tools. Companies use Radian6 to avoid snafus precisely like this one.

We live in transformational times. Companies like Comcast are among those who are using the new conversational tools to improve their reputations. Others, like U-Haul, are ignoring the challenges for change.

One course seems much wiser than the other.

CHAPTER 5

Customers Take Control

A major change in the Conversational Age from the Broadcast Age is that more decisions are being made faster at the front lines of business, where a company's representatives interact most with its customers.

This is a reversal of the command-and-control system of yore, where most important decisions were made by a few very senior people at the top of the organization. Historically, the decision makers were geographically the farthest away from where the relevant information was available. Even in organizations headed by the most responsive of leaders, the process was slow as information traveled from point of action uphill to point of decision, then back down again. The bigger a company got, the slower it got.

The Internet has been flattening corporate structures for some time now. Social media has accelerated the process, and the recession has speeded up the process still further.

Many companies have discovered that it is smarter, more popular, and ultimately more profitable to make more decisions out at the edge of an organization rather than in executive chambers. It allows large organizations to become more agile.

Best Buy, the world's largest consumer electronics company, has used social media to let in-store rank-and-file staff help and train one another through an internal social network for floor help called Blue Shirt Nation. It is "generally making each other smarter at the point where Best Buy interfaces with customers," cofounder Gary Koelling told me.

Robert Stephens (@RobertStephens), CEO and founder of Geek Squad, Best Buy's 15,000-member tech support service, told me it has also built its own behind-the-firewall information-sharing social network, which has resulted in fewer mistakes, better profit margins, happier customers, and improved employee retention.

Does the home office feel threatened or reduced by such front-line social media tactics? Not at all. Michele Azur, vice president for emerging customer channels, told me the reverse is true. "Empowering employees and fighting bureaucracy is a Best Buy business strategy."

Best Buy has also started using Twitter. Barry Judge, the chief marketing officer (@BestBuyCMO) has been there since mid-2008, and Bianca Roland (@BestBuyTulsa221) shows how a local store manager can use Twitter to interface with customers.

These are tough times for store chains such as Best Buy. There has been a shakeout of major brands and Best Buy, although having its own sales troubles, is considered by most business observers to be the likely brick-and-mortar survivor.

I think Best Buy has a smart strategy. It may be one of the companies that realizes it is not in control of its destiny. Their customers are in control. Their future depends on how close they can get to their customers, and how fast they can learn what their customers want from them in terms of both goods and services.

In fact, the customer has always been in control of the fate of enterprises in a great many categories. But throughout the Broadcast Era, neither the companies nor the customers fully realized that fact.

Customers actually have far greater impact on one another than any market campaign could dream of accomplishing. We simply trust our friends more than we trust an ad message.

Social media gives us more friends and colleagues who cover more ground and have far greater collective knowledge and wisdom. As Yossi Vardi, the Israeli investor who founded ICQ, the first Internet-based instant-messaging service, told me when I interviewed him for *Naked Conversations*, "social media is conversations on steroids."

Those social media steroids have really beefed up the collective muscle of us customers, as this chapter illustrates. As a matter of fact, so did the last chapter. Let's look back for a second.

Would you prefer to fly on an airline that apologizes for canceling your flight by tweeting you a free ticket for your next trip, or one that leaves you hungry and without information for seven hours on a snowy tarmac and never actually apologizes at all?

When you are about to visit somewhere you've never been, would you trust a hotel based on what its Web site says about itself, or what a friend tells you or shows you with digital pictures or video clips? When you want a special meal, would you trust a restaurant ad over what people who ate there say on a user-review site such as Yelp.com?

Social media has very clearly accelerated a process that has been going on for some time, whether companies see the value or not and whether they like it or not.

Decision making has not just moved to the corporation's front line, it has started to cross that front line and land in the hands of the customer that company was formed to serve. There is no going back.

In marketing, some PR agencies and advertisers have witnessed the shift, and have adjusted their core strategies from trying to put messages into "target" minds to realizing their best approach is to engage existing and potential customers in conversations.

Some marketers may still try to use spin. More often than not, that spinning will do no more than make themselves dizzy. The definition of marketing is reverting back to what it once was, and that is the building of relationships with customers.

Spinning and targeting are simply outmoded. They have become ineffective and inefficient tools of an era that is rapidly closing. If you try to use old tools in new times, you may find the results are the reverse of what you wanted to achieve. And Twitter has turbocharged conversations that already were on steroids.

> @pkedrosky: bloomberg, fox business, and cnbc all have live tv setups in lobby at beverly hills hilton. like matter, antimatter, and doesn't matter.

A Really Big Headache

The Motrin Moms ad campaign lasted one weekend in November 2008, but it is likely to be remembered and studied by marketers for years to come. McNeil Healthcare, makers of Motrin, an ibuprofen-based painkiller, would probably prefer that everyone just forget about the incident altogether.

Motrin Moms was an integrated advertising campaign involving print and online ads. But what got noticed and caused the makers of Motrin such a huge headache was a video clip component that they uploaded onto YouTube. The social video site was an important part of the strategy. They were following potential customers who had migrated away from traditional media.

Like H&R Block, Motrin has seen a need to reach out to a younger adult demographic, so YouTube was a vital component. They were not advertising to their established base so much as trying to attract new customers.

The ads poked fun at wearable baby clothing—slings, backpacks, and other garments designed for hands-free baby toting. In a playful style, the ads asserted these items could cause aches and pains that Motrin could relieve.

Most people who saw the ads during their brief run did not find them particularly offensive. The only ones who felt offended were some of the very people that McNeil was trying to attract.

It started really with the posts of Jessica Gottlieb (@JessicaGottlieb), who tweets, blogs, and is active on Facebook. Gottlieb is a "mommy blogger," one of the largest of all social media global neighborhoods.

Another tweeter pointed Gottlieb to the ads and she responded moderately enough, saying Motrin wasn't being "particularly supportive of mothers and that during tough times mothers would be smart to buy generic ibuprofen." A few minutes later she was asked to clarify what was wrong and she wrote that "picking on new mothers is vile."

From there, a groundswell incident occurred. (Charlene Li, who wrote the foreword to this book, and Josh Bernoff coauthored *Groundswell*. The title describes an event that occurs when a seed lands on fertile soil in social media and grows faster than Jack's legendary beanstalk.)

Word passes from one person to another on social media platforms, and as it does, the speed of communications increases. On Twitter, a user-invented feature called a hashtag is the accelerant. The hashtag "#MotrinMoms" (note the "#" sign) was added onto almost all the tweets on the subject. The hashtag meant that anyone who wished could use Twitter Search and find all the posts related to the Motrin ads; in a few hours there were thousands. In fact, #Motrin-Moms became the top Trending Topic in Twitterville that weekend.

The controversy spread onto mommy blogs. On Facebook 1,300 people joined a new group called Boycott Motrin. Response videos were posted on YouTube as well as Flickr. One YouTube video was a near-perfect parody of the original Motrin ads. The narrative voice and look were almost identical. While the voice in the Motrin Moms ad says, "I'll put up with the pain, because it's a good kind of pain. It's for my kid." The parody ad, cleverly replacing baby carriers with breast implant surgery, concluded, "I'll put up with the pain, because it's a good kind of pain. It's for my husband."

By that same morning, coverage found its way into publications as diverse as the *New York Times*, *Scientific American*, and *Computerworld*, onto network TV, and was generally ubiquitous in the media and on radio talk shows.

Monday morning, Kathy Widmer, vice president of marketing for McNeil, officially apologized on the company Web site. She apologized a second time four days later.

"We realized through your feedback that we had missed the mark and insulted many moms," she stated. "We didn't mean to, but we did." She also gave sage advice to other marketers: "When you make a mistake, own up to it, and say you're sorry. Learn from that mistake." But she failed to mention how imperative it has become for companies to be part of social media conversations.

There was no Internet during most of the twenty-five years that I was a communications consultant. When my clients had a crisis, we had at least a week to work out a strategy and begin implementing it. McNeil had listened, responded, and reacted in just a few days. That may sound impressive to someone schooled in traditional marketing. When the decision maker saw what happened on a Monday morning, she responded quickly and said the right words. Her two posts stemmed an angry tide, and the issue tapered off nearly as abruptly as it had started.

Gottlieb herself said Widmer's words had satisfied her. "They have the voice of authenticity," she wrote. She added that the event had been "no tsunami, just a set of big waves on the beach. Those waves are now receding and it is time to move on."

But storm damage remained. The company was current enough that it had been watching social media even if it was not participating. But they had made a mistake. The people who watched for social media comments had taken the weekend off. The potential customers who got offended, however, engaged in conversation over that weekend. And no one from the company was listening.

Nobody from Motrin's organization saw the Motrin Moms as they self-organized. From Friday night until early Monday morning, they had posted hundreds of text and video replies to the Motrin ads, all while the marketing people were enjoying a pleasant autumn weekend.

Once Motrin joined the conversation, the crowd dispersed. As David Alston said after his ordeal with U-Haul, once he felt someone was listening and felt bad, he was mollified.

But scars remain on U-Haul's image, and I believe the same happened to Motrin in a very short period of time.

Mommy blogger Erin Kotecki Vest (@QueenofSpain) summed it up: "What is relevant to all of us is how the game has changed. I realize you may be shocked by this, but there was a time it was necessary to educate companies and other bloggers on just how influential the moms online are. That time has passed."

It's not just moms. It's people who care on any subject. If they are in Twitterville, it's easy to find people who share your interests, and that's how global neighborhood form. Hashtags and Twitter Search are a few of the carpenter's tools you can use to build or join as few or many neighborhoods as you wish.

> @nejsnave: A request. Can we stop using the drinking the kool-aid metaphor 4 sm? It's just not being used properly. PEOPLE. THE KOOL-AID WAS POISONED.

Pepsi Bites a Bullet

Some people considered the Motrin Moms campaign to be on the edge. If that were true, then what became known as the Pepsi Suicide ads went well over it. If Motrin Moms offended a few people, these soda ads offended almost everyone who saw them.

It started in Germany. A lifestyle magazine published just three ads touting Pepsi Max, a diet drink with one calorie per bottle.

The ads were intended for an avant-garde readership who likes it when advertisers stretch boundaries. Traditional advertisers like niche markets. They can customize ad messages to fit the tastes of a specific group of people with much in common. At least, that's the way it used to work.

BBDO Düsseldorf, Pepsi's German ad agency, decided it would be fun to spoof suicide for this targeted audience.

The creative team designed a cute blue cartoon character that, the ad claimed, represented the "only one very, very, very lonely calorie" in a Pepsi Max. Each of the three ads depicted the calorie attempting a variety of suicide methods including hanging, poisoning, slashing the blue calorie's little blue wrists with a straightedge razor, and firing a bullet through its head. You could see the bullet speeding out the far side of the calorie's head, trailed by splattering blood.

The ad guys would very quickly discover that when you try to attract one demographic on the Internet, you are likely to be as victimized by Jurassic Park syndrome as the Odeo guys were with TWTTR. It took less than twenty-four hours for word to burst out beyond the intended niche.

A tweeter named Chris Abraham (@chrisabraham) caught wind of the ads. He pointed them out to Matthew Creamer at *Ad Age*, who picked up the news and ran it as the lead story in both the online and paper versions of his publication on January 19, 2008. Abraham then used his Twitter account to point to the article. His post was retweeted dozens of times in a short period. Unlike the Motrin Moms ads, there were no defenders of the ads at all.

Suicide is the number eleven cause of death according to the UN

World Health Organization, who reported in 2006 that one in every forty deaths is self-inflicted. In 2000 alone there were one million suicides worldwide, more than the number of soldiers killed in any war since 1945.

In 2004, 32,439 people committed suicide in the United States. One of them was the older sister of Christine Lu (@christinelu). So when Christine saw Creamer's article, she promptly tweeted a terse response: "Dear Pepsi & BBDO—seeing as how my sister committed suicide, using it to sell soda isn't funny to me. Sorry."

As Lu told me, Twitterville response was immediate, but it was less visible than it had been during the Motrin Moms incident. Out of public view, she was getting countless e-mails and direct messages from people who had suffered a loss similar to hers. "People don't like to talk about suicide," Lu said. "It's a painful and personal topic for those affected by it."

I was among those who had sent Christine a private note telling her of the pain I sometimes still feel from a loss of a twenty-year-old cousin more than forty years ago.

However, someone else was more public. B. Bonin Bough (@boughb) tweeted his experience of having lost his best friend to suicide. He happens to be the director of social media for Pepsi. Bough apologized on behalf of his company. Minutes before, another PepsiCo International communications manager tweeted a public apology to Lu, and informed her that the ads would be taken down. The BBDO ad agency had been terminated.

Looking back a few months later, it's interesting to me that the Motrin Moms ads are still discussed, but as far as I can tell, the Pepsi Suicide ads are apparently forgotten.

Is it because even in today's transparent society, suicide remains one of those few subjects most people don't wish to discuss in public?

That would be one plausible explanation, but there is another.

Unlike Motrin, Pepsi had joined the conversation. B. Bonin Bough had joined PepsiCo just five weeks earlier. But he was a social media veteran, and understood how it worked. He also had already established himself in Twitter and as a blogger.

He rapidly joined the conversation. He showed a personal reason why he cared. He had already established credibility, and people were willing to take his word for it. The company had acted quickly in spiking both the ads and the team that had come with them.

But there is a single common point between both of these stories, one that could not have happened at all before social media and one that still might not have occurred until after Twitter.

The user has gained control.

Classic marketers had tried traditional attention-getting tactics in social media venues, and the desired result had backfired on ad people who did not understand how conversational media worked. At least one person from Pepsi however, had been watching social media, and saved his employer from a potentially damaging crisis.

The other company took the weekend off.

> @jaybecton: I'm listening to the Dixie Chicks voluntarily. HOW WILL I EVER GET TO HEAVEN NOW?

Driving Fans onto the Right Path

I am a recovering publicist.

I used to own a Silicon Valley PR firm called SIPR. One day a Chicago law firm sent me a cease-and-desist letter directing me to stop using my four-letter name, which was an acronym for "Shel Israel PR." They represented a food company who distributed pork rinds. The company used the same four letters in its logo and had been using them prior to my agency's existence.

I had to hire a lawyer. He wrote a letter saying that I would agree not to go into the pork rind business if the Chicago company stayed out of technology PR.

I never heard from the company again. But the incident cost me money and sleep. Like most small business people I have never felt kindly about large businesses sending cease-and-desist letters to small ones.

So when I learned that Ford Motor Company had sent a C&D letter to the Ford Ranger fan site demanding $5,000 in financial compensation, my gut instinct was the same as the angry voices expressing views in Twitter and on blogs.

But there was one catch: Scott Monty (@scottmonty). Monty had recently joined Ford as their top social media officer. He and I knew each other through participation in the Society for New Communications Research. We were both from Massachusetts. We knew many of the same people, and we were also both Boston Red Sox fans. This is relevant because we tend to trust people we know and with whom we share common interests.

But more relevant than that was his established track record on Twitter. He had been there for nearly two years, had over 5,500 followers, and had posted over 8,000 updates. In all that time, I had never heard anyone accuse him of speaking a falsehood.

Scott had credibility with me and with others who followed him. While I tend to sympathize with little guys when it appears big guys are pushing them around, I did not know the Ford Ranger fans. In fact, I did not realize that the Ford Ranger actually had fans.

So when Monty asked people to hold off until he could investigate the matter, I was among many who were willing to cut him some slack.

Monty had first learned there was an incident just before he went to bed at 10:30 PM. He was awake with coffee in hand, checking

Twitter at five-thirty the next morning. The story had spread as he'd slept. The Ford Ranger fan site owner had been trying to drum up sympathy. Now other fan sites wanted to know if Ford planned to come after them as well.

Monty knew a major PR headache when he saw one. He understood that speed was essential in stopping a wildfire. He gulped down his coffee and drove to his Dearborn office.

In his first few minutes at the Ford Motor Company's campus, he told me, "I realized that this was not just confined to a couple of sites or Twitter. Our customer service people had received over a thousand e-mails overnight expressing anger at Ford." He started tracking down the legal people, confirming that an incident had indeed occurred.

He determined that a letter had been sent to The Ranger Station (therangerstation.com) demanding a payment for trademark infringement and that the site stop using the Ranger name in its URL. But, Monty was told emphatically, Ford had good reason to pursue the issue.

While he had been fact finding, the Twitter amplification engine was revving up. Ford was being called a bully. Some of the worst blasts were coming from some of its usually loyal fans.

That was when Monty logged onto Twitter and asked people to hold off: there was "more to the story." That slowed it down a couple of notches. A little later he added to the tweetstream that there was counterfeiting of Ford trademark properties involved. That froze the conversation. He had bought some more time.

A few years ago "some time" in a PR crisis used to translate into about a week. Monty figured, with this being on Twitter, he had bought Ford a few hours at best.

He used those hours mostly on Twitter Search. He needed to understand who was saying what about the incident. He used Twitter Search to separate facts from noise. First Monty had to filter out all the Ford mentions not relevant to the issue. It's surprising how many references to Gerald, Betty, Harrison, Lita, even Henry and Edsel Ford you find in Twitterville.

Every time he saw someone posting about the incident, he jumped into the conversation, confirming there was an incident but there was more to the story, and repeating his request for time to dig out the full story.

At about 4:00 PM, Monty finally got authorization to post Ford's version. It was a long and polite post. His key point was, "What was not mentioned was that TheRangerStation.com was selling counterfeit Ford-brand merchandise on the site. . . . We cannot let something like that pass."

He got the site owner to confirm that he had omitted the counterfeiting part when he had told the world about the C&D letter. Monty also announced that Ford would license its name and trademarks to fan sites and other sites, so long as counterfeit goods were removed. Since TheRangerStation.com was now complying, Monty wrote, Ford was encouraging it to keep its name, and the $5,000 demand had been withdrawn.

Almost simultaneously, the Ranger fan site owner posted a notice confirming Monty's side of the story.

Monty tweeted links to both his and the fan site statements. He asked people to retweet the links so that misinformation could be squelched, and hundreds of Monty followers did precisely that.

Monty could go home for dinner that night. It had been a hell of a day, but the entire disaster had been turned around in less than a day, mostly through the efforts of one social media professional.

"Would this have worked for Ford if we didn't have a Twitter presence?" Monty asked. "It would have been far slower, and the response would have had a much smaller impact. Searching Twitter throughout the day kept me in the loop with what was being posted and where—it was the Country Store, where people came in and out and shared their gossip, and there I was, sitting by the pickle barrel."

There is another fundamental issue: if your company finds itself in a reputation crisis, it is highly likely to spill into the social media. It is very smart to join Twitterville and establish your credibility before your company's reputation depends on it.

PART 2

What They're Doing

CHAPTER 6

The Twitterville Marketplace

Previously, I talked about the activities that seem to have become Twitterville's building blocks. Very few of the incidents occurred because people were intending to create what is now a community of over thirty million people discussing thousands of topics every day.

These building blocks are for the most part, for just the downtown business section. I use a big tent definition of business that includes anything from a home office to a global enterprise. I also include government, the media, and nonprofits.

The following chapters look at each of these sectors. I've tried to find success stories of companies from a broad cross section. I hope some will be useful to you; many may at least be interesting.

I've already told you about a few global companies. In fact, any business entity that is using social media or the Internet is now considered a global company. This section profiles five large and branded entities, each of which is using Twitter in a decidedly different fashion, each of which has achieved significant success for their brand and their business.

But first, I want to back up a few decades to give you some

historic perspective on what happened before Twitterville, and how things have evolved.

Two Oceans, One Screen

I was seven years old in 1951, when my parents bought our first TV set. The neighbors watched with us as two burly guys brought the big box with a small screen carefully into our living room. A third guy climbed onto our roof and attached an eight-foot-high antenna.

Ours was the first set on the block, and it gave us status. The antenna made our house—for what would be a very short time—the tallest one on the block, sort of a feather in our cap. Neighbors asked to come see this amazing device.

Until then, our living room had been a place where people sat face-to-face and talked, laughed, and argued with each other. Now our furniture was rearranged so that we all faced this new, mysterious screen. We talked among ourselves less. Instead we passively watched programs broadcast from three channels coming from as far as sixty miles away.

We didn't mind the snow that flecked our black-and-white screen. We watched a kids' puppet program called *The Howdy Doody Show,* and I still remember all the characters.

One of these shows was actually taking place in California on the other side of the continent; we all marveled that somehow we could be sitting in New Bedford, Massachusetts, watching a comedian named Milton Berle live from California.

There were several other factors at work here. One was our family's presumption that we were seeing content for the price of a TV set, while sponsors and advertisers had a different—and more correct—viewpoint.

Second, and more important, was that our world had abruptly

become a lot bigger. Until then, most of what we saw and talked about happened inside the geographic confines of New Bedford.

But now we were being entertained by other people in other places. And families in Mississippi and Nebraska and North Dakota were all seeing and talking about the same thing at the same time. This changed our culture in many ways. It made us see our similarities and sometimes it made us understand our differences. TV reorganized American culture along the lines of who watched what program at 7:00 PM on Sunday nights.

Before my family got a TV, I thought Mississippi was a different world than New Bedford, Massachusetts. But now I had something in common with people there: we both watched and laughed at the same TV content. If we met, TV gave us a common ground.

Also, we were likely to share knowledge and perceptions of the ads we saw as we watched what we thought was free entertainment.

All of this struck me when I was that young. I remember the defining moment for me. It came on a Sunday night in November 1951, when the legendary newscaster Edward R. Murrow debuted a new program called *See It Now*. I was among those who viewed something no one had ever seen before—the Atlantic and Pacific oceans on the same screen at the same time.

To my way of thinking, that moment is a significant dot on a continuum that began a lengthy and amazing progression to Twitterville, and is why businesses are joining in such accelerating numbers. It certainly was not the first dot on that continuum, which probably happened when our ancestors were in caves. And most certainly it will not be the last dot.

Yet it was a point that started making people in diverse places feel that it was normal to share information and entertainment from far away.

Not only did people adjust, so did businesses. In 1951, when TV was stampeding into American homes, you had to be very big to take advantage of the new technology through sponsorship. By 2007 you could be a one-person operation using Internet technology to have a global presence. Branding could become a personal thing.

By the time we got to Twitter in March 2007, it was normal for people to talk with other people in public in a place that was farther away than the Atlantic is from the Pacific. That place is the Internet; you can't really touch it or feel it, yet as Charlene Li told you in the foreword, Twitter is "a conversation." And as *Cluetrain* readers will note: that's what markets are.

In 1951 television changed marketing. It was an apex in what is usually called mass marketing. Yet TV was not an actual market-place, because it afforded no direct interaction. If you didn't like what the marketer was saying, you could shout at your TV set, but the marketer never heard you. You could take a refrigerator break, or eventually use a mute button. The best TV technology has gotten to in terms of user empowerment is the TiVo fast forward button.

But television did change the marketplace. In many ways it became the expediter of today's mass-merchandising systems—the chains, the franchises, and the big-box stores.

In 2007, with less drama than Edward R. Murrow used, Twitter formed a new marketplace in the hallways of SXSW. It was far from the first disrupter to mass marketing, but it would reveal itself to be the most disruptive to date because it was so up close and personal.

And that's why so many companies of all types and sizes are rushing into Twitterville even as I write these words. For the most part, it is making personal brands of company representatives more important than the corporate brand itself, as a subsequent chapter points out.

> @pistachio: Resolutions born of criticism and self-loathing are almost always bound to fail. You have to care deeply for the person you want to help (you).

Golden Moments

Every market has unique characteristics. Television's was that you could sit in a studio in Burbank, California, and put ads in front of the eyes of people all over the world. This was a golden moment in broadcast or mass media marketing.

Twitterville is a golden moment in a new approach, one that I call massive micro marketing. It is a conversation, rather than a monologue. It's also more personal. In Twitter, what the community thinks of an individual usually has more value in more cases than does traditional brand identity.

But as another chapter will examine, some enterprises have brought brand strategies into Twitterville with great success. These seem to have kinder, gentler approaches to branding and the best of them usually let you know that your conversation is with a real human and not a logo.

Let's start by looking at some of the world's largest companies and see how they use Twitter to demonstrate a very local touch.

CHAPTER 7

Global Companies, Local Touch

I n 1999, when Nick Swinmurn was shopping for shoes in a San Francisco mall, one store had the right size, but not the color he wanted. The next had the right color, but not the size, and the third was out of stock altogether.

He muttered the magic words that have started many great companies: "There's gotta be a better way." Looking for that better way took him to the Internet, where he founded Zappos (zappos.com), a name derived from "zapatos," the Spanish word for shoes.

Zappos soon became the largest online shoe store, but that was just a start. Over the next decade, it started offering accessories, clothing, watches, eyewear, and more. In terms of revenue it went from an annual return of, in Swinmurn's words, "nearly nothing," to grossing over $1 billion in merchandise sales in 2008.

The company had a couple of outlet stores for a while, but mostly its presence has been online. Its merchants have almost never been able to interact face-to-face with a customer. Nearly all its transactions take place over the Internet or by phone.

Yet customers gush about the close, personal service they receive from Zappos. They keep coming back. They urge their friends to try Zappos. Researching this chapter, I went to Twitter and asked for

Zappos horror stories. What I received were fifteen testimonials, a report that one customer suffered a paper burn while opening a Zappos package and a warning that I should stop picking on those great folks at Zappos.

So what is this company's secret? Why do Zappos's customers serve as its volunteer corps of company champions instead of just buying shoes and sunglasses?

According to Tony Hsieh (@zappos), the CEO and the driving force behind the company's unique corporate culture, Zappos is "a service company that just happens to sell shoes." It's an interesting statement, and as you drill into it, you find every aspect of the company is focused on providing superior services to customers despite facelessness on both sides.

Hsieh told me he never set out to build an e-tail monolith. Instead he built a culture.

"We hire people who are passionate about customer support," he said. "I don't much care how they feel about shoes. We believe that if we get the culture right, then most of the other stuff—like great customer service and building a great brand—will happen naturally."

To create the culture he felt Zappos needed, he moved the company from San Francisco, with its deep technology talent, to the Las Vegas area, where the human-resource pool is deep in call-center experience.

Hsieh is tightfisted in spending promotional dollars. He and Zappos team members attend a few industry events, but the company has consistently maintained a near-zero PR budget. "I prefer investing money in improving customer experience to marketing," he said.

When recruits start employee training, they receive a company "culture book" rather than an employee handbook. Training lasts four weeks; half of it is spent talking with customers, under supervision, in the call center. This includes new senior executives.

Hsieh then tries to get everyone who successfully completes the course to immediately quit. He offers each a $2,000 cash incentive to just go away and never come back.

"I want people who feel like they belong here. Who want to be a part of this culture," Hsieh explains. Some people take him up on the deal. Over 90 percent stay.

Hsieh was yet another business observer in the SXSW 2007 hallways. Along with Ricardo Guerrero and Lionel Menchaca, he too stumbled upon Twitter. Like the others, he saw very little business benefit at first, but enjoyed getting an inside line on conference parties.

Back home after the show, he talked with a few friends on Twitter. Unlike Guerrero, he noticed an immediate benefit. He could stay closer with people who mattered to him on Twitter than he had been doing via e-mail, phone, or other social media platforms.

Hsieh figured if Twitter could help him get closer to his friends, maybe it could do the same for Zappos and its customers. So he injected Twitter into company culture. He showed the new tool to some staff members, and encouraged them to join his Twitter conversations. Next he went after recruits, introducing Twitter in Zappos orientations. Once these seeds were planted, "Other employees just gravitated to it naturally," Hsieh recalled.

By the end of 2008, there were 435 Zappos employees on Twitter, about 30 percent of the company. They talk with one another and to customers. If customers or prospects visit the Zappos.com static Web site where transactions take place, the site encourages those visitors to join their Twitter conversation.

Like Binhammer, the Zappos employees don't just talk shop, and they never shill product, but they do answer company and product customer questions. At first glance, a skeptical visitor might think this is a waste of employee time.

But when you think about it, the banter is pretty much like a showroom salesperson who begins a conversation saying, "Nice day, isn't it?" In the real world we don't start very many business conversations with business. Buyers and sellers often spend a little time getting to know each other before getting around to transaction talk.

There's also a good likelihood that potential customers do a little lurking, just like Binhammer and Menchaca did when they were new to Twitterville. Newcomers can watch the Zappos tweetstream and get a sense of its culture. They can assess the credibility of Zappos sales operatives before they make a call, place an online order, or ask a question in Twitterville.

"Twitter allows us to both build and expose company culture internally to employees and externally to customers. Part of the Zappos brand is about forming personal connections, and that happens through the telephone as well as through Twitter," Hsieh said.

Here's a company that almost never has a face-to-face encounter with customers. And here's Twitter allowing this company to give a close personal touch to customers whose eyes they never see—and vice versa.

But what about the reverse situation? What about a company whose customers have been accustomed to sitting across from a company representative year after year?

Could Twitter be any help to them? You bet.

> @palafo: @scottsimpson I'm more interested in the new Amazon Kindle Nano: a $12, single-title device printed on "paper."

A Taxing Situation

The poet T. S. Eliot wrote that April is the cruelest month. This is evidence that he was born and raised in the United States, when federal and state taxes are due.

This has been the traditional harvest time for H&R Block, America's granddaddy of tax preparation services. Historically, the company has had no trouble getting closer with its customers, most of whom have been coming to H&R Block for years, usually in a strip-mall storefront located close to where they live. They sit face-to-face with an H&R Block representative—again, often the same one they have been seeing for years. Some still arrive carrying shoe boxes filled with receipts and tax records.

Those are not likely to be Zappos shoe boxes. While the prototypical Zappos customer is young and comfortable using online transactions, the prototypical H&R Block customer has, until recently, skewed older and has also been much less comfortable in digital environments.

H&R Block has an aging customer base, which is not good for any company in the long term. I call it the Cadillac factor. For years, General Motors's top-of-the-line car was the symbol of luxury for a generation that came of age in the 1950s. Like the rest of us, each year that generation got older. Eventually they got too old to drive, and started dying off. Those who achieved affluence in the generations that have followed came to view Cadillac as an old man's car, and opted to buy other luxury brands.

H&R Block understood the perils of following that road. By the early 2000s the company's image had become tied to older taxpayers, a surefire way to lose younger demographics who will live and pay taxes longer.

That brings us to the third and most important point. Those younger taxpayers are more easily found on the Internet than they are in strip malls. They are more prone to have electronic check-paying systems, and are often more comfortable filing their own taxes.

H&R Block seemingly ignored all this for over two decades, opening a huge window of opportunity for TurboTax, acquired in 1993 by Intuit. Now the world leader in personal financial software, Intuit holds over 75 percent of the online tax preparation market as of April 2009.

Those numbers become more daunting if you are after younger tax preparers, who presumably are more prone to file online.

In 2007, with an eye toward establishing an online presence, H&R Block recruited Paula W. Drum (@pauladrum), a veteran Internet marketer. Almost immediately, she began an ambitious social media campaign that would encompass blogs, Facebook, Second Life, MySpace, and YouTube.

In 2008, almost as an add-on, H&R Block started tweeting as @ HRBlock. As has so often been the case, the company's initial strategy was to use Twitter as a broadcast mechanism to distribute H&R Block messages.

"Big mistake," Amy Worley, who started the Twitter program, told me. "We'd just post updates out to the world and then go away. Nothing happened."

After a while, Block started talking less and listening more. It abandoned its original drive-by tweeting style and began to engage in other people's conversations. Drum told me that they soon discovered "there's no place like Twitter for connecting with customers online." They began to use the direct message feature to give free, private taxpayer tips.

But the more time H&R Block employees spent in Twitterville, the more business value they found. They started to learn valuable information by joining other people's conversations—where they learned from people more knowledgeable than they were about these issues. "Listening made us a lot smarter on how to succeed with online strategies," Drum said.

The results are still too early to measure in terms of market share, but Drum is certain that Twitter has played a fundamental role in reversing the Cadillac factor. H&R Block is building an online business that is gaining momentum. "We are having conversations with more and more young adults, and I'm certain that many are becoming customers whom we can retain for years to come," she said. The fact that this company is using social media while TurboTax (to date) is not positions H&R Block as being more digitally savvy than their competitor.

H&R Block has faced a second issue that the company believes Twitter will help. It currently has a seasonal business, but Twitter has given them a way to engage people in tax-related conversations year-round, and in these conversations the company gets to point to their expanding array of digital products, which include TaxCut, a direct TurboTax competitor, as well as online consulting services covering timely financial issues such as mortgage, banking, and investment guidance.

These days, people are thinking more and more about tax-related issues year-round. Drum says the economy makes more people want to talk with them.

"Sometimes we use Twitter just to give a person moral support," Drum said. "Twitter lets us demonstrate that we care. We answer questions. We solve problems. We are able to humanize our brand," she said.

Drum says a large percentage of H&R Block's Twitter followers are between the ages of twenty-five and forty-five. As a matter of fact, these were the people that Block followed into social media to begin with. "The interesting thing about the newer generation is that they are not technology adopters—they are technology expectants who want to interact with businesses on their own terms." In short, if you want younger people for customers, you need to find them online and let them use the technology tools they have grown up using comfortably."

Drum also warned traditional marketers, "Twitter is a bad place to try to broadcast mass messages. You are just never going to have the same reach as a television ad. What Twitter does offer is a golden opportunity to listen to people and find out how they perceive your brand."

@TomTravel2: Think about it, none of us follow the exact same people so we all see a unique set of Tweets no one else sees. Twowflakes of a sort.

Live-Tweeted Surgery

While I was writing *Twitterville*, unexpected events kept popping up in unlikely places. Among those that caught me by surprise took place at Henry Ford Hospital in Detroit, part of the larger Henry Ford Health System (HFHS).

Doctors at Henry Ford were about to perform robotic surgery to remove a prostate cancer, which in itself was not unusual. But this procedure would be described live over Twitter.

The primary purpose was for medical education. Simultaneous to the procedure would be a urology conference at the Bellagio hotel in Las Vegas attended by 450 medical professionals.

The idea to live-tweet the surgery came from an HFHS brainstorming session on how to communicate to this audience. They decided to stream it in public, allowing anyone who wished to follow the tweets.

No, the surgeon did not have a scalpel in one hand and an iPhone in the other. Dr. Khurshid A. Guru, the primary surgeon, didn't actually touch the patient. His hands were on the controls of a medical robot that would perform the procedure with greater precision and less intrusively than a human could.

Two tweeting doctors were in the operating room, sufficiently physically removed to ensure no breech of the sterile procedure. They watched on a large 3-D monitor along with other members of the surgical team, and posted about each step of the successful surgery. Conference participants—indeed, anyone else—could ask questions in real time, and the two tweeting doctors replied.

A third tweeter in the operating room was William Ferris (@BillFer), who answered most of the nontechnical questions that came in. Ferris is HFHS web manager, a social media champion, and the guy who brought Twitter into the organization. He explained to me that the health-care industry was becoming a lot more active in social media than I had thought was the case. HFHS was using blogs, podcasts, YouTube, and most recently Twitter.

A significant portion is directed toward patient conversations. For example, a certified nurse-midwife leads a patient-support group on menopause via an HFHS blog (menopausesupportblog.com).

Up until the surgery, however, HFHS didn't do much more with Twitter than link to press releases, promote classes, and point to other hospital-related content.

Ferris told me that live tweeting allowed direct engagement with conference participants, but it also provided an archive for future reference. HFHS used a hashtag (#HFOR) so people could go back later and see the entire conversation as it took place, just as #MotrinMoms followers did.

But, as Ferris noted, education is not just for medical professionals; it's also for patients, who can now follow a road map of what will happen in the operating room.

Henry Ford Hospital has subsequently performed three live-tweet surgeries, one in which a patient's cranium was removed while he was still conscious. They have added both YouTube and TwitPic components to their social media coverage.

The ultimate result, Ferris said, is that the hospital is "humanizing surgery," something that almost anyone who has either undergone surgery or watched a loved one go through it would consider an improvement.

While the primary purpose may be educational, Ferris readily notes that the PR benefits have become clear. The hospital is seen as an innovator at a time when most people see a need for innovation in health care. It is included in news stories about a rebirth in Detroit in a post-automotive economy. "Medical and related organizations have some of the same goals as most other organizations, such as recruitment and brand building, which aren't industry specific at all."

In short, live-tweeting surgery is good for business. Henry Ford's first such surgery generated attention first on Twitter, followed by mainstream press coverage. By May 2009, five additional hospitals had begun to live-tweet surgeries and other medical procedures. Most are incorporating video components as well.

The Hospital's Fault

Ferris was right. There is a good deal going on in social media and health care. And the applications are quite diverse.

Moving a hometown hospital off an earthquake fault line and selling it to a hospital chain is pretty far removed from live-tweeted surgery, but that's what happened in the quiet community of Castro Valley, California, where the most earth-shattering events are usually caused by the Hayward Fault, an earthquake line that gets active every few years.

Since 1954, the local Eden Medical Center, which was built close to the Hayward Fault, has withstood numerous large and small tremors.

By 2008, however, there was a question of how many more the aging facility could withstand. Everyone involved agreed that it was time to build a new facility. Except that economic down times had come to this suburban unincorporated community of about sixty thousand, and hospitals are expensive to build—costing in the United States an average of $2.5 million per bed.

Castro Valley followed a health-care trend and turned the responsibility over to a hospital chain, Sutter Health, a $5 billion enterprise that owns twenty-six hospitals and numerous clinics in northern California. The operation is a moneymaker with a good reputation in managing health facilities.

But there is something that does not necessarily love or trust $5 billion corporations when it comes to caring for someone you love. Understanding it needed to build community trust, Sutter turned to two local communications firms, headed respectively by Cathryn Hrudicka (@CreativeSage) and Shelly Gordon (@g2comm).

The two immediately started using social media tools including Facebook, LinkedIn, FriendFeed, MySpace, and YouTube as well as existing Castro Valley networks to educate the community. They set up a Twitter account, @SutterEdenMed, that would serve as the front line of its communications campaign. Hrudicka and Gordon were transparent about the fact that they were paid communications officers contracted by Sutter Health.

"We used Twitter to chat with people about all the issues involved in the building of a new hospital and medical center," Hrudicka explained. "To advocate for the Environmental Impact Report; to inform people about our blog posts and other social network discussion topics; to inform people about key community events, town halls, and hearings; and to communicate with the media."

They even used it to recruit local staff for other Sutter facilities at exactly a time when jobs in northern California were becoming scarcer.

"We received many comments from people who were impressed with how we used social media to keep our community informed and to honestly respond to concerns, issues, and questions," Hrudicka said.

In the spring of 2009, the ground breaking for the new facility began with little or no opposition. Partly because of Twitter, the community understood the need for the project, and supported it.

When I tweeted that I was writing about a twittering health-care facility, I caught immediate flack. I was sent links to blogs explaining why health services should not engage in social media, that it was illegal for medical people to give advice online, and so forth. This last statement is not exactly true; my doctor uses secure e-mail to give me medical advice, saving us both time and expense. Not all health-industry community issues are sensitive or diagnostic in nature. Health facilities and health care are issues people talk about. To me it makes a good deal of sense that the health-care providers join the conversation where they can better hear, and respond to concerns of the people they serve.

The @SutterEdenMed Twitter account picked up followers from the health-care industry in North America as well as in twenty-five other countries, which would indicate a hunger for greater health services information on social media.

> @Spin i've been working on genealogy stuff the past week; It's like the social networking of dead people.

Rubbermaid's Lethal Generosity

As personal and sensitive as health-care issues can be, I couldn't think of any reason why anyone could possibly feel passionate enough to tweet about dish drainers. So I was surprised when a few people in Twitterville kept pointing me to the company that makes the old-tech gizmo that many of us use to air-dry our dishes.

Newell Rubbermaid (@Rubbermaid) is a $6 billion, seventy-year-old manufacturer of bins, racks, boxes, dividers, the aforementioned dish drainers, and assorted miscellaneous items designed to save space. Mostly Rubbermaid sells merchandise through a broad global supply chain of independent retailers. Historically its only communications with end users has been through brand advertising, reserving customer conversations to local retailers.

The folks at Rubbermaid probably understand that although their products are useful, even reliable, they just don't evoke much passion. Yet there is a group who really does care a great deal about such things.

The National Association of Professional Organizers (NAPO, at napo.net) is a community of people who organize home and office spaces for a living. As you might expect, NAPO is neatly divided into geographic chapters who meet and hold periodic national conferences.

Until Twitter came along, however, there wasn't a way for NAPO members to get together in between these big conferences.

Enter Jim Deitzel, Rubbermaid's e-marketing manager. He's principal writer for the company blog, and was an early and active user of Flickr and YouTube. Like almost every early business user, he sidled into Twitterville by starting an account, then doing almost nothing with it for several months.

Although the account is called @Rubbermaid, people who go to the page see "currently tweeted by Jim Deitzel, a way to reveal the human on the company end, while leaving the door open for future changes." Making clear who he is is part of Deitzel's strategy he told me. "I wanted people to know who they were talking with, and I wanted them to get to know me personally. It's in Rubbermaid's interest for people to know they can count on me, not just a logo, to answer questions, talk about partnerships, and just feel connected."

As is almost always the case, he tweeted at first to point to other Rubbermaid content. Then one day in May 2008, Deitzel started wondering where professional room organizers hung out online.

He stumbled across a couple of them on Twitter, and started engaging them in conversations; through them he discovered still more organizers. Eventually he posted a list of all the professional organizers on Twitter. Since that required a lot more than 140 characters, he blogged it, then used Twitter to point to the post.

Giving people recognition usually generates gratitude. He got it enthusiastically. Organizers who were not yet on Twitter joined just to be part of the conversation.

This is an example of what I call lethal generosity, a phenomenon used by the smartest of companies. In social media the greatest influence invariably goes to the most generous participants, not the loudest. So if you join a community where a competitor exists, or is free to join, and you give more to that community than the competitor, the other player is forced either to follow you or to abstain from participating in a place where customers spend time.

Deitzel did not form a room-organizer community on Twitter. He found one. All he did was provide a little glue that made it cohesive. Then the community gave him influence—he could not simply take or declare influence. It just doesn't work that way.

The result was that he and Rubbermaid became the professional organizer neighborhood's Twitterville community center.

When a competitor eventually finds the NAPO Twitterville neighborhood, it is unlikely to be able to displace Rubbermaid from its leadership position. The competitor can choose to spend money to sponsor the next NAPO conference, perhaps with a big display banner. It can advertise in a trade publication, or it can even join the Twitterville organizer neighborhood. However, it would have to "out-generous" Deitzel to displace his prominent position.

Deitzel has also learned the reciprocal nature of Twitter. When he blogged about a home garage makeover project, he had gotten a few suggestions. Most people, it seems, like to be asked about something they know about. So when Deitzel decided to reorganize his home pantry, he reached out. He posted a blog with pictures showing that he clearly needed help.

When he pointed to the blog post on Twitter this time, he got plenty of suggestions. When he completed the project (using an array of Rubbermaid products, naturally), he posted a second blog with a little video showing his spiffy renovated pantry. He thanked people for their help, and got numerous reviews along with a few additional useful suggestions.

At no point has Deitzel ever used either the blog or Twitter to boast of Rubbermaid's superiority in any way. Instead he braids

Twitter and his blog together as interactive helpers for anyone facing organizational challenges.

One NAPO member that Deitzel met in Twitterville is Lorie Marrero (@ClutterDiet). As part of his Twitter outreach program, Deitzel invited organizers to be interviewed for the Rubbermaid Web site. Marrero jumped on it, and a phone chat soon followed. Marrero agreed to be interviewed for articles on organizing closets being developed by Rubbermaid's PR agency, which used her as an expert resource. Rubbermaid posted the articles online and mailed them out to the company's huge mail list, which of course helped Marrero's business.

Deitzel has since done the same for numerous other professional organizers. He has also helped Marrero and others to get better deals as resellers, despite the fact that professional organizers tend to buy in low volume.

None of this would have happened without the Twitter piece of Rubbermaid's strategy. Said Marrero, "Twitter has made a huge difference in my relationship with Rubbermaid."

> @HowardOwens: I can still get very romantic about newspapers, but romanticism no longer plays a role in my thinking about the business.

Molson's Golden Giving

Molson uses generosity as a key component of its social media strategy, but it has an entirely different customer base than Rubbermaid. It helps its brand by being generous to many who are in great need.

Generosity is not what most of us expect when we talk about big brewing companies and branding campaigns. It's usually more about events in a roaring stadium or young people partying on beaches.

That's why I was surprised to learn that Molson Canada, North

America's oldest brewery, has an active branding program that helps feed homeless people and invests more in safe transportation on New Year's Eve than on alcohol-centered events.

But Molson, or at least Molson's small social media team, headed by the affable Ferg Devins (@MolsonFerg) seems to have passions that run in two directions. First, he's clearly a marketing guy who wants to sell beer. But second, he believes in supporting Canadian communities, particularly those who need the most help. In our conversation he mentioned the company motto, "Proud to do our part," often enough to convince me it guided a benevolent social media branding strategy.

Although Molson rarely initiates a community generosity project, it often helps local organizers reach its goals. For example, when Toronto's Daily Bread Food Bank (dailybread.org) announced at the beginning of the 2008 winter holiday season that contributions had been sparse and unless something changed, homeless people would go hungry.

Austin Hill (@AustinHill), perhaps Canada's best-known social entrepreneur, jumped on Twitter urging others in the Toronto area to help him do something about the situation. Almost immediately a small neighborhood formed to raise money for the food bank. It was called HoHoTO (@hohoto), and primarily through Twitter, it planned and started promoting a fund-raising event to be held in Toronto's trendy Mod Club a scant two weeks from the announcement date.

Tonia Hammer (@ToniaHammer), who brought Twitter into Molson, was the first in her company to plug in, bringing Devins's attention to the project soon after. The two were already known in the Toronto Twitter community, so when they offered Molson's help, the community accepted it as sincere, rather than a cheap attempt to grab publicity.

The Molson team spread the word, using Twitter to urge a widening audience to attend the event and contribute financially. Their efforts produced more attendees and sponsors. To that, they added a top-off, something they had done for other causes as well. Their deal was that whatever amount got raised, Molson would top it off to the next big round number, thus doing their part as the company slogan claimed.

HoHoTO was attended by six hundred Toronto-area Twitterville enthusiasts and their friends. The top-off gave the food bank a total of $25,000, an amount that made a difference to a good number of homeless people. Molson was soundly praised.

A few weeks later, when budget problems this time led the Greater Toronto Transit Authority to cancel its traditional New Year's Eve free-ride program to save $85,000, Molson launched a campaign to replace the public cutbacks with private sector donations, starting with its own $20,000 contribution.

In a smart act of lethal generosity, Molson publicly invited arch-competitor Labatt Breweries to join the campaign. Labatt followed Molson's lead.

Not only do the two companies compete for beer buyers, they also compete for talent. So when Malcolm Bastien (@MalcolmBastien), who had worked for Labatt the previous summer, showed up in Tonia Hammer's tweetstream to say he admired Molson's efforts to save a Toronto ride-share program, he may have also inadvertently promoted Molson's recruiting cause.

"That's so cool you do Molson community stuff. I worked at Labatts just over the summer. Need I say more," Bastien, who had returned to college, wrote. He made clear that Labatt did not have any social media programs.

Molson Canada is involved in similar programs nationwide. It contributed in 2008 to the Edmonton Food Bank. In Winnipeg, it teamed up with the Winnipeg Blue Bombers football team in a Free Ride Home program. All the time they were talking it up for these causes on Twitter.

"When Tonia first turned me on to Twitter I thought it was a bunch of mumbo jumbo. Now I realize it moved us from talking *at* the community to talking *with* the community," Devins said.

Observed Tris Hussey (@TrisHussey), a social media journalist and consultant, and one of Canada's most prolific and respected tweeters, "The Molson folk get it from the top down. They keep in touch and step up to the plate. The whole team rocks."

A later chapter will deal with fund-raising for goodwill projects, some of them quite remarkable. There will be other stories of raising money in a short time period, other food banks, and significant acts of generosity.

I've included Molson here, because their generosity is so clearly attached to a large company's branding strategy. Yet it is transparent. The result is that people feel good about the company, while the faces of the company on Twitter feel good about themselves; a few less people go hungry, and a few more people arrive home safely.

I found about two-thirds of the shops of Twitterville are represented by real people, a strategy that I recommend.

Yet other companies take a different view, and are doing quite well by ignoring that level of transparency as the next chapter will show you.

CHAPTER 8

Seeing the Wizard

Chances are you're familiar with *The Wonderful Wizard of Oz*. Dorothy, Toto, and her friends are out to find the wizard, who is reputed to have special powers and great wisdom. He turns out to be just a regular guy, hiding behind a curtain and deceiving people into thinking he's more than human.

To me, the story's best twist was that the so-called wizard turns out to be not only nice, but actually wise. He has no magic himself, but he gets Dorothy and Toto up and away (okay, Dorothy's magic slippers help a little, but you get my point).

The Twitterville business neighborhood seems to me to be a bit like Oz. You see corporate logo images where human faces should be, and names of recognized brands where tweet authors' names should be. Some of those authors came out from behind their curtains to speak with me. I found them generally to be pretty nice. But, like the wizard, none of them seemed to possess much magic.

They represent companies that decided to join Twitterville so they could extend traditional brand strategies. More often than not, they represent brands you probably know.

I call them "logo" or "branded" tweeters. They are quite popular, despite the fact that I don't think much of the approach. In my view, it is better on any given day to talk with a human than, say, a Coke bottle.

This chapter is intended to give you a sense of the logo tweeters, and for you to decide for yourself what is more beneficial and effective for you and your company—a person or an iconic symbol. But please understand this is not an objective report. I come to logo accounts with an established point of view.

> @Ed_Dale: Twitter is not "getting" followers—it's creating a reason to be followed—you are in the hands of your market—that's how it should be.

The Trumpet-playing Tweeter

With over 200,000 followers in June 2009, @Starbucks was among the most popular of all logo tweeters. The account is primarily unidirectional, offering occasional in-store promotions, including discount Starbucks Gold Cards. However, when a customer asks a specific question, @Starbucks very often answers it, and usually promptly.

The voice behind the @Starbucks curtain belongs to Brad Nelson. Our conversation took place over the course of a week with the exchange of thirty-three e-mails. It took a while to get it started, because Nelson needed PR permission to talk to me. Once that occurred, I found him to be as candid and as likable as anyone I spoke with in researching *Twitterville*.

Nelson revealed to me a loyalty to Starbucks, where he has worked since 1998. I also learned he had a passion for playing trumpet and keyboard in a Seattle rock band called the Preons (ThePreons.com). During our many conversations, he admitted he was spending a lot of personal time building his band's Web site. And like so many twenty-somethings, you could tell he'd really rather be a rock star than the @Starbucks tweeter, but Nelson made it very clear that he loves his day job and he is passionately loyal to his employer.

He began at Starbucks in 1998, when he was still in high school. He started as a barista, a concocter of espresso drinks. By the time we spoke, he had been elevated a few levels; he was part of Starbucks's music business team based in corporate headquarters.

Starbucks picked Nelson to be the voice behind the curtain when it joined Twitter in August 2008. It remains an add-on to his regular music business duties. His easy conversational style works well, and the logo tweet account has been popular from the start.

He sees his company's Twitter presence as a natural extension of CEO Howard Schultz's favorite public statements: "Starbucks is more about people than coffee."

Nelson said, "Twitter lends itself so easily to a casual and conversational tone—much like what you'd find in a Starbucks—and it is a natural and obvious way for a brand to participate in the conversation."

This sounded good, but still I wondered: if Starbucks's CEO says the brand is about people, why doesn't Starbucks encourage its own people to tweet under their own names, thus helping to humanize the brand? Nelson is exactly the kind of young, passionate, informed person who tends to do well in Twitterville.

Personally, I'd rather see his face than the Starbucks mermaid.

Are Brands People?

There are those who see the issue differently. While I was researching this chapter, an argument over logo tweeting flared up in Twitterville. The pot had been stirred by Dr. Mark Drapeau (@cheeky_geeky), consultant to the U.S. Department of Defense. Drapeau posted a blog on Mashable.com, one of the tech industry's most influential blogs, taking a dim view of branded tweet accounts.

"Twitter is about people sharing information with other people," he wrote. "So how do one-dimensional organizational brands fit into this mix? When you really think about it, they don't." Drapeau went on to argue that Twitter charge for allowing logo tweeters, or better yet in his view, "ban them altogether."

While I am not big on branded accounts, I am even smaller on banning content. I'd rather let people decide for themselves.

Besides, the logo tweeters have a fair amount of support from real people and tens of thousands of people who visit logo tweeters every day.

When I posted that I thought logo tweets just don't work as well as having a real person—or people—represent a brand, Kris Colvin (@KrisColvin), managing director of Fuel Labs, a brand identity design firm based in Kansas City, expressed a different view. "I just love seeing my little brand logo twittering. But that's just me."

The irony, I thought, was that Colvin, who makes a living designing brand identities, uses her own name when she tweets. The final twist came just as I was finishing this chapter, when Colvin alerted me that Old Navy had just started a talking mannequin account (@SuperModelquin), which made me wonder how many people enjoy talking with dummies.

Another strong proponent for logo tweeting is Lon Cohen, (@Obilon) a writer-consultant, who sent me a lengthy essay arguing the case for branded accounts. He came to the conclusion that "brands are people too."

As evidence, he outlined the lengthy history of "humanized brands," spotlighting the ageless Betty Crocker, who in 2003 was replaced on her brand logo by a spoon. Crocker was born fully grown in 1924, when General Mills sponsored a live "womanly talk-radio show." Her last name belonged to a corporate executive, her first was selected because it sounded "warm and friendly," and her signature was the work of a corporate secretary.

She acquired her first face in 1936, and it was put on the backs of cake-mix boxes and into ads. She has always been dressed in a tasteful wine colored dress or dark suit. In 1945 *Fortune* magazine named Crocker the second-most popular woman in America, just after Eleanor Roosevelt. By 1986 there had been seven Betty Crockers, sustaining a never-aging image. Of course, each Crocker was a professional model of a particular age, whose contract would be terminated when her physical appearance ran its natural course.

In 1955 Crocker was seen in a series of TV ads giving viewers the impression she was baking those yummy brownies in her own suburban kitchen, rather than at a factory in the Midwest, as was the actual case.

Cohen argues that brands like Betty Crocker have become part of American culture, and are essential to marketing. He believes they will live on even as we move from the Broadcast Era into this new Conversational Age. I agree because there still is TV as well as magazines, and such ads still sell products.

But they are playing to steadily diminishing houses; the return on the sponsorship investment just isn't what it used to be, and probably never will be again. Betty Crocker is not human; she is a contrivance used to sell mass-produced cake mix.

In fact somewhere around 2002, General Mills removed Crocker's ageless white suburban face from its ads and packaging, while letting the signature remain intact. The target demographic had shifted, and her image was turning out to be less appropriate than the spoon that replaced Crocker's face in logos.

Brands are not people, but in Twitterville, it seems to me that brands can be enhanced by letting people represent them in their own voices and showing their own faces. It adds a certain human touch to a company's brand.

I can't prove it, not yet, but I'm betting more people prefer talking to real people than they do to little logos.

But let's get back to Starbucks's Nelson who, I thought, presented a stronger case than Cohen or Colvin. He argued for discoverability. "I don't think that you can underestimate the importance of an easy-to-find URL or account name. Starbucks would not have built up one of the largest Twitter accounts if it were called @BradNelson, since most people don't know me.

"The thing about peoples' relationship with Starbucks is that they don't think of it as a big company they don't know. They tend to think of it as their local coffee shop, the place they hang out in their neighborhood. Starbucks is the people they know who work there. So @Starbucks probably means something to them, when @BradNelson doesn't."

He has a point. But why not follow the Dell team approach and let him tweet as @BradatStarbucks, and encourage other Starbucks employees to join the conversation? Or at least take the Rubbermaid approach and say the tweeter is currently Brad Nelson. Would that help or hurt the Starbucks brand in Twitterville, and would that not be a better reflection of the Starbucks CEO Schultz's contention that Starbucks is mostly about people?

> @copyblogger: I think I need a Twitter hiatus . . . this is getting too compulsive. I'll see you in five minutes.

Voices Behind the Grocer's Shelf

Marla Erwin's (@MarlaErwin) story is similar in many ways to Brad Nelson's. She's one of two primary authors of the @WholeFoods logo account.

She got the job because she pushed for a Whole Foods Twitter account during her job interview that landed her a position as interactive art director for the natural food grocer's Web site. That job takes enough time and energy that she does her @WholeFoods tweeting from home at night. Why bother? "Because it's my passion," she told me.

Like Brad Nelson, I found her open and transparent. I fully agreed with her perception of Twitter's value proposition to Whole Foods. "It gives a clear and immediate picture of what our customers are thinking, and gives us a chance to respond more directly than we can in any other venue," she told me. What she hears in Twitterville directly impacts Web site design and functionality.

Like Nelson, Erwin finds Twitter good for quick marketing promotions, such as walk-in discounts offered only to people who see a tweeted offer.

And finally, like Nelson, she is dead certain that behind-the-curtain tweeting is the right strategy for the well-recognized brand she represents: "We haven't seen any disadvantages at all." She estimated that only about three people out of ten thousand had ever complained about her anonymity.

She gave three reasons for using the branded tweet approach.

1. **Authority.** Whole Foods has more authority in the public eye than does Marla Erwin. By using the brand, she speaks for an entire company and not just an individual.
2. **Boundaries.** On their personal Twitter accounts, Erwin and Wendy Hsia, the other Whole Foods tweeter, discuss such diverse topics as tattoos and politics. Keeping their names off @WholeFoods frees them to voice personal opinions without endangering the brand.
3. **Continuity.** Someday the two current tweeters will be replaced, which means their anonymity makes the changing of the guard seamless to the visitor (just

like when one Betty Crocker model was replaced by another).

She thinks account visitors are sharp enough to realize they are not talking to an actual logo—as she felt I had implied—and that people didn't care who she was.

"If you contact an airline, it is more important that you get the right tickets than knowing the identity of the person on the other end of the phone line," she argued.

Additionally, Erwin expressed strong feelings that there was plenty of humanity displayed through @WholeFoods. For example, during the 2008 Gulf Coast hurricanes, stores remained open in hard-hit areas so people could obtain free safe water and buy groceries, which had become scarce. She used Twitter to keep the communities informed about locations and to give emergency information updates.

I liked Erwin and her passion about her position. However, one of my rebuttals for her position in using a brand name is not the elimination of said brand name, but a more transparent approach to show who the speaker is and what that person's other job responsibilities are. I think when the authors are replaced, regular followers will sense a change, and the new authors will not always understand the history of conversations with regular customers. And again, Jim Deitzel has resolved this by using the word currently in his @Rubbermaid account.

In talking to Erwin, I found it interesting that she was also a Web site designer. She was not a grocer; her passions were closer to interactive designs than in the benefits of growing organic food. I also felt she had a certain feistiness in dealing with my skeptical inquiries. I liked that, and would probably follow and recommend the account if I saw it in her Whole Foods tweets. Yet there she seems consistently mild-mannered, quieter, and from my perspective, less interesting.

> @mancevic: If a tree falls in the forest and it's not on twitter, does it still make a sound?

There's a Beef

These are changing times in ways that transcend just economic difficulties. There are also issues of health and environment. Many people have changed what they eat, and their attitude toward how and where food is raised.

For those who see no need to bother changing lifestyle, Carl's Jr. is a good place. While other fast food brands have moved toward more wholesome cuisine, Carl's is sticking with fat-filled tastiness.

"We don't worry about what the 'food police' are saying about fat grams or calorie counts," Beth Mansfield told me. "Apple slices? Maybe if they were fried."

Mansfield is Twitterville's "@CarlsJr." She also has her own personal account (@BethMansfield), where she impresses me as a smart professional marketer. She also makes it clear that she's a mom in her forties.

But on the @CarlsJr account, she displays a certain "attitude," a West Coast swagger that you usually associate with young, edgy guys, between ages eighteen and thirty-four. That, of course, is the burger franchise's target demographic. It has been for years.

In 2008, Carl's Jr. took direct aim at this demographic with the help of celebrity heiress Paris Hilton, who appeared in a televised ad for the chain clad in a scant, clingy black leather leotard, slathering suds, then hosing an elegant car while biting into a succulent Black Angus Beef Six Dollar Burger while a bluesy version of "I Love Paris" fills the soundtrack. The ad certainly stirred conversations. The eighteen-to-thirty-four male demographic noticed. So did TV censors, who banned it.

So Carl's Jr. posted the Paris ad on YouTube, where you can view it if you click on a button declaring you are eighteen or older. By May 2009 it had been viewed five hundred thousand times.

While the Hilton campaign was involuntarily retired from general audience viewing, the marketing edginess consistently remains in Carl's Jr. campaigns. That's why Mansfield assumes that young, edgy male style when she sits behind the curtain and speaks as @CarlsJr.

She does it well. And that's why, she argues, her name and photo just wouldn't work for the @CarlsJr account.

I completely agree. But it begs the question: why doesn't Carl's Jr. just go out and hire an authentically young and edgy guy to tweet for them?

In fact, why doesn't the company use Twitter to run a contest looking for someone to tweet for them? Then Mansfield, a talented communicator, could enhance the brand by tweeting what it's like for a forty-year-old mom to manage such an almost out-of-control edgy guy.

Mansfield made clear she is a traditional marketer. She came to Twitter with the old-fashioned approach of aggregating customers by delivering messages. Yet she too has started to see the advantages of listening and to joining conversations.

She uses Twitter Search to quickly catch any mention of Carl's Jr. So if someone tweets to a friend to meet at the local franchise, Mansfield catches it and follows as fast as the JetBlue guy in the previous chapter joined a passenger's conversation.

She also trolls for media opportunities. When I talked to her, she was planning a corporate communications campaign to support several new Carl's Jr. openings in Texas. After she found one Houston-based editor, she searched his Twitter follower list on the reasonable assumption that editors and reporters are likely to follow each other—and she started following the additional Texas press members as well.

Mansfield also understands that increasingly, the desired customer will never visit the company's traditional Web site, and that command-and-control message delivery just isn't as effective as joining conversations. "They are very quick to do so on Twitter. Someone needs to be listening and responding.

"I would have never been able to comprehend just a year ago, what Twitter can do. The Motrin Moms dustup was an eye-opener for a lot of executives that Twitter wasn't just an anomaly or something on your to-do list, but was, in fact, an important cog in the marketing wheel."

It makes her see the PR profession from a new perspective. "It's an evolving field in which practitioners must adapt to succeed and social media strategy is something so fluid, that it changes weekly.

"Today I send a press release out on Business Wire (a publicist's subscription-based distribution service). I also send it to media and bloggers using e-mail. Then I post it on PitchEngine.com as a social media release; post it on our company Web site; tweet about it, cross-post to Facebook; and if it involves a commercial, post it to YouTube. Things have sure changed."

Yes, things have surely changed, and marketing continues to transform from message sending to just getting closer to customers.

It will be interesting to see how Carl's Jr. evolves in the coming years.

Evernote

Evernote is a hot Web 2.0 company—maybe not as molten as Twitter, but certainly hot. All Web 2.0 companies use open-source technology that lets you move your productivity from your computer desktop to the Internet.

Evernote is sort of an Internet-based shoe box for just your use or to share with friends. You can clip Internet text, audio, and video content on any subject into one shoe box. You can open as many of these shoe boxes as you want and then retrieve or review all contents from anywhere that allows you Internet access.

Like other Web 2.0 companies, Evernote eschews most traditional marketing to find customers while maintaining a high profile in social media. The company is active on Facebook, YouTube, FriendFeed, LinkedIn, and three microblog platforms including, of course, Twitter.

So I was surprised to discover that a company built on an open-source culture was successfully using mostly a traditional, single direction approach in Twitter. My surprise increased when I discovered that this promising young company had amassed nearly twenty thousand followers by May 2009.

The logo tweet account stays on message. Its posts are all about why and how you could use Evernote. It never asks followers for feedback.

Most of Evernote's posted links send followers only to other Evernote social media sites.

Andrew Sinkov, Evernote's lead marketer and principal tweeter, made it clear when I talked to him that Twitter is at the center of the growing start-up's integrated social media strategy. He updates frequently, and he credits Twitter as an essential component of the company's ability to grow and thrive.

But Sinkov's view is almost the exact opposite of everything I might advise a company to do. Listening to Sinkov, I have to assume he thinks Evernote doesn't "need no steenkin' conversation."

We talked by e-mail, where he described Twitter as a "powerful broadcasting tool" that he uses for marketing messages, user tips, or perhaps to point to an "interesting article," which almost always spotlights Evernote.

Still, he claims Evernote is using Twitter "in an incredibly personal way, akin to receiving an IM message from your close friend," he told me.

I think Sinkov and I may treat our "close friends" differently. I usually inquire about how their families are doing, and what is going on in their lives. My friends and I banter about sports, books, movies, and weather. Sometimes we kid each other. More often, we provide a listening ear and if we can, offer words of support.

Sinkov seems to treat his "close friends" as an audience. "We would not reply publicly to messages, nor would we comment on things unrelated to our product. If successful, we felt that this approach would help build a positive relationship with our brand."

It reminds me of a comment by Steven Maturin, a central character in the fictional Master and Commander series by Patrick O'Brian, my favorite novels. "I thought I had been invited to dinner," Maturin says. "But I discovered I was merely the intended audience."

Evernote's approach has near-military logic behind it. "Each message has a value and a purpose. We tweet only during hours and days when the greatest number of users will be online," Sinkov told me, which must be difficult in the Internet's 24/7 global environment. It's always noon somewhere.

Evernote's logo tweeting strategy is designed to block conversations. "If we had tied Twitter to a person, then there would be a natural tendency towards conversation, and our feeling was that the signal to noise ratio would become unfavorable."

I wonder how many businesses consider customer comments to be noise. Yet I cannot refute that the strategy is working for the company. Evernote is growing, and if you search Twitter elsewhere, you find customers recommending the product.

Even with this policy, Twitterville users have managed to lead Evernote into new market opportunities. For example, the company noticed a large number of adoptions in religious activities. Church leaders post sermons on Evernote, which can be shared with congregations. Divinity students use the service to store and share research notes. The most unexpected tweet came from an individual who recorded his sins in Evernote so that he could remember them for confession.

There are companies whose social media approaches I have disagreed with, two examples being Apple Computer and Google, who seem to me to be pretty command-and-control in their approach. Yet I use the products and services of both companies with gusto. They make great products, and at the end of the day, your relationship with a commercial entity is more about products and services than conversations.

Sometimes you just want to buy a product or book a ticket and in Evernote style, you don't want no steenkin' conversation. Then the interaction can be conducted in other venues, including static Web sites. Twitter works best for conversations. It was designed for that, and your business approach should be to keep that in mind, or so it seems to me.

The next time I write a book I will probably use the Evernote service, despite what I think of their Twitterville approach. They make a great product that will help me be more organized and productive. I need that. But if something comes along to compete with Evernote, I'd be quick to switch, since I will not have a chance to develop a real interactive relationship with the company.

My Evernote lesson is quite simple: it remains far more important to have a great product than it is to be great in social media activities.

@jordanepstein: Make it fun, empower people to simply and easily make a personal difference, and get commitment.

Mayo Clinic

Mayo Clinic, the renowned center for diagnosis and treatment of complex illnesses, had the best reason I heard for logo tweeting: self-defense.

Lee Aase (@LeeAase), Mayo's manager of syndication and social media, is the voice behind the curtain for the clinic. He grabbed the @MayoClinic handle after a British woman commandeered the Mayo Clinic name on MySpace, where she created a logo nearly identical to the Mayo Clinic's, except for one detail: When you looked closer at the logo, you saw a guy strapped to a medieval electric chair being electrocuted. Obviously the site owner was not a Clinic admirer.

"We generally prefer to not have an electric chair associated with our brand, so we wanted to prevent that from happening on another platform," deadpanned Aase when I talked with him.

But when they started @MayoClinic, they had not thought through how to use it, so they just channeled news from the company's blog (newsblog.mayoclinic.org).

But once in Twitterville, Aase started looking around and seeing the conversational strengths of the platform. Twitter also interested Mayo Clinic in other social media tools.

Mayo's iconic account makes more sense to me than the other branded accounts I've discussed. There is good reason to take up the spaces of social media before people not on your side usurp your brand. Many companies have registered logo account names at Twitter without ever planning to use them, just to protect themselves from identity larceny.

But what makes Mayo Clinic particularly interesting is what happened after Lee Aase spent extended time in Twitterville, watching the dynamics of conversation, noticing that companies can almost touch customers in the virtual space that is Twitterville. At some point, @MayoClinic identified Aase as the wizard behind its Twitter curtain.

Aase has become a leading proponent of social media in health care. He speaks at industry events. He also is champion of a movement that would allow doctors to not just talk with patients in Twitterville, but by using the private direct message feature, give free medical advice. By so doing, medical practitioners can save providers and patients time and money by reducing the amount of visits.

> @danmcquillan: Collaborate across silos: are you nuts? That's like asking the tongue to taste itself.

Converging with the Diva

The logo tweet issue reminded me of something that erupted when Scoble and I were writing *Naked Conversations* and marketers started producing "character blogs."

Character blogs are akin to logo tweets, in that real people are sequestered behind fictitious creations. In *Naked Conversations*, we spotlighted Moosetopia, a blog that featured a talking cartoon moose proficient in making awful puns. Moosetopia was the creation of an executive at a company that sold gourmet flavoring to ice-cream manufacturers; it made no sense to Scoble and me that those customers would want to talk with a cartoon moose any more than it makes sense to me for people to want to talk with an iconic Coke bottle.

Back then, I spoke with several character blog champions. I came to like and respect some of the humans behind the characters as much as I came to like the people behind brand tweets in this chapter.

My favorite was Toby Bloomberg (@TobyDiva), an online marketing maven based in Atlanta, Georgia. I met Bloomberg in 2005, during a call-in podcast in which we were both being interviewed. The podcast host asked if character blogs were acceptable. "Absolutely not," I asserted, while simultaneously Bloomberg declared, "Of course, they are."

Our conversation deteriorated from that point, most likely leaving a confused audience and an unresolved issue. While the issue remains not completely decided, Bloomberg and I now seem to have taken at least a few footsteps toward convergence.

In 2005 Bloomberg had created a character blog for her client Gourmet Station, a lifestyle-products e-merchant. The fictitious blog author was an urbane woman named T. Alexander. Ms. Alexander seemed to spend her life savoring wine, food, and a Gatsbyesque lifestyle.

We gave Bloomberg her say in *Naked Conversations,* and she presented a strong case for character blogs, which I did not buy, and said so in the book.

I decided to check back with Bloomberg to see how her views may have evolved over four years. She was still consulting Gourmet Station, and she informed me that Ms. Alexander remains the blog's central character. But humanization had seeped in. Eight real people now regularly contribute alongside the fictitious Alexander.

It turned out that T. Alexander had succeeded in some ways. Bloomberg told me that the character part of the company blog engaged customers and built loyalty.

Yet Bloomberg now concedes that character blogs have limitations. For example, people are less inclined to hold serious conversations with the character icon. When a serious issue arises, the company CEO, Donna Lyons-Miller, steps in to handle it. And I have to wonder how much more credible that CEO would be in a crisis if she were the primary blogger all the time, and people knew her better because of it.

Where Bloomberg once believed that blogs were yet another arrow in the marketer's quiver, she now sees it as a more general business tool that can be used for multiple corporate purposes, particularly customer support.

"Social media not only influences the way we interact with customers, but with people within the enterprise. Equally important is letting customers know they have been heard," she told me.

But when it comes down to the issue at hand—branded Twitter accounts—"I vote for the people stepping out of the brand shadows and sharing their true identities."

Bloomberg said she didn't mind "character tweeting" but that it was important to see the person behind the icon. This, she believes, is more important on Twitter than on blogs.

"I get uncomfortable on Twitter when everyone is mashed into one identity," she said. "I have no idea who is talking. It then becomes the voice of the enterprise and not the voice of the individual." And like me, Bloomberg doesn't much care for the contrived and collective enterprise voices.

"To me, that dilutes the power of Twitter. It becomes a dull yawn," Bloomberg said.

Bloomberg and I still differ in our respective views. But where there was a chasm in 2005, there are just a few feet of space between us now.

This is key to what I think will happen over time to branded Twitter accounts. Like just about every business thinker I spoke with, the branded tweeter people are learning the advantages of listening and the importance of transparency and authenticity as well.

Lee Aase came to Twitterville to stop someone from making a mockery of Mayo Clinic's brand. He discovered a new channel for communication that could have significant impact on conversations between health-care professionals and patients.

As even the Twitter guys learned when they were still the Odeo guys, the road to success has detours. Branded accounts are a starting point.

It will be interesting to see how they evolve over time.

CHAPTER 9

B2Bs Are People Too

Nearly all the business stories that I've told you so far have been about businesses using Twitter to get closer with end users. A lot of people seem to think that Twitter is too lightweight for business-to-business (B2B) interaction, the conversations conducted between, say, Ford Motors and its dealerships or parts suppliers. The folk, the argument goes, don't have time for frivolous chatter.

But when you think about it, nearly all business conversations start on a friendly note. "How was your weekend?" or "Did your son get accepted at college?" just seems to build stronger relationships than, "Are you going to buy something today?"

I did not find as many B2B examples as I found examples of companies tweeting to end users. But I did find a lot of them, and they were as diverse and compelling as any I found in business.

Let me tell you about just five B2B companies that are about as different from one another as companies can be. Each uses Twitter differently from the others. At least one of these ways might be useful to you.

@gapingvoid: I work extremely hard doing what I love, mainly to ensure that I don't have to work extremely hard doing what I hate.

IBM: A Thousand Twittering Experts

IBM is the world's largest computer company. With the possible exception of Microsoft, it is also the world's "tweetingest." As of February 2009 there were more than a thousand IBM tweeters, and that number is growing at a steady clip.

This is a company that sells virtually nothing through retail. Yet IBM employees are involved in thousands of conversations in Twitterville every day.

Whom are they talking to? Who authorized employees to spend part of their workday following and talking on Twitter, and how does the company make sure that not one of these employees says something to embarrass the company? Who manages and sets the rules for this brigade of tweeters?

No one at IBM corporate headquarters decided that employees should tweet. No one controls what, when, or how employees use Twitter. There remains no official IBM policy directly applicable to Twitter. Employees can talk with anyone they wish, about anything they want, and anyone who chooses can follow what is being said.

IBM employees mostly use Twitter to talk with one another. They also talk with their partners, customers, vendors, media, analysts, and other members of the company ecosystem. Overwhelmingly they are using Twitter to have the conversations relevant to their jobs.

And IBM is absolutely delighted with the results. Twitter saves time, brings employees and customers closer together, and makes the company collectively smarter.

Big Blue, as it is often called, has about 360,000 employees residing in 140 countries. Nearly one-third of them telecommute. Many belong to work groups whose members live in different countries. Some report to managers whom they have never met face-to-face.

IBM is a vast and diverse organization, involved in more businesses and services than most people—even inside the company—can name.

It should come as no surprise that IBM has long been an innovator in using video, audio, and text social media tools to keep this huge and often mobile workforce as cohesive and efficient as possible. During tough times, when travel becomes a scrutinized expense, online conversations become even more valuable.

Adam C. Christensen (@adamclyde), manager of social media communications at IBM's world headquarters in Armonk, New York, told me that Twitter spread within IBM organically. "There was no top-down mandate. One employee started using it one day and influenced another, and so on." Now Twitter is being used by company employees at many functional levels, in a variety of departments, all over the world.

IBM needed no planning meetings when Twitter came along. Employees already knew it was consistent with IBM's long-term mandate to make the enterprise more agile and responsive by moving responsibilities from corporate headquarters out to the edge, where IBM interacted with its partners and other members of its ecosystem. The strategy is not unlike what Best Buy has done with Blue Shirt Nation. Except that at Best Buy, employees are just sharing information. At IBM, employees are not just trusted to make decisions; they are directed to do so without consulting headquarters.

IBM's thinking is that the average employee talking publicly about his job better represents the company "than a couple of guys sitting in corporate." Christensen, who happens to be a guy sitting in corporate, also said that IBM shuns the social-media-luminary approach some companies use. "We aren't interested in creating a few rock stars to be the face of IBM. Our social computing guidelines are very specifically designed to encourage and enable everyone to be active and open. This is true on all platforms, and certainly so on Twitter."

IBM doesn't even think about using Twitter for sales or customer support. For the company it's an "ad hoc communications platform." As employees build personal networks of fellow IBM colleagues they trust, Christensen maintains that more trust is found in the Twitter network than in traditional enterprise-structured communications systems.

What has simultaneously occurred is that more than a thousand IBM tweeters have become company citizen journalists, spreading IBM information faster and more effectively on Twitter than when it travels on the company's intranet or blogs, Christensen told me.

Yet Christensen thinks Twitter's crowd sourcing may be an even greater benefit to IBM. "Twitter makes employees smarter. At the core, we are comprised of people who are paid to be experts. Their ability to learn from colleagues inside and outside the company has massive positive implications," he said. "Twitter is the best platform for developing relationships with smart people wherever they are, at whatever company, and at whatever level they operate."

Bartlesville Finds Twitterville

The people who run United Linen & Uniform Services (@United Linen)—located in Bartlesville, Oklahoma, a city of thirty-seven thousand 42 miles due north of Tulsa—probably know more about doing business in tough times than any other company discussed in *Twitterville*.

United Linen started in 1936, a point in the Great Depression when the dust bowl states were particularly hard hit. Gerald Saddoris, a salesman, and his wife, Lenna, were having trouble getting by, so they started taking in laundry from neighbors.

They did well enough with it. As the bad years fell away, the business steadily improved. It grew beyond their home and into facilities that now wash fifteen million pounds of tablecloths, napkins, uniforms, and even doormats a year.

It has remained a family business, passing through three generations of Saddoris family members. George's grandnephew Mat has been in charge since about 1990.

The company's small truck fleet serves restaurants in Oklahoma and parts of Arkansas, Missouri, and Kansas. They employ about 140 people. They tend to promote from within. The bookkeeper, for example, started out years earlier, pressing shirts.

This geographic region is not usually known as a hotbed for early technology adoption. For that matter, neither are family-owned regional laundry services. Credit for that goes to Scott Townsend, who started off as a route driver and is now director of marketing, where he has built a multiplatform integrated social media program.

Townsend employs Facebook, MySpace, YouTube, a video publishing site called Viddler (viddler.com), and a blog to talk with customers. Each platform directs visitors to the others.

Townsend seems to understand that if you present it right, almost any story can be useful and interesting to some audience. The company blog (unitedlinen.typepad.com) features a seven-part video series on restaurant-quality napkin folding. If you watch the entire series, which is posted on YouTube, you will be able to master folding napkins into swans, crowns, the always-elegant lily, and my favorite, the rosebud.

Townsend posts such valuable nuggets as: if you were to take all the napkins United Linen launders in a single day and lay them down end to end, they would stretch for twenty-four miles. To illustrate how far that is, Townsend posted a Google Earth map of that distance stretching over northeastern Oklahoma.

How did this company become so resourceful in social media? There are elements in the corporate culture that hint at it—transparency, for example. The company posts its financial balance sheet every month so that employees know how the company is doing.

Additionally, Townsend said, United Linen is a relationships-based business. The company organization chart seems to be built around the small team of United Linen Customer Service Representatives (CSRs), whose job it is to interface with customers.

In 2006 Townsend and the senior team stepped back and took a long view. "We had been in business for seventy-three years. My question was, where will we be in another seventy-three years?"

Townsend wondered if, moving forward, he might use social media to extend the CSR role. If so, the company might be able not only to better serve existing customers, but cover more physical ground with its service.

Unlike most business social-media efforts, Townsend started with Twitter. He tried posting game results for the company-sponsored United Linen Braves baseball team. The idea struck out. It turned out that the local cell-phone provider did not support the SMS code necessary to post Twitter messages.

Townsend explored other social media possibilities. He moved onto Facebook, which succeeded because "it fit our personality." From there, the company played with still other social platforms.

Townsend finally circled back to Twitter, where he used it at first just to point people to their other social media content. He encouraged customers to join Twitter to talk with the company. That became handy. When an ice storm hit in late 2008, @UnitedLinen used Twitter to warn customers that deliveries would be delayed. If the company had had to call each restaurant, some clients would not have learned of the problem in time.

But why should a regional linen laundry service care about global conversations at all? By following other marketers on Twitter, Townsend has discovered articles and blog posts that have influenced him and molded United Linen's approach.

"Twitter has helped shape the way we market to our customers because of what we have learned from other marketers posting on Twitter," he said. "Twitter is a great educational tool. If you want to learn more about marketing, start following some marketing profes-sionals. If you want to learn more about stay-at-home moms, start following them."

While United Linen may have geographic constraints on its cus-tomer base, it now has unlimited access to people all over the world who have ideas about social media, marketing, new technologies, and customer service.

And because United Linen is in an area where social media adop-tion is still emerging, the company has become a recognized evangelist in getting their customers to use Twitter to communicate with them.

> @Wossy: I twit, therefore I twam.

Mailstreamer in the Tweetstream

Even though a series of acquisitions has brought Pitney Bowes into global software and services business, this company remains best known for its core, which for the last one hundred years or so has focused on postage meters and all aspects of managing and handling physical mail, a process Pitney Bowes calls "mailstreaming."

Some might say the company has a stodgy image, one that seems incompatible with social media. Yet in recent years, Pitney Bowes, which has about thirty-six thousand employees, has become ex-tensively involved in conversational media, using it internally to collaborate and externally to glean new ideas from business thinkers whom they might not otherwise encounter. Finally, and most im-portant, the company uses social media to present a more human face to its global network of business customers.

That human face very often belongs to Aneta Hall (@AnetaH). While her title is emerging media manager, she usually describes herself as an "agent of change." Either way, she has been the driving force for social media at Pitney Bowes.

According to Hall, Pitney Bowes needs to go where new customers can be found; increasingly, that means social media spaces. She strongly prefers people to logos in social media.

"I often deal with social media participants who are neither willing nor comfortable engaging with a brand," Hall explained. "The way to overcome that is surprisingly easy: present yourself." In her view, putting a person in front of the logo makes people feel better about the logo.

Hall first learned about Twitter in July 2008 at PodCamp Boston, an industry insider event attended exclusively by social media enthusiasts. At the registration table she did what she always did at a conference. She filled in the two blanks on her name tag with what she thought was the obvious content. She wrote: "Aneta Hall, Pitney Bowes."

She was the only one of more than a hundred attendees to follow that old-school approach. All other attendees had entered their Twitter handles instead. They had not mentioned their companies, and often not even their own names.

During the conference itself, nearly everyone was live tweeting the event as Greg Reinacker had started doing way back at SXSW 2007. Hall realized something new was happening and she didn't quite understand what it was. One of the new things was that attendees were getting one another's Twitter handles from the name tags and then communicating via Twitter during the event. By not entering her Twitter handle, Hall was being excluded from conversations that turned out to be an integral part of the conference experience for the other attendees.

After the conference, Hall became immersed in Twitter. She started following and conversing with people all over the world who, like her, were not the inner circle of social media, but professionals in established enterprise environments grappling with how social media could loosen and improve entrenched environments.

These professionals shared ideas, experiences, and gave one another support in what was often an uphill battle. It became a global neighborhood of enterprise social media champions, and its membership keeps growing.

The value of Hall's Twitterville evangelism has begun to make headway with Pitney Bowes's senior decision makers, who have learned from Hall that Twitter gives the company faster feedback than is possible in other channels.

Additionally, other Twitter users see Hall helping Pitney Bowes customers. It demonstrates that someone at the old mailstream company has passion for helping customers.

Finally, Twitter gives Hall a new venue to demonstrate Pitney Bowes goodwill initiatives. She has used Twitter to raise awareness of a joint effort with the American Red Cross to send mail to members of the U.S. military engaged in combat zones.

Pitney Bowes's story is not nearly as dramatic as James Buck's brief Egyptian saga. But it demonstrates how Twitter has begun to seep into some of the most staid enterprise cultures, and in so doing, changes them for the better.

The Bottom-up Analysts

One of the fundamental changes from the Broadcast into the Conversational Era is the flow of decision making from top down to bottom up. Instead of having a small group of senior executives attempt to command and control what is said and done, companies are finding it smarter, faster, and economically wiser to let decisions be made by employees on the front lines, where the action is and where most market intelligence is gathered.

For big companies like IBM and Pitney Bowes, this is challenging. They must adjust systems and business models that have been up and running for decades.

It is a necessary adjustment, caused by the upheaval of many factors, particularly the move from proprietary enterprise software that is confined securely behind firewalls to software that is free, resides on the Internet, and can be used, shared, or tweaked by almost anyone who wishes to do so. This in itself has a tremendous flattening effect on the enterprise.

RedMonk is a unique analyst firm. It seems uniquely structured to help companies adjust to bottom-up strategies. Its headquarters display no granite counters, no fashionably attired receptionist, and no impressive art on its lobby walls. It is based in Twitterville.

There are a grand total of four team members residing in three countries on two continents. They rarely see one another face-to-face, communicating instead through myriad Internet tools.

Yet all this smallness seems to have attracted some very big players. RedMonk's client roster includes Adobe, IBM, Dell Computer, Hewlett-Packard, and Nortel, to name just a few.

The firm is different in just about every way from more traditional analyst firms, with whom they often compete.

For one thing, RedMonk shuns the services that are the bread and butter of the analyst business. It doesn't conduct proprietary research. The partners don't sell research reports. Whatever market intelligence they gather, they give away, usually by posting it on a team member's blog. Anyone can use or share RedMonk's content or add to it as they see fit. They would, of course, like some attribution when you do.

RedMonk is the world's first open-source research firm. As I've mentioned, such software is always free, just like RedMonk's market intelligence.

The companies who contract them are hardware and software giants whose roots are in proprietary enterprise software. These are companies whose business models may be at or near the end of their lifecycles, in part because of open source and Web 2.0. This creates all sorts of challenges.

If you're a new company like Twitter or Evernote, open source allows you to grow fast and gain customers, although it makes it puzzling how to monetize what they offer.

Older, larger companies have business practices that have been shaped and refined by enterprise software models designed to provide recurring revenue from installed bases. For them, moving into an open-source business model is tantamount to traveling through a wormhole in outer space, being unsure where you come out.

That's where RedMonk comes in. They advise companies on how to meet the challenges being fomented by the open-source movement.

"Essentially, we are paid to give our opinions," cofounder James Governor, a Texan who now lives in London, told me. As it happens, there is a little more to it than that. They bring a new perspective to old companies, helping them develop new business models based on open-source technologies.

Traditional analyst firms, such as Forrester Research or Gartner Group, also offer consulting services regarding such transitions. But they approach it from an historic top-down perspective. Such consultants usually play to the enterprise's central information officer (CIO).

RedMonk stays focused on what happens from the perspective of the software developer who creates the technology the company will run on. Theirs is a bottom-up perspective and it often looks different from that perspective.

"We serve people in the enterprise who choose and deploy tools, often without asking for permission from their higher-ups," Governor told me. These are the company code writers and Web engineers, who are focused on building online communities, the new enterprise marketplaces.

There is another aspect to RedMonk. They don't even try to speak with one voice. They thrive on showing they are four smart individuals, and they do it mostly in Twitterville.

"Twitter is where we hang out the most," Governor said. It is, in fact, where the team members interact with one another. They often start or join conversations that lead to new business engagements.

They also have started using Twitter Search more often than Google searches. There are three primary reasons for this.

First, Google usually gives you the most visited results first, rather than the most relevant results. This often produced an outdated or obsolete entry. Only because Google keeps sending people there, the outdated site keeps rising in popularity.

For example, if you search for "Shel Israel" the fifth entry down will show you ItSeemstoMe, my abandoned blog where I last posted in 2006. There is no mention on the first page of entries of *Twitterville*, which has been the subject of most of my blog posts, talks, and media interviews since November 2008 and is far more relevant to anyone checking me out. It will take months before Google starts elevating *Twitterville* references in search results for my name.

Yet if you check me out on Twitter Search, the most current information is on top. Often a topic I mention is findable there less than a minute after I post.

Second, Google is being gamed by a growing number of search engine optimization (SEO) professionals. SEO is relatively new, and has legitimate usages. Essentially, SEO people study what people search for, and then insert keywords into a company's Web-based content so that it appears more prominently than a competitor's.

SEO therefore may help a company get found legitimately, but it also can cheat by slipping in popular buzzwords that let a company float up a Google search results page when they really don't deserve to. The company wins, but the user gets less relevant results. There are those who feel SEO has corrupted Google Search results. Governor argues that Twitter gives you cleaner results, because so far, Twitter Search is harder to game by SEO manipulation.

The third reason is, to my thinking, the most compelling. Governor says Twitterville "is a marketplace of ideas, thoughts, and prejudices. It's where people live declaratively, which creates opportunities and challenges for companies of all shapes and sizes."

To translate, Twitter lets you ask people you know about things they know. While Google uses robotic spiders to crawl the Web and give you keyword results, a Twitter user can simply ask friends about products, services, or anything else. For this to work, of course you need to be on Twitter for a while and to have built up some number of followers. But the result is that people you know are helping you. It is unlikely that an SEO professional will ever be able to game that aspect of Twitter.

"Twitter is the new Google," quipped Governor. He has a point. Twitter has characteristics that portend to disrupt many other popular online services.

Craigslist is another company that should be taking careful notice. Since the recession hit in late 2008, a good many people have announced they were hiring or looking for a job exclusively on Twitter. No fewer than twelve job market Twitter accounts existed by February 2009, and there were several reports of people who found jobs because of Twitter.

But RedMonk is probably the first company to have made its offer directly and transparently on Twitter and to have its offer accepted in a public reply. It also created a subsidiary for the world's smallest global analyst firm.

In 2008 Governor started a new blog called GreenMonk (greenmonk.net), which analyzes sustainable energy practices in the enterprise. It takes particular note of how sustainable energy practices favorably impact the bottom line.

At the realization that sound energy practices were good for businesses, Governor began thinking that what started as a blog related to a personal passion could emerge into a new business unit. However, to do it he needed to find a fourth team member—an enterprise expert who also understood and cared about green issues.

Enter Tom Raftery, a respected IT consultant based in Cork, Ireland. Pilar, his Spanish-born wife grew sick of Ireland's cold winters, and persuaded him to give up his partnership in an appropriate technology data-storage company to move to her warmer hometown of Seville, Spain.

Raftery agreed to move for love, but he saw barriers to moving to Spain. For one thing, he didn't speak Spanish. He started blogging and tweeting about his employment dilemma, and Governor caught the tweet.

Governor and Raftery had actually met a couple of times, but they had never talked in any depth. Through an extended Twitter-based dialogue the two found they were kindred spirits with shared passions.

Governor recollected, "Tom was the obvious candidate. We made him the job offer on Twitter, and he accepted through Twitter."

The power of Twitter as a job market seems to me to be because it is community based. On Craigslist you see ads that are often left up long after the jobs have been filled.

But on Twitter people you know recommend you for jobs to people they know. The best way to get a job in the real world, most people seem to think, is through personal recommendation. This dynamic carries over into Twitter better than it does anywhere else.

> @jasonfried: Don't talk about monetization or being transparent—talk about making money and being honest.

The Twittering Recruiter

Sodexo, the leading food services provider to North American health, college, and military facilities, has actually turned Twitter into its major recruiting tool. It uses Twitter to find and attract chefs, facility engineers, environmental service managers, dietitians, district managers, and even vice presidents. And despite cutbacks elsewhere, Sodexo was in hiring mode, with a 2009 plan to add 5,000 managers and professionals as well as 2,000 recent college grads to its existing cadre of 120,000.

Sodexo started using Twitter as an executive recruiting tool in 2008 (@SodexoCareers). It also had at least twenty company recruiters active on Twitter by February 2009, with expectations that the number would steadily grow. The recruiters help one another out. When a candidate mentions a willingness to relocate, recruiters use Twitter to share the lead with colleagues in that part of the country.

Arie Ball (@Arie_Ball), a thirty-year company veteran and vice president of Sodexo's Talent Acquisition Group, came up with the idea of a tweeting network of company recruiters. She had spearheaded other Sodexo social media forays, including YouTube and Facebook recruiting efforts, as well as participation in a Second Life virtual job fair.

Ball champions using social media to fill top-level positions "to connect with individuals in a more authentic way, and share information about our company, culture, work environment, and career opportunities. Social media provides a way for us to share who we are and open a dialog for exchanging views," she told me.

Unlike most companies, where Twitter usage starts on a grassroots level and then grows organically, Sodexo took a strategic approach. Ball launched Twitter during a presentation at a national recruiting team meeting with a live demonstration onscreen as she talked. She then orchestrated a Twitter training program for the recruiters.

Although the program was still nascent when I talked with Ball, she already had examples of Sodexo finding talent that it would not otherwise have connected with.

When Ball tweeted that she was headed to Tampa, Florida, she received a note from a Tampa chef who had interned with Sodexo years earlier. The chef was interested in returning to Sodexo, impressed by the company's forward-thinking use of the site. Twitter allowed the chef to check the pulse of the company, revealing employee and customer interactions, and, perhaps critically, Sodexo's sound financial state. Ball forwarded the chef's résumé to the Tampa Sodexo recruiter and he was hired.

This all happened in less than a day's time. Ball could think of no other way for this to have occurred, had it not been for Twitter and Sodexo's involvement in it.

In the last few chapters, I've looked mostly at big companies who have talked with a wide variety of customers. I've given you numerous, diverse examples of how Twitter has helped such companies in ways that massive, expensive marketing campaigns could not achieve.

Only a few of these examples—Evernote, RedMonk, and Twitter itself—have involved companies too small to be able to spend much on advertising, PR, or branding campaigns. We'll look at a lot more small companies in the next few chapters.

CHAPTER 10

Small Business, Big Footprint

It is really no surprise at all that there are so many small companies—often very small ones—that have come to Twitterville.

Why wouldn't they? A new business located in a spare bedroom or less-than-prime former industrial space can build a network of customers all over the world at little or no cost. It can find itself getting talked about and written about by people and organizations that can help a small business become much bigger. Some companies seem to have been designed with Twitter in mind, and they are thriving because Twitter exists.

> @ronlaudadio: Twitter: Writing or sharing cool stuff >
> Builds RESPECT > Grants ACCEPTANCE from others to
> Self-Promote > Profit!

Conversations You Can See

Perhaps Seesmic would have existed anyway, but it would not be the same without Twitter. And it would not have come so far, so fast in terms of adoption without Twitter. Its charismatic founder would not be so well known and so often covered in both social and traditional media.

Seesmic (seesmic.com) is often described as a Twitter for video lovers. It is an extremely easy way to record, upload, and share a brief video clip. It is easy for others to respond with either a text or video comment.

By September 2009, when this book is published, Seesmic users will have allowed tens of thousands of users to post more than a million video clips, nearly all produced by amateurs using nonprofessional equipment—often just camcorders built into or clipped onto their personal computers or on their phones.

Loic Le Meur (@Loic), a serial entrepreneur with a track record for finding the right opportunities at the right time, moved from Paris to San Francisco in 2007 to start Seesmic.

Usually the videos on Seesmic are of everyday people sharing thoughts and opinions. But Seesmic has the potential to accomplish much more. and I suspect it will.

In January 2009 Le Meur attended the World Economic Forum. He interviewed former UN secretary-general Kofi Annan for Seesmic. People from all over the world joined in to ask questions. "This is how people can add video to a Twitter kind of conversation," he told me. It also demonstrates the potential for professional-quality video programs using Seesmic technology. Even more important, it demonstrates a new form of interactive video citizen journalism that could be quite powerful.

To establish itself as the most conversational video platform, Seesmic has integrated itself as closely as possible with Twitter. Its entire launch was conducted on Twitter without spending a cent on traditional advertising and PR.

In April 2008 Seesmic acquired Twhirl, a desktop Twitter application that makes it easier to integrate Seesmic content with Twitter in terms of uploads and sharing, and renamed it Seesmic Desktop. Launched in the late winter of 2009, Seesmic Desktop makes Twitter feel like a built-in Seesmic component. If you are a tweeter who wishes to post videos as easily as text messages, Seesmic Desktop is pretty seamless.

While Twitter was an obvious venue for generating word of mouth among social media enthusiasts, Le Meur went further. He turned Twitterville into Seesmic's test lab.

Before the technology was ready for public scrutiny, he opened a Twitter account and used it to recruit "a few volunteers to test an early alpha version."

Alpha product testing is usually a private affair restricted to professional software testers, where bugs are fixed and improvements to functionality are made.

By using Twitter instead, Seesmic would be tested not by professional technologists but by the sort of people likely to adopt the product when it was ready for public use. Also, instead of having a small team of paid lab professionals to kick Seesmic's tires, he hoped to get a few hundred people trying out Seesmic and giving feedback.

A few days after inviting people to sign up, Le Meur had several thousand requests to join. He let them start playing with Seesmic a few batches at a time. Their comments were posted not in proprietary reports but on Twitter, where they could be reviewed by Seesmic's tech team along with anyone else who wished to read them.

What if the tech press saw some negative comments? Le Meur couldn't care less. He was having direct conversations with his user base; press coverage was welcome, but it was secondary in importance. Previously, companies counted on the press to reach users. With Twitter, Seesmic was going directly to the customer. Ironically, this seemed to increase editorial interest in Seesmic.

This dialogue with customers changed how the product was built and what would be in it. Usually technologists decide what bugs will be fixed first and what features will go in early. In this case, the users decided.

This collaboration between the Seesmic team and its customer base became a Twitterville global neighborhood. People who cared about citizen video hung out there. They shared information and ideas with a company. They became passionate about Seesmic. They recommended what to repair. They shared tips on getting better results. They encouraged friends to visit the Seesmic neighborhood.

The Seesmic neighborhood is a noisy place. "Buzz started to grow way ahead of any of our plans or expectations," Le Meur told me. He has succeeded in keeping it enthusiastic and highly active not by promoting Seesmic, but by giving back to the community. Le Meur said, "Giving credit and thanking Twitter users for their feedback is very key. Your community does not want a lecture. It wants conversation."

And like H&R Block's Paula Drum, he warned companies away from trying to use Twitter the same way a company would use mass media.

"I think many brands [that] use Twitter only to broadcast will fail. They try to use Twitter as traditional media, and it simply does not work."

This is why Seesmic is more likely to succeed in a social media venue than, say, CNN. The broadcaster may understand video broadcast, and it may be able to incorporate chat technology. But it does not understand community dynamics and conversational media. Ultimately, Seesmic's position is strong because it is built on a community culture. It does not think mass media; it thinks conversation.

Using Twitter has been just about all Seesmic needed to get onto the playing field. It is included in almost all public conversations on citizen-generated video. The company's marketing budget remains close to zero, and there are no plans to change that.

It should be noted that Le Meur had one advantage over most other entrepreneurs considering Twitter for a launch: he was already an industry luminary, having founded Le Web, one of the most popular social media conferences in Europe, in addition to launching four previous Web start-ups. He brought a strong personal network to Twitterville when he arrived.

Not everyone wishing to use Twitter to get a company started will have the luxury of being well-known on two continents at the outset. But the point that matters is that it is wise to get into Twitter and social media as early as you can, and before you want Twitterville to help you design, distribute, and market a product. Build your relationships and reputations as soon as possible. Then, when you want help, people will already know and, ideally, trust you.

A Community of Stock Pickers

StockTwits is a Twitter-based community for people who are still brave enough to invest in stocks and currencies. While Twitter can sometimes be a venue for touchy-feely, what-you-had-for-lunch kinds of communities, StockTwits is more a place for hard-nosed, pragmatic people to share information and, ideally, profits.

StockTwits is an information-based community. Members share what they know about publicly held companies. The conversations are held often in a candid, cut-the-crap style that no Wall Street analyst would dare use.

But while Wall Street analysts seem to be losing credibility these days, some pickers in the StockTwits community seem to be gaining it.

And while you have to pay to get most Wall Street analysts' reports, StockTwits is free to anyone who follows the Twitter account. Most of the seventy thousand members do not offer analysis but simply follow some of the several hundred people who do.

To become part of the StockTwits community, you have to sign up at the company's Web site (stocktwits.com). You enter a stock portfolio so that the community knows what stocks interest you. Then, on Twitter, you follow @StockTwits.

On the Twitter account you will see any and all discussion regarding stocks or the sectors that interest you. StockTwits starts you off with about sixty people who recommend stocks in the area you want to follow. You can discover new people and add them, or filter out people whose opinion you do not like.

This filtering and tweaking system is important. The sum-total wisdom of seventy thousand people is far greater than any single Wall Street analyst, but it would be overwhelming if every time you wanted to buy a stock, you got seventy thousand opinions.

While I advise that just measuring the number of followers on a Twitter account will often mislead you, it makes sense on Stock Twits. The better a community member's track record on stock picking, the more people tend to follow him, according to StockTwits cofounder Howard Lindzon—making it relatively easy for new community members to decide whom to trust.

"StockTwits is about reputation and trust. You earn that. You can't show up the first day and have it," Lindzon says. "If you are talented, though, the community is set up to promote the best traders as fast as possible. StockTwits is all about building a farm system for ideas generators. Ideas that will make the community members money."

This is still a nascent community, but it is growing fast. In the long term, the most popular stock analysts here may be more than a little disruptive to the traditional institutions that have recently lost their luster.

The StockTwits company itself is comprised of just two people—Lindzon and Soren Macbeth. They met online through their blogs. Neither Macbeth nor Lindzon were nearly as well-known as Le Meur had been when they launched their venture. But both did have street credentials with investors. Macbeth was a successful currency exchange player and Lindzon, a former hedge fund manager, was a successful entrepreneur. Lindzon cofounded Wallstrip (wallstrip.com), a daily business news satire video series that was acquired by CBS in 2008.

Lindzon told me he saw an opportunity when Wall Street's reputation and financial positions simultaneously foundered in 2008. Until that time, stock-picking influence and expertise were controlled and dispensed by the world's largest financial institutions and their approved mouthpieces. And, until the crash, most investors were happy making their decisions based on a small group of designated "experts."

Lindzon said the crash gave StockTwits the chance to "reaggregate the people who love stocks" and create a marketplace for new analysts and traders "to develop audiences built on trust, transparency, and performance."

Macbeth and Lindzon believe that agile, interactive, online communities shall supplant centralized investing institutions. These communities will share news and ideas through social media. The top-down structure of investment analysts will be replaced by more credible peer-to-peer interaction.

StockTwits is another example of a crowd-source company. The wisdom of crowds not only lets community members find the most successful stock pickers, but it seems also to be a good safeguard against abusers such as penny-stock spammers who have, in the eyes of many, destroyed the credibility of Yahoo! Finance, to name just one. "Reputation makes it harder to just walk away," Lindzon says. "You must protect your reputation in the finance business. The reputation mechanism also turns every wannabe analyst into a potential superstar—if he or she is good."

StockTwits is the first community of its kind, and is unlikely to be the last. Lindzon did not share with me any plans for monetization, but after this community reaches a certain critical mass, there are lots of options that may be available. Perhaps StockTwits will simultaneously help his emerging band of next-generation analysts monetize as well.

It is an interesting business model, one likely to be copied by other entrepreneurs. A community of people who share passion, data, news, ideas, and opinions could be formed around subjects from politics to literature to sports. The potential is endless.

Network computing is based on something called Metcalfe's Law: The power of the computer network grows exponentially as the number of nodes increases. On Twitterville, we have become the nodes. And the more of us there are sharing what we know and think on any given subject, the more powerful we become.

> **@Zeldman:** Your tweet that linked to the exact same tweet on FriendFeed that linked to a two-word post by Kottke linking to actual content was awesome.

A Creative Marketplace

Founded in May 2008, crowdSPRING (crowdspring.com) works quite simply. A potential buyer comes to the site and requests bids to design a logo, Web site, or other graphic work, stipulating a deadline and a maximum fee she is willing to pay.

Then members of crowdSPRING's global talent pool of more than 12,000 freelancers and small agencies located in over 140 countries bid for the work. The bidding process is simplified. There is no written proposal. Instead, bidders just submit sample artwork.

The crowdSPRING Web site is a graphic design marketplace. It gives artists everywhere the opportunity to bid for work anywhere, work they wouldn't have otherwise known about. Conversely, it lets buyers find the best talent for the job at a fraction of the cost that top-priced design houses demand.

The average project gets more than seventy work samples and bids for each buyer to review. Buyers and sellers then haggle back and forth until a deal gets cut. The negotiation can be as public or private as the buyer wishes it to be. Once a deal is made, crowdSPRING handles the necessary paperwork. Upon completion, the site tacks on 15 percent for commission.

Some crowdSPRING users are well-known—at least in the social media community. Author-investor–serial entrepreneur Guy Kawasaki (@GuyKawasaki) held a T-shirt design competition for Alltop.com, his social media reference service. Charlene Li paid a mere $400 for a new logo for Altimeter, her recently formed consulting firm.

Some big brands have also found their way to crowdSPRING. Epic Records contracted a designer for a Judas Priest album cover through crowdSPRING. Spreadshirt (spreadshirt.com), an online custom T-shirt company, has bought new product designs from them.

ConAgra, the branded-foods giant, tends to launch products the old-fashioned way: privately, until an official date arrives. Still, they saved money by using crowdSPRING to find a product-box artist— all password protected, so that no one would see their selection prematurely.

CrowdSPRING cofounder Ross Kimbarovsky told me that Twitter is at the very core of the company's marketing strategy, helping it find both buyers and sellers. He and partner Mike Samson are both active on Twitter, as are several other employees. Many of crowdSPRING's first customers came through Twitter.

Like so many of today's entrepreneurial efforts, crowdSPRING began with a zero-dollar marketing budget—which has yet to increase now that the company is off the ground. Instead, the founders invested personal time on Twitter. Through Twitter they have met and interacted with thousands of people, and from those thousands have attracted several hundred customers, Kimbarovsky told me.

Readers who have hired graphic designers the traditional way know the selection and revision process can be tedious. Twitter speeds it all up. Within minutes of a Twitter project announcement, Kimbarovsky says, there are immediate responses from bidders. Every step of the project goes faster than in a traditional search-design-produce process. No one seems to miss the paper proposals that talk about the great past contributions of the designers and why they would be so happy to get the new business.

Kimbarovsky also likes what Twitter does for crowdSPRING's image. This young company is perceived to be "on the forefront of the online world," he says. "In other words, it would be a brand failure for us to *not* be on Twitter. How can you claim that you're blazing a trail for a new online world and then sit on the sidelines?"

Not only that, the online presence camouflages the chinks in this start-up's veneer. "We appear to be much larger, more organized, and more impressive than we really are, just because we can beat the big guys to the punch by being faster, more nimble, and more active," he confided.

CrowdSPRING uses Twitter to pick up new business before mainstream design houses see that the business is even there. Instead of buying direct mail lists and sending postcards to people who will redirect them to local landfill, the company lets the customers come to them. "We put our ear to the ground and listen as hundreds of people a day tweet, 'Boy, I could sure use a logo for my new business.' It doesn't get any better than that."

Tweetups at The Groundz

We've discussed global companies who use Twitter to present a local feel to customers, and in this chapter I've given you a few examples of very small companies using Twitter to establish global presence. But there are also a growing number of local companies who use Twitter just to reach highly localized audiences. (Ev Williams and Biz Stone have both stated that they see local-to-local as Twitter's most promising aspect.)

The Coffee Groundz is an establishment where they really do care about what you had for lunch—or breakfast, or even dinner if you happen to live or work in Houston.

J. R. Cohen, manager of the independent café, hopes that if your day brings you anywhere near Midtown Houston you'll have at least one of those meals at his place, that you enjoyed it, and that you will tell friends about it as well.

Cohen's job is, in part, to get more locals to hang out at The Coffee Groundz than at the competing Starbucks down the street. Social media and Twitter are part of the competitive battleground. For example, Starbucks has Wi-Fi, but you have to pay for it. The Coffee Groundz offers customers free access, and there are plenty of outlets for power-hungry laptop users to boot.

In September 2008, about a month after Brad Nelson started @Starbucks, Cohen became the café's tweeter in residence (@CoffeeGroundz). He chatted with a few customers, but nothing much happened until Halloween morning, when one hungry regular, Sean Stoner (@MaslowBeer), a faithful Coffee Groundz customer, was late to work and very hungry. His route took him near the café; out of desperation, he sent a direct message to Cohen asking if he could pick up a breakfast burrito at the drive-through window. "What do you want on it?" Cohen tweeted back.

And thus, as blogger Erica O'Grady wrote as a guest poster at the popular Pistachio Consulting blog (pistachioconsulting.com), it was "the first time that Twitter had ever been used to place a to-go order."

Cohen thought there might be a business opportunity in the online attention the incident generated. He tweeted about the café's

willingness to accept to-go orders. Pretty soon more cars were queu-
ing up at the drive-through window. To-go tweeting created a small
but sustained spike in business.

This started building The Coffee Ground's popularity among
Houston-area "Twitterati." The café started to become the destination
of choice when Houston Twitter users wanted to hold get-together
events called Tweetups. These are held all over the world, and have
an interesting dynamic. People who have met only in Twitterville
plan and attend an event where they can actually meet in real
life. Even among the most ardent social media champions, there is
still nothing quite like a face-to-face meeting. There is sometimes
the very strange sensation that you are meeting an old friend for the
first time.

The Houston-area Tweetups draw more than two hundred
people to The Coffee Groundz about once a month. Each time there
are some people who have never been to The Coffee Groundz
before. Some invariably become regulars. The events are at night,
when the Groundz serves dinner, drinks, and ice cream; the extra
revenue adds up.

"This is a big, big deal," Cohen says. "I think that without Twitter
and the buzz it has generated for us, it would be impossible to make
The Coffee Groundz a destination and have people drive a long way
to get here."

And that success begets more success. A presidential election
night party at the Groundz was arranged by one tweeter; more than
250 people showed up. The unique Twitter angle has also generated
news coverage, with local TV and radio covering how business people in Houston are using the platform.

@CoffeeGroundz had about 6,200 followers in June 2009, a lot
fewer than @Starbucks's 200,000. But in the hometown battle, Cohen
is highly likely to have more Houston tweeters following him than
@Starbucks does. The Coffee Groundz has unquestionably gained

more incremental business through Twitter than has his branded competitor.

When you are a global brand, it may be difficult to have the local touch of companies that make clear where and who is the tweet author. There's an interesting twist. Brad Nelson had presented a reasonably persuasive argument why he tweets as @Starbucks rather than as himself, the way Dell handles its branded tweets. The answer may be that Brad Nelson in Seattle was preemptive to the Starbucks guy in Houston, who now has his own brand stopping him from joining a local conversation.

> @createdbymom: Twitter is future of biz, bringing biz back to being between people, rather than faceless corporation superpowers—exciting!

Searching for a Twitterville Plumber

There's simply no business more local than a plumber. And when plumbers adopt social media, it seems to me evidence that conversational tools are moving from the tech sector and into—if you'll pardon a pun—the mainstream.

When we wrote *Naked Conversations*, Scoble and I searched for a mythical blogging plumber. While we never found one, we came pretty close when we uncovered a blogging lawn-sprinkler repair guy in Boise, Idaho.

For *Twitterville*, I searched for a tweeting plumber and came at least as close. Scott Becker of Suffolk, New York, is Twitter's Online Handyman (@OnlineHandyman). He gives tips to people on all sorts of handyman tricks, and seems to be quite an expert on plumbing issues.

Becker also uses video and a Web site. While he is a local

guy with a local business, he is building up a global reputation on home repair at a time when homeowners are looking for help on how to do it themselves. That may help him enter new businesses in the future or perhaps write a home repair book. It certainly helps position him as the go-to handyman in the Suffolk, New York, area.

Becker is not alone. @HandymanSeattle seems to be enhancing his own reputation with the same approach on the other side of the country. A few miles away there's the Do-It-Yourself Answer Guy (@DIYAnswerGuy), who serves Washington State's Olympic Peninsula.

Over in West Grove, Pennsylvania, Sal Pizzurro has started his own Twitter account, @SalPizzurro, to promote his Chester County general contracting practice. While he doesn't post much about plumbing, he seems to be the area's expert on stump grinding.

There are a growing number of local contractors using Twitter. While the number of people who follow each of them is relatively small, their conversations show that they are mostly potential customers.

Where is it all going? Picture shopping for a plumber or handyman. You need to make a judgment to hire someone. You can do it through your local Yellow Pages, where you see a line of type, or perhaps a small display ad. Or perhaps you can find someone through an online listing service, which usually provides no more information than the phone directory.

Or you can discover a local guy doing a local service who tweets. On Twitter you can see his personality, his areas of real passion, his conversations with current or past customers. You can also use Twitter Search to see what others have to say about him or her.

Twitter gives potential customers better information about what these guys are about. Now local repair people, artisans, service providers, and merchants have a new way of building their reputations and a new way of talking with customers and prospects.

It may take a little time, but it's more effective and less expensive than any other available option.

Evolution of a Foodie

Danny Gabriner not only depends on local customers for his business, he does not yet actually have a business. As of May 1, 2009, he still had a day job as a CNET/CBS analyst in the global media company's San Francisco offices.

But his passion is elsewhere, and his hope is that by the time you read this book, he'll be making a living that is more closely linked to what excites him: food. And if that is indeed the case, he owes getting started to Twitter.

Gabriner, age twenty-three, is a "foodie." Until early December 2008, Gabriner had to be content just to write about food on a personal blog, which he abandoned shortly after joining Twitter. From the day he started tweeting, his foodie credentials have spiraled upward. He has used Twitter to effectively build relationships and reputation, as well as to start constructing the framework for a new business.

He's coupled his Twitter account, @Gastronomer, with a new blog, Gourmet Gastronomer (GourmetGastronomer.com), and in the San Francisco Bay area he has become prominent in both online and foodie community events.

Gabriner started using Twitter with the intention of becoming a professional food connoisseur, but he had no road map for getting there. His first step was to look for people on Twitter who shared his interest in food. He searched Twitter for gourmet terms such as "béchamel" and "soffrito." At the time there were about 4.5 million people on Twitter. About a dozen had used at least one of these words.

It was a start. Gabriner could see who these dozen people were talking to. From there, he could start building a global neighborhood of tweeting foodies.

Next he started exploring Tweetworks (tweetworks.com), a Twitter adjunct that lets you find groups on a multitude of subjects. There he found and started following a few dozen foodies at a time. He found more tools, which provided more names, and the process accelerated. Soon he had several hundred people in his foodie neighborhood.

This small effort started to change his life. Now, when he wanted to talk about food, there were people who cared what he had to say, who could contribute new insight and information into the conversation. Like so many others, Gabriner learned the powerful synergy between blogs and Twitter: "One is very fast but constrained to shallow content. The other is longer and deeper but does not draw traffic as easily."

Gabriner invited six other food lovers that he met on Twitter to become regular guest bloggers at Gourmet Gastronomy. The Gastronomers, as the group became known, decided to hold a macaroni-and-cheese recipe competition, which he named the Mac and Cheese–off. Gabriner used Twitter to invite contestants and received ten responses. Each contestant got to post a recipe and picture on Gastronomy. He used Twitter to send people to the blog, where they would vote. His blog traffic skyrocketed from a few dozen per day to several thousand.

By mid-January, six weeks from his starting point, these activities had already elevated Gabriner to a point of prominence in a viable and sizable global neighborhood that had not previously existed. He was a noted online food enthusiast.

But when it comes to food, there's just so much you can do on the Internet. The Tweetups held at The Coffee Groundz were succeeding because there's nothing that beats a face-to-face meeting for most people. With food, looking at a picture will only take you so far.

To succeed, Gourmet Gastronomer was going to have to bring real people and food into the same venue simultaneously. So Gabriner produced a giant party in his hometown of San Francisco.

The event was free, except for Gabriner. But now he had a process that could be turned into a business—if people will pay to eat and party at Gastronomer events. The formula is to announce a contest on his Twitter account, post the best entries on his blog, then get people together to sample and judge the winners. If such an event can work in San Francisco, then they can work all over the world, wherever people are social and enjoy food.

When I last spoke with Gabriner, he and his group of Gastronomers were planning a "Soup Off." The three leading soups will be served up, and party attendees will pick their favorite. He just might charge them for the privilege this time—or the next.

With the exception of The Coffee Groundz, and my Twittering handymen, you may have noticed that the people and businesses that I profiled in this chapter share one additional aspect in common.

None has yet developed a business model that is clear to the observer. While they may have them, each is still supporting their businesses either from investor dollars or, in Gabriner's case, a day job.

As of this writing, this is also true of Twitter. Perhaps it is a perspective developed in Silicon Valley, where I have seen this happen time and time again: if people follow their passion and find others to do the same, then communities form. And as they grow, the appropriate path to monetization becomes clear, as it did for Google, Facebook, and other companies. It is the build-it-and-they-will-come approach, and it is not for traditional thinkers.

But it is for those who wish to turn dreams into reality. It involves high risk in the hope of higher gain.

Twitter has lowered the costs of building global communities to nearly zero. It can help a local handyman or a global video platform.

It can build communities of independent investors who can change the shape or future of Wall Street.

There are a great many skeptics of the transformations taking place. They try to apply old models to new approaches and fold their arms, saying it cannot be done.

The late senator Robert Kennedy once said, "There are those that look at things the way they are, and ask why? I dream of things that never were, and ask why not."

I think Kennedy would have liked the vision of the Twitterville entrepreneurs I've discussed in this chapter.

CHAPTER 11

Personal Branding

I t is apparent that the term "brand" has come to mean many things to many people, but it's rooted in shaping how customers and communities feel about a company. Brands are emotional. When you see a company logo, ad, or press release, or when someone hands you a business card, the action is intended to evoke something akin to power, sexuality, romance, warmth, or loyalty. This differentiates one company brand from another. Chances are, the impression you get from a Mercedes logo is different from the one you get from a BMW or a Porsche, although all three are luxury automobiles. This is true of branding perceptions in beer, wine, clothing labels, restaurants, and so on.

Branding has been around for centuries. The modern interpretation of it goes back to a book published in 1957 by Vance Packard titled *The Hidden Persuaders*. The work sold over a million copies and ignited a controversy that continues to this day. On the one hand, it became a bible for Madison Avenue advertisers. On the other, it raised questions about the morality of such subliminal messages as selling cigarettes by persuading young people that it makes them sexier.

Contrary to the tweeter who took issue with me, branding has nothing to do with commoditization. It has everything to do with differentiation.

I have previously argued that we are in a transformational time; a new Conversational Era is eclipsing an aging and dysfunctional Broadcast Era.

Hidden persuasion prevailed during the Broadcast Era. People often used devious methods to devise messages that they could surreptitiously plant into our foreheads. They spent massive dollars in the one-directional campaigns.

By its very definition, the Conversational Era requires two-way communication. This book is filled with examples of companies that came to Twitterville to talk and have learned the great value in listening.

Here's the thing: brands do not listen. People listen. And not only do they listen, they respond. When this happens, you think better of those people—even if they do not or cannot give you everything you asked for. At least they tried. After all, they're only human.

Personal brand has a lot to do with seeing real people trying and succeeding, or trying and failing, then trying again. While in recent times we have lost a lot of faith in corporate brands and corporate branders, social media has brought forth the concept and the ascent of personal brand.

Personal branding has to do with how we feel about people, and it involves the humanization of corporations that allows us to see and converse with the humans who actually work for them.

Personal branding is nothing new. Our ancestors trusted Og to succeed in the hunt and Guk to build good fires. The tribe knew whom to trust or mistrust based on tribe members' past performances.

What's new is that social media has amplified and accelerated the process. Each of the six individuals I discuss below are known and trusted around the world. Each wields influence in fields where they are passionate. Each derives a clear financial benefit from their activities in Twitterville. Some work for themselves, and others work for or with large organizations.

I picked these six out of the more than thirty million personal brands available in Twitterville as of June 2009.

Some of these are better known than others. But what they say on Twitter, whom they follow, and who follows them shapes their reputations, their fortunes, and the fortunes of their employees.

If you are on Twitter—or are about to be—the same holds true for you. In Twitterville, you are what you tweet.

> @UpbeatNow: ThinkTweet: What would be your strategy if you chose to make 90% of your tweets memorable?

Resurrection of a Dinosaur

He's called New Media Jim (@NewMediaJim) in Twitterville, but his day job makes him an "Old Media Jim." Jim Long has been an NBC cameraman since 1993. He's often assigned to the White House, where Barack Obama is the third president he's covered.

Long has traveled around the world more times than he can count to provide NBC viewers with coverage of the president, cabinet secretaries, and other top-level executive branch dignitaries.

"I have the coolest job in the world," he told me. "History passes through my lens."

But he's also reasonably certain that one of these days, he will wake up from this dream job to discover he has been assigned to something radically different and less lucrative. Traditional broadcast media just isn't what it used to be. There have been several rounds of layoffs, and there is scant evidence that the worst of these has passed.

For a decade now, advertising and audience have been migrating from old media to new. The price of a thirty-second network spot covers an awful lot of Web ads.

Sooner or later, Long figures, he's going to have to follow the money onto the Internet.

"I look at what's happening and I realize I am quickly becoming a dinosaur," he said.

I wouldn't know Long's story if I had not found him on Twitter. By the time I actually met him face-to-face at SXSW in 2008, we were old friends.

Long had over thirty thousand followers as of May 2009. Many share my view of him as an old friend even if they have never been in the same room with him. They root for him. If he sticks with NBC, they want him to prevail. If he leaves, they want to help him get going in his new endeavor. He's part of the neighborhood, and the neighborhood is on his side.

Long's personal brand is good for NBC. And that brand is largely driven by his activity on Twitter. On several occasions, I've tuned in to NBC because he tweeted that he would be behind the camera of a government event, and I'm sure I'm not alone. People tell Long all the time how his tweets have brought them back to the network.

Is this neighborhood of Jim Long fans enough to save a faltering broadcast network? Of course not. But it can help NBC by extending the broadcaster's word-of-mouth network. Long's followers have influence, and each follower has feet on the street. When earthquakes rocked the Midwest in 2007, Long found eyewitnesses near the epicenter tweeting as dramatic events unfolded, while NBC's traditional network of local affiliates seemingly could not. To enhance their coverage, the network ran Twitter screen shots supplied by Long.

Long's preference would probably be to help NBC make the transition from old media into new media, letting him keep on with what he has been doing as he teaches the organization how to switch over. But that does not seem to be where the decision makers want to take NBC.

"At the end of the day, there will be a time when NBC will no longer want to pay a guy like me," he told me. Layoffs at NBC, like at many companies, are removing the most experienced people, such as Long, and replacing them with less experienced junior staff members.

That's why, in his spare time, Long is leveraging his personal brand into new media. When the day comes for him to go off on his own, he will use a personal brand built on a decade and a half experience behind an NBC camera to construct something new online. And he has already put the virtual bricks into place. In the spring of 2008, Long and a partner founded Verge New Media (vergenewmedia.com), an online video production service for niche markets.

In November 2008, Verge entered into a joint venture to form Crafty Nation (CraftyNation.com), a social network devoted to the crafts community. Users can post blogs, pictures, and episodic videos, which Long's team produces.

Because Long is often Crafty Nation's cameraman, the video quality is on par with NBC's coverage of presidential events. And in a start-up, Long's rates are competitive with other freelance video professionals.

The videos and site are ad supported, and the advertisements are contextual—for a video on bead making, you will likely see an ad for a bead supply company. And despite the economic situation, Long is sanguine about the site's prospects. He believes that the worst of times are actually the best of times for his target niche. "Do-it- yourself activities have always thrived during recessions," he told me.

Long acquired his experience from an old media job, but he built a global personal brand through Twitter, and he is poised to thrive at a time when many of his colleagues are being made obsolete.

The Power of Generosity

Jeremiah Owyang's (@jowyang) personal brand played a big role in landing him his current job, as well as his previous one. The next time he needs a job, chances are he'll get multiple leads simply by tweeting his availability.

If you Google "online communities," Owyang is prominent in the results you will find. As a senior analyst for Forrester Research, he covers all things social media. He prepares reports for large companies, often about the small companies that are disrupting their markets with digital innovations.

Charlene Li performed a similar role at Forrester for nine years. When Li sought a replacement, naturally she began the search online. She entered several keyword variations for "social media marketing." Owyang came up more often than anyone else. That alone did not get him the job, of course. Owyang works hard and produces a lot of useful content; otherwise he would not be the top result for so many relevant search engine queries. But his social media activities—and what others had to say about him—clearly had a greater influence than the old-fashioned ritual of a résumé and writing sample.

When Li met Owyang, he was an online strategist for PodTech, a now-defunct podcast producer. He landed the PodTech job because of his personal brand too. Owyang decided to position himself as a Web thinker and strategist and build his brand from the ground up, using social media.

Owyang and Forrester have brands that depend on each other. Because Forrester is a respected technology research firm, Owyang became a recognized expert by joining the team; he was often interviewed by the top-ranked mainstream media on social media issues. Simultaneously, Forrester enhanced its brand by bringing in Owyang, who had so successfully constructed his personal brand.

I mentioned on Twitter my plan to interview Owyang, and re-ceived four e-mails extolling his generosity. The response from Les-lie Carothers (@tkpleslie), founder of the Kaleidoscope Partnership (tkpartnership.com), was typical. "When I first started and he had no reason to help me, he did," she wrote. Since then, she said, his writing has served as a mentorship for her.

Owyang was my first case study in what I call lethal generosity, a term I used when I told you about Rubbermaid and Molson Canada a few chapters back. In social media, the people who are the most generous to their communities almost invariably acquire the great-est influence.

I first met Owyang in December 2006, when he was employed at Hitachi Data Systems (HDS). He was eager, smart, and relatively unknown. He was hungry to understand how social media could help both him and his employer.

HDS was not the easiest place to evangelize social media. The parent corporation is a Japanese-based global enterprise with a traditional top-down structure. Social media is the opposite, due to its tendency to disrupt traditional structures.

Owyang explored paths of least resistance at HDS. His first major success was to create the Data Storage Wiki. This served as an industrywide site for all vendors, purchasers, and managers of data storage. He carefully established it as a community tool. He went out of his way to treat the site as the possession of the industry and not of his employer. He invited all HDS competitors to join in. But HDS had started it, and the data storage community knew it.

This led to an interesting choice for the competitors. They could ignore the Data Storage Wiki, and thus stay out of a communitywide conversation that involved their own customers and prospects, as well as analysts and others who cared about data storage. Or they could participate in the wiki and help bolster the HDS thought-leader position. Owyang's generosity had placed the competitors right between a rock and a hard place.

This is lethal generosity. Being helpful to the community and being inclusive of all participants is authentic, not devious. Yet it can have a very strong impact on the position of a competing company or individual.

The wiki forged the foundation of Owyang's brand and could have also contributed to the HDS brand. Social media sites are among the fastest-growing consumers of data storage. But when Owyang left HDS, it meant the end of most social media participation for Hitachi. No one replaced him. The Data Storage Wiki went into atrophy and, without fanfare, disappeared from the Internet altogether.

I interviewed Owyang in January 2009. He told me that Twitter is the core component of his social media strategy—and he uses about a dozen tools quite regularly.

When it comes to your own personal branding strategy, Owyang told me, "Have an objective. First, define a very clear career mission. What is it that you're trying to solve for your clients or employer? Don't focus on the minutiae of tools; instead, think of the greater problem and solution you'll provide."

He went on: "Stick to your plan. Be consistent and be ready for the long haul. Building my own personal brand has taken years, and I studied those who did it before me and emulated them. Integrate the tools. Don't just focus on one but learn to use them all in tandem."

> @anamariecox: If you haven't had a glass of bourbon rimmed with Bacon Salt, you are missing out. Also, you are healthier than me.

Twitterville's Mayor

I once suggested that Chris Brogan (@ChrisBrogan) should be Twitterville's mayor, because he is among the community's most generous participants, making him also among the most influential.

Brogan is one of a small handful of Twitterville thinkers who have made themselves available and useful to both community new-comers and long-term residents. Like most mayors, the guy seems to be everywhere.

Brogan's life was considerably different prior to Twitter. A few years back he was a telecomm guy, starting with Verizon when it was still New England Telephone and NYNEX. That got him into the guts of wireless technology and business strategy.

"I have no professional background in business communications, except that my entire career was founded on it," he told me.

"Social media was a way to express my thoughts, to share in two-way streams what mattered to me, and to find people with like minds to share a voice. The more I become immersed in this technology and with people who embrace it, the more I'm finding value," he said.

While I have no examples of Brogan being lethal in his generosity, as Owyang has been, he is certainly a leader in what I call Twitterville's cult of generosity. He has written more blog posts giving tips on how businesses should use social media than anyone I know—with the possible exception of Owyang.

But he has also been active in more Twitterville goodwill fund-raising activities than any member of social media's business community.

In February 2009 he gave away his hair so kids could get laptop computers they could not afford. It started with one of many social media "ego lists." *Ad Age* posted a Power 150 list of social media blogs. When someone tweeted Brogan, asking if he expected ever to be top-ranked on the list, Brogan replied that if he ever made the number one position, he would shave his head in honor of the shiny-domed author Seth Godin—who was number one at the time, and whom Brogan credits as his mentor.

Then Brogan, of course, made it to the top of the list; he posted a video on his site announcing he would shave his head—which he has since done. But instead of focusing on his *Ad Age* popularity, he posted a headline saying he was shaving his head for charity.

In fact, Brogan, who had already donated significantly to the One Computer for Every Child program in Africa, asked people to make small contributions for needy kids in the United States to get laptop computers. For this One Laptop per Child (OLPC) program, Brogan promised to match each dollar that others pledged, up to $10,000. He would then ask either Dell or HP to donate double the amount he had raised.

All this generosity has bolstered his personal brand. And that bolstered brand has caused his revenues to rise despite the recession. Brogan consults for big corporate brands on social media strategies and programs. He told me he makes twice the money today than what he earned as a telecomm guy less than three years earlier.

Inheriting a Tweeting Talent

Laura Fitton's personal brand is also very closely integrated into Twitter. In fact, prior to starting on the platform in April 2007, no one knew about her at all.

"I was under a rock," she told me, and the rock was in Pennsylvania. She had been actively consulting for corporate clients on communications issues for fifteen years, but between 2005 and 2007 she had two complicated, nearly back-to-back pregnancies. When her life stabilized, she found herself a stay-at-home mom.

These days, Fitton sits on the best-attended panels at the most prestigious industry conferences. When a session ends, she is usually surrounded by more attendees than the other panelists. She is on the short list of people whom old media journalists talk to when writing about Twitter. You see her in social media venues being asked her thoughts on just about everything.

When I spoke with her in May 2009, she was working on a start-up called One Forty (oneforty.com) so named for the maximum number of characters in a tweet. If she raises the $140,000 in investment capital, the company will attempt to serve as a Twitter marketplace where people can find Twitter applications, reviews, and, perhaps most important, execute transactions.

If you've heard of Fitton, it's highly likely to have happened since her arrival on Twitter, and it's just as likely that you know her as @ Pistachio. In a very short period, Fitton's brand has exploded solely through becoming one of Twitterville's most followed residents. And in the process she has acquired major-name clients, such as Johnson & Johnson and Ford Motor Company.

"If it seems like I came out of nowhere," she told me, "that's because I did." But her path followed a logical—and extremely rapid—progression. She started watching social media, particularly blogs, while she was at home. One post in particular strongly extolled the virtues of Twitter.

A few days later she attended a Tweetup in Boston and met several Twitterville community leaders. One of them was Brogan, who became her mentor.

Fitton followed his advice, and by early 2009 she seemed to be on the dais at every social media gathering. She was guest speaking at Harvard University and consulting on social media strategy with major corporations. She has since become a specialist in residence for SHIFT Communications, a national independent PR firm active in social media. She's active, like Brogan, in countless goodwill fundraising activities.

"All my work now comes from people I know through Twitter: all of it," she told me. "Not only do all my clients come from Twitter, but by the time someone contacts me, they thoroughly understand how my mind works and have already decided I am the one for the project."

What's more, she found time in her newly busy schedule to coauthor *Twitter for Dummies*, a handy how-to book for Twitter beginners.

How did so much happen in so little time?

Well for one thing, it may have been in her genes. Fitton stumbled across a 1974 diary kept by her late great-grandmother Pratt, who was then ninety-nine years old and living in the Pond Nursing Home in Wrentham, Massachusetts.

"I noticed the entries were short little tweetlike bursts," Fitton said. "It's lovely; she tweets about weather, collecting stamps, making afghans, and how she gradually gets to know the nurse Ruth."

The diary has entries about spending hundreds of hours creating a hand-crocheted afghan and the satisfaction and relief Pratt feels when her daughter, Pauline, receives it with gratitude. Pratt talks a lot about the Red Sox opening game being rained out in 1974. That same year, the team sent her an autographed baseball for her birthday.

Fitton was touched by how the diary allowed her, so many years later, to have an intimate view of her great-grandmother, who died at age 101 in 1976.

She took entries from the diary and created a Twitter account, @ggpratt, where you can see how the diary entries work so well in a Twitter format.

> @cshirky: New Illinois politics motto: "We're Louisiana, but with more snow . . ."

The Luminary Brand

Like Jim Long, Veronica Belmont (@veronica) thought her career would be behind the curtain, not on center stage. Educated in audio production and new media studies at Boston's Emerson College, a cross-country student jaunt landed her in San Francisco, where she fell in love with the city.

Getting an internship there at CNET, the tech media subsidiary of CBS, was the "cherry on top," she told me.

In a little over three years from her CNET start, Belmont has become among the best-known faces in tech sector video. With over 675,000 followers as of June 2009, she was the fifty-fifth most popular tweeter worldwide. She is by far the most followed person profiled in this book.

Her brief career has seen a prolific string of increasingly popular programs. She began at CNET as a video producer for the First Look from the Labs series. She then became the audio producer of the once-popular podcast *Buzz Out Loud*. One day she decided to correct one of the hosts while he was on the air. That was her online broadcasting debut, and it was well received, so her interjections became an increasingly frequent part of the show—until she became the third host.

Her role as a producer-host expanded to include two additional CNET podcasts: *MP3 Insider* and *Crave*.

In July 2007 Belmont left CNET to host and produce Mahalo Daily (mahalodaily.com), a new start-up formed by social media luminary Jason Calacanis (@JasonCalacanis). The podcast soon became one of the most popular of all tech sector video programs.

She moved on to costar in two online video programs: *Tekzilla* (revision3.com/tekzilla), produced by Revision3 Studios in San Francisco, and *Qore*, Sony Computer Entertainment America Inc.'s subscription-based gaming program.

Belmont has also made numerous guest appearances on other video shows and in the social media world; her face is almost instantly recognized on video. She is generally referred to simply as

Veronica. People say "I was watching Veronica last night" rather than referring to Tekzilla.

"It never would have happened without Twitter," Belmont told me. Twitter seems to serve as her manager and her publicist. She uses Twitter to connect all her social media output. She also uses it to instantly gather audience feedback, asking followers what stories they want her to cover.

Belmont is one of an extremely small handful of people in social media who have cultivated the "luminary personal brand." Luminary brands look pretty much like a movie star's brand. Of course, like most movie stars, Belmont needs to have talent, and most people agree that she does. But so do a great number of other aspirants, many of whom would love to replace Belmont in video stature.

Belmont's competitive edge rests in the popularity of her personal brand. This is a business model that is useful to very few people, whose livelihood depends on fame.

Social media generally works differently than mass media, and very few people are wise to pursue a career based not just on talent but on follower counts. If Sony wants people to subscribe to a game video, then having her as the host is an asset, and she will be compensated accordingly.

Twitter is to Belmont what Nielsen Rankings are to *American Idol*. It is a public metric of her brand value. She is not the most frequent of tweet posters, although she tweets several times a day. While she often posts about her blog and her various video shows, she spends about equal time sending followers to other sites through links.

Belmont expresses ambivalence about the privacy she needs to maintain. When you meet her face-to-face she is quite open and candid. Ironically, her celebrity has made her more cautious as a public figure. Most Twitter users are not as closely scrutinized as Belmont. What she says about a product can substantially help or hurt a brand. What she shares about herself can just as significantly shape her personal brand and thus her revenue.

Addressing a Big Animal Behavior Problem

Dr. Mark Drapeau (@cheeky_geeky), whom I mentioned in chapter 8, does not have Veronica Belmont's celebrity. He's a scientist by training, an expert on animal behavior. His past endeavors have included the Honey Bee Genome Project.

Drapeau's expertise in animal behavior got him a consulting contract at a U.S. Defense Department think tank, where he was assigned in 2008 to study social media. His fieldwork brought him to Tweetups in several cities, where he began meeting and engaging with some of Twitterville's most active members. People seemed interested in him, perhaps because of the novelty: you just don't meet many government-contracted animal-behavior experts at Tweetups.

In April 2008 Drapeau started tweeting, covering all sorts of topics, not just government related. "I use my Twitter network to connect people with news I find interesting," he told me. "If it interests me, then it might interest them." He has become a regular guest columnist on Mashable (mashable.com), one of the tech industry's largest and most respected blogs, and True/Slant (byvoices.com), an online citizen-journalism site.

In contrast to the popular conception of a government bureaucrat, Drapeau likes to take a stand. I've already mentioned his opposition to branded accounts, in which he argued on Mashable that branded Twitter accounts should be banned from Twitterville. "Behind every Twitter account is a person," he wrote. "But some of these people 'hide' behind organizational brands, obscuring their persona and therefore reducing authenticity and transparency." Strong stuff.

Through his prolific tweeting, Drapeau has developed a personal brand that puts him at the intersection of social media and the federal government. It's a neighborhood growing in dimension. The Obama administration has made e-Government an initiative for every department, division, bureau, and agency. These new technologies are supposed to make our government more efficient and responsive. Right now, there are a long list of people who need to figure out social media strategies and a short list of knowledgeable consultants who can help them.

Drapeau is now one of the few go-to guys on the red-hot topic of government and social media. That's the brand he's built for himself through Twitter, steadily growing in influence and authority with every tweet. "Merely by talking about what I do every day, Twitter has made me more popular," he told me. "People find my combination of science research, government consulting, and happy hours with a dose of humor interesting, and I'm happy about that."

I wondered what being an expert in animal behavior has to do with solving the challenges of e-Government.

"Unless you're a computer programmer or venture capitalist, social software has very little to do with technology," he contended. "It's about people communicating with each other, and when we talk about ecosystems of people communicating and messaging or spreading memes, that's the language of evolutionary biology, ecology, and animal behavior. Social media is just a big animal-behavior problem."

Drapeau has a point. At the most primal level, humans are just animals. Our behavior isn't all that different from other primates. We organize into packs, and we compete for prominence in those packs. We depend on other members of these packs. So perhaps global neighborhoods are just another way of forming them.

> @dsilverman: oh noes!! may have to unfollow @ijustine. she's got an animated GIF as her icon and it's in my Following montage, giving me epilepsy.

Humanizing the Humans

Not so long ago, when you handed someone your business card, your company logo would have the greatest impact on your recipient's perception of your personal brand.

Increasingly, when someone meets you, reads what you say online, hears or sees you in a podcast the impression that person has of you impacts what that person thinks of your company.

At the height of the Broadcast Era, Aneta Hall of Pitney Bowes would have been far from the only person in the room who put her name and company on her ID tag. Now, in some circles, your Twitter handle means more. An individual brand now impacts a corporate brand.

Historically, branding efforts rarely focused on the real people in a company. If employees were represented in ads, for example, actors would portray them. And the branding efforts attempted to convince audiences of a company that did not exist, a company where employees seemed to think in total unanimity and speak in perfectly choreographed harmony.

In the fast-emerging Conversational Era, personal brands are building or destroying corporate brands. Social media is amplifying the personal brand, and that is happening faster and more dramatically in Twitterville than anywhere else. It is a community of millions of personal brands. They are shaping the present and future of individuals and the companies they represent.

Some smart corporations have come to understand that their credibility rises as they reveal the humans who actually work for them. And the fact that these employees share an umbrella does not require them to agree at all times on all issues. Most people find it comforting to discover that there are real people with real views behind the branded curtain.

In a previous chapter, we discussed a small handful of companies that so far have succeeded with branded Twitter accounts. But other than that handful, Twitter is comprised of millions and millions of people who are building personal brands. What you think of them is shaping what you think of their companies—whether that company is a freelancer in a home office, a television network, a consulting practice, or a political campaign.

CHAPTER 12

Braided Journalism

O n the day I started writing this chapter, the *Rocky Mountain News*, winner of four Pulitzer Prizes, died at the age of 150.

Much was written about that paper's great moments. Even more was said about the decline of newspapers. Some speculated that social media was killing newspapers. As a touch of irony, the announcement that the *News* was closing was recorded and uploaded to YouTube.

Few doubt there will be more newspaper closings, particularly among metropolitan dailies. There will also be more commentary speculating on social media's role in the decline of traditional media.

Compounding matters are a few loud voices in social media who cheer the demise of newspapers and traditional broadcast media. I am not among them. I do not think the world will be a better place without professional news-gathering organizations.

Perhaps one day a blogger, tweeter, or Facebook poster may be added to the more traditionally credentialed White House press corps. In March 2009 Garrett Graff (garrettgraff.com/blog) was awarded a one-day pass to attend an Obama news conference. He later posted that he found the room shabby and the event uninteresting. Others of us might have appreciated the chance to report on what was said.

But this day is not imminent. Even social media champions like me see the problems of admitting bloggers to cover a White House news conference anytime soon—unless they represent a recognized and credible news organization. For one thing, there's just too many of us, and selecting attendees is too complex.

There are legitimate reasons why accredited journalists often are assigned to cover government events, wars, and natural disasters while social media writers stay home.

Yet as this chapter demonstrates, there have been some remarkable exceptions, which show that the either/or division between traditional and citizen journalists may not be the direction in which we are headed.

Instead, I see a convergence of old and new media in our short-term future. And in that convergence I see great possibility.

I call this convergence "braided journalism."

There are three strands to braided journalism, each comprising a great many fibers. The strands are coming together, intertwining, and changing the way people get information.

1. **Traditional Media.** Organizations that pay professionals to gather and report on that which is timely, interesting, or useful. Their roots are in printed and broadcast media. They pay people to go out and get content that will be reported and published. As these organizations move online, they remain traditional, publishing news to derive ad revenues.

2. **Citizen Journalism.** This, quite simply, is the reporting of news by amateurs. Very often, these reporters stumble upon something newsworthy, and they share what they see with others. Citizen journalists have been around

since the beginning of recorded time. A key point is that they are amateurs who report news for free because they believe others should be informed.

3. **Social Media.** This simply involves places on the Internet where people communicate and collaborate. It is the newest and shortest of the three strands. Not everything posted to social media involves reporting, but it is where traditional and citizen journalism touch and braid into the very fiber of social media. Something new and different is forming, which includes and encompasses both the professionals and the amateurs

Let me explain where I'm coming from.

I started my career as a journalist for traditional newspapers. They were remarkable years. I was barely twenty when I began, but because I represented newspapers, I was allowed free access to concerts and movies; mayors dropped everything to answer my questions; police granted me access to restricted areas. I was impressed by both the power and responsibility given to a reporter. The pay wasn't much, but at least I was compensated for my content.

As a newspaper reporter I was part of an organization. I had editors who challenged my facts and refined my writing. When it was a big enough story, my editor assigned a news photographer to join me at a news scene.

And then there were the stringers—people on call who covered minor meetings and outlying areas that we full-timers could not always reach when news broke. They were paid even less than us staff reporters, and when budgets began to be slashed, stringers were the first to get the boot. In general, they were not professional-quality writers. But they knew the facts and nuances of their hometowns.

News organizations started to contract in the 1970s. The costs of newsprint, union demands, and delivery-truck fuel all started cutting too deeply into revenue.

That was a headache in itself. But when the Web came along in the late 1990s, it became a Motrin headache, and the advent of social media made it one very big, throbbing migraine.

The pain was not caused by any single monumental incident, but by a series of them that mounted in frequency and intensity over decades. Perhaps the first pang came in 1988 when Brad Templeton, (ideas.4brad.com), an online joke collector, started ClariNet, which called itself the first online newspaper. In 1993, it became the first dot-com and was the first online news organization to require paid subscriptions.

ClariNet never earned much more than lunch money compared to most daily newspapers of the time. But it demonstrated that you could organize, search, and find news faster and easier on the Internet. Newspapers recognized then that they might have a problem, but shrugged off any action because the number of people who used the Internet to get news was so small.

Besides, for established newspapers to migrate from one business model to another is a challenging, time-consuming endeavor. It's not just the mechanics. It's also cultural.

The eminent *New York Times* business-technology reporter John Markoff once likened bloggers to the "CB broadcasters of the 21st century"—the guys who chat their way down highways, serving up miscellaneous tidbits with uneven accuracy and questionable relevance.

Markoff's characterization may not be flattering, but there is truth to it. Yet I think he vastly underestimates the value of the CB broadcasters. Sometimes something very important happens on a road and will have an impact on more than just a few "good buddies."

Markoff is undisputedly among the best of breed in contemporary professional journalists, but in his disdain, he seems to have overlooked peers who get paid to "report" on aliens who come to Earth and impregnate movie stars.

Besides, it wasn't the professional media people who decided the trends—it was the readers and viewers. And where they went, the advertisers would surely follow.

By 1995, Yahoo! had come along and broadcast started to see ad dollars slipping away. Then came the free classifieds offered on Craigslist, and the headache really started to be debilitating.

In essence, the traditional news business model was broken. That $100 a year in per capita subscription was a lot more expensive for readers than free online. And $2.20 per line for a classified in the local paper was no longer such a good deal.

Much focus was placed on such issues, but what got overlooked was old journalism's irreplaceable asset: credible, effective, branded news organizations. The value was not in the paper but in the content. The reader was moving online, and many newspapers dragged their feet to follow them.

> @jayrosen_nyu: @scottros The sad fact is many pro journalists doubt that blogging gave people a printing press; they think it gave everyone a vanity press.

From Cave to Twitterville

Citizen journalism has been around since our ancestors lived in caves. Tribe members used blood and berries to paint stories of hunts on the walls. This was a form of citizen journalism.

Citizen journalists are nonfiction storytellers. The people who do it today may be a little taller than their cave-dwelling ancestors, but otherwise people haven't much changed since then. However, their tools have vastly improved. And the better the tools, the more people can use them. Connected technology takes less time and moves a lot faster than cave painting did.

Modern tools predate the Web. In 1991 Rodney King, a black man, drove through a red light in Los Angeles; police pursued him. Instead of pulling over, King sped up, he would later say, because he feared the Los Angeles police.

When King was finally pulled over, he was dragged from his car onto the sidewalk, where several LAPD officers repeatedly struck him with batons and viciously kicked him.

Watching from a distance and in shadow, George Holliday videotaped twelve minutes of the beating on his new camera. Holliday then copyrighted the tape, and licensed copies to local TV stations that broadcast excerpts the following night.

Few people think that Rodney King was the first black man to be dragged and beaten by police, but this time George Holliday was nearby and he had a handheld camcorder that would provide persuasive evidence contradicting the official reports

Holliday had no intention of becoming a citizen journalist on that night, but he had a camera and just happened to be where news was happening. The tape led to riots, investigations into LAPD discrimination, a change in police chiefs, and a change of public perception on how police sometimes treat minorities.

Flash forward almost eighteen years. It is 2:00 AM, on New Year's Day 2009. A skirmish breaks out on a BART car, the San Francisco Bay Area's subway system. When the car stops at Fruitvale Station in Oakland, several BART police pull four youths from the train and scores of New Year's Eve celebrants get off to watch the incident. Several officers crouch over Oscar Grant, the only one of the four youths not handcuffed. He is lying on his belly when one of the officers steps back, draws his gun, takes aim, fires, and kills the young man.

But the tools had changed since Rodney King's day. They had become smaller, cheaper, and more ubiquitous. Three BART passengers had whipped out video cameras, and they recorded the shooting death of Oscar Grant from three separate angles. The clips found their way onto local TV and YouTube, where two million people saw them over the next few days.

Most citizen journalists become so by coincidence. You may become one tomorrow on your way to work.

The Social Media Strand

Social media started in the late 1990s, but was mostly the purview of technology enthusiasts until about 2005. Before that, the tools were too difficult for most people to use. As they got easier, adoption accelerated.

If social media sites are not yet ubiquitous, they soon will be. According to comScore, the online data research firm, the top twenty social media sites had a total of one billion users by November 2008. There is, of course, a great deal of duplication on these lists. For example, I'm a registered user of six of these sites, and I assume comScore counted me six times.

In any case, a lot of people have adopted social media, many of them found themselves in places where news happened, and because of social media, they had venues to report what they saw without much notice from traditional media.

Evelyn Rodriguez (@Eve11) is one good example. She did not visit Thailand in 2004 to become a citizen journalist. She was there for beaches and fun when a tsunami assaulted Phuket, where she was staying. The first wave was over a hundred feet tall, and miles wide. It caused considerable death, destruction, and suffering. Rodriguez was not injured, but she underwent considerable hardship, ending up in a refugee camp for a short while.

She was among the first to relay eyewitness reports as a citizen journalist. She used social media to distribute her reports days before any traditional Western journalist ventured into the area. She was not alone. A Dutch vacationer video-recorded the second wave as it flooded a beachfront restaurant, engulfing an elderly couple clinging to a rail. The footage was uploaded to YouTube, where it has been viewed thousands of times.

Unfortunately, natural disasters seem to be a great venue for citizen journalists using social media. People are very often present when something awful happens.

When Hurricane Katrina struck the U.S. Gulf Coast in August 2005, the worst hurricane to hit North America in recorded history went virtually unrecorded by traditional media. Instead national press interviewed federal officials in Washington, D.C., a thousand miles away from the damage. Local media either shut down or had no electricity to broadcast.

Blogger Ernest Svenson (@ernieattorney) was there. He experienced a saga of unpleasant events. He blogged about what he saw and gave his readers a real sense of what was going on. When the storm interrupted Svenson's Internet connection, he relayed text content via cell phone to a friend in Florida, who posted at his blog on his behalf.

New Orleans is just south of Lake Pontchartrain, the second-largest saltwater lake in the United States. When the lake flooded its banks, Slidell, Louisiana, a folksy city of about twenty-five thousand, was inundated, and nearly all residents scattered in haste.

Brian Oberkirch (@BrianOberkirch) a technology marketing consultant, was living in Texas when Katrina hit. But Slidell was his hometown. He had family and friends there.

Oberkirch started the Slidell Hurricane Damage Blog (slidell .weblogswork.com) to report on what happened, and more important, to find missing people, pets, and property. As residents of the community fled to other parts of the country, they found one another through Oberkirch's blog.

I don't know if any newspaper ever had a stringer in Slidell. It remains one of those places that outsiders tend to overlook. But when disaster struck, one person stepped up to keep a community connected.

The Risk of Shedding Light

Much of citizen journalism is far from dramatic, but is the work of everyday people reporting "hyperlocal news" of interest to very few people—for example, @UnitedLinen's coverage of local baseball games. But there are those who sometimes volunteer to shed light on events that others would prefer to conduct in the dark—such as Rodney King's beating.

They often do this at considerable risk to personal safety.

In Saudi Arabia and Iran, bloggers have been tortured and executed for offending government or religious leaders. In Egypt a twenty-one-year-old student was imprisoned for four years after he criticized the country's leader and Islam.

Egyptian powers also managed to get Wael Abbas (@WaelAbbas) fired in 2005 from his job as a freelance journalist because his reports irritated them. Instead of stopping, Abbas turned to social media. Since 2006 he has posted hundreds of hidden camera videos depicting police brutality, government corruption, and harassment of "Westernized" women on YouTube.

In 2007 he became the first blogger to receive the Knight Foundation Award for Journalistic Excellence. He does all this at great risk. Abbas told me he has been detained, stalked, threatened, and followed by police. He noted that it is not unheard of for Egyptian police to pick up people who are never seen again.

Abbas is prepared to face such a fate. If his voice is muted, he predicts he will be replaced. "People need to know what is occurring," he told me. "Who does the telling really does not matter."

I was among people all over the world who were concerned in April 2009, when Abbas got into a dispute with a neighbor who was a police officer. The policeman broke into the Abbas home, where he beat up both Wael and his mother. Abbas went to the local police station to file a complaint. He was told to go away. When he refused, they threw him into jail, where he followed James Buck's lead from exactly a year earlier. He tweeted his situation from inside a jail cell, and people all over the world picked it up. Like Buck, he was freed twenty-four hours later. Abbas had no State Department help. He just had Twitter, where many voices were raised on his behalf.

"Many voices" is a phrase I heard many times when I visited China and met prominent members of that country's blogging community. It refers to how bloggers hope to avoid government crackdowns. With an estimated 250 million Chinese using blogs, forums, Facebook, Twitter, and China-based social media platforms, China has more people on social media than any other country.

Like everywhere else, most Chinese social media content is neither newsworthy nor challenging to the government. There is more flirting online, by far, than talk of human rights.

Yet there are envelope-pushers. In November 2008 I was a guest speaker at a Chinese blogger conference where some participants expressed pride at how many times authorities had temporarily shut down their blogs because of so-called offensive content.

They were clearly amused when I asked if they feared imprisonment, pointing out that such occurrences did happen, but very rarely. More often an offending statement will simply get a blogger's post blocked without comment or explanation. When this happens the censored blogger gains a certain prestige among dissident social media practitioners.

Isaac Mao, China's first and perhaps most famous blogger, told me in an interview that Westerners often perceive the Chinese government as an all-seeing entity, but in fact there is simply too much to censor online for the government to keep up.

As one blogger explained, "Too many voices. Too few ears and eyes."

I was repeatedly told that while no one knew for certain, there was a common belief that the Chinese government employed thirty thousand censors. This seemed like a daunting number at first. But when you examine it closer it soon gets less so.

These censors, I was told, are assigned to cover all the content produced by 1.3 billion Chinese. They review all the books, magazines, movies, radio and television broadcasts, speeches, lectures, and leaflets in search of offending statements.

By September 2008 there were an estimated half-billion Chinese with Internet access. Most content that offends the government is posted in online forums, where speakers are usually anonymous. While it can be done, it is not easy for censors to track down offenders who post from Internet cafés.

Twitter has many Chinese interested in two areas. First, China's growing Web 2.0 community is embracing Twitter because it is an easy way to join conversations that are relevant to their work and to let them understand what others are doing. Second, the dissident community has used Twitter because it is difficult for the censors to keep up. As more people enroll in Twitter and post more and more comments, it gets increasingly difficult for censors to track an offending post to its source.

The dissidents also understand that censors use keyword searches on the Internet. They work around that as well by changing a character in the phrase being searched. For example, if a Chinese tweeter wishes to make fun of the government anthem of "social harmony," she changes a character and the word becomes "river crab." Censors miss it, at least thus far, but tweeters don't. As of April 2009 I could find no case of a Chinese tweeter being blocked, nor has Twitter been taken down—yet. This is subject, of course, to change at any minute.

When I visited China, insiders estimated there were an additional twenty-five million social media posts on blogs, Facebook, Twitter, and localized platforms, topped off with about forty thousand user-generated videos per week. Not surprisingly, the nation's censors are also assigned to review scores of millions of daily e-mails.

"Too many voices. Too few eyes and ears."

Activists also seem adept at outmaneuvering the censors, who primarily search for offending keywords such as "Tibet." Instead of using that nation's name, bloggers talk about "mountain people," which a keyword searcher will miss, but blog followers can figure out it refers to Tibet.

But the government can be provoked into taking broader steps if they feel they are being outmaneuvered. A few weeks before June 4, 2009, the twentieth anniversary of Tiananmen Square's historic confrontation, the government simply shut down all international social media platforms. They were restored on June 8, and Chinese social media aficionados celebrated the restoration in a string of major city Tweetups.

Rerouting for Safety

Some citizen journalists use social media to make trouble; others do it to achieve the opposite. In Kenya, few people have their own computers. In outlying areas they don't even have cell phones, but there's usually one in each village that people share.

When violence followed Kenya's disputed 2007 election, Erik Hersman (@WhiteAfrican), an American missionary's son who is now an online entrepreneur for African-made products, created Ushahidi, (ushahidi.com), a site offering location-based information on violence. When there was trouble, flames on the map indicated hot spots, and the site offered routes Kenyans could use to by-pass them.

Converging on Twitterville

By early 2008 the writing was on the wall for newspapers and some broadcast media. Halfhearted attempts and dabbles in social media were not enough. They would need to follow readers and advertisers online or perish. The downturn in the economy accelerated the process.

Big media started to arrive in Twitterville in early 2007. Like so many of the companies I've told you about, they came intent on talking, but the savvier ones would soon discover there was greater benefit in listening.

CNN was perhaps the first big media company to arrive, or so people thought. @CNNBRK posted headlines of fast-breaking news with links to CNN sites. After @CNNBRK eclipsed @BarackObama to become Twitterville's most popular account for a while, many in Twitterville were surprised to hear that @CNNBRK had been a citizen-generated feed until the news organization acquired it in April 2009.

Still, CNN has had its own innovations. News anchor Rick Sanchez started @RickSanchezCNN. When he is on the air, Sanchez often reads comments and answers questions that come in on Twitter, thus integrating it into live TV broadcasting.

Other media companies have successfully followed suit. *The New York Times,* NPR, BBC, and the UK *Guardian* all had one or more of the top twenty-five Twitter accounts in June 2009.

But something else started to happen. The traditional media discovered social media was a great place to find news. While their own ranks of "feet on the street" had thinned over the years, here were millions of feet on a great many of the world's streets.

Such was the case in May 2008, when nineteen-year-old Casper Oppenhuis de Jong (@CasperODJ), staying in Chengdu, China, walked into the Bookworm (chinabookworm.com), a combination bookstore-bar-restaurant that is popular among visiting Westerners and expats who want to access free Wi-Fi. Suddenly the building started shaking. Oppenhuis de Jong knew it was an earthquake. He had felt them before, but this one was different.

"It got a lot more intense," he told me. "Everybody ran outside because the Bookworm was situated right under a residential tower."

The main shock lasted for nearly three minutes and the street became flooded with people, young and old.

This was the Szechuan Earthquake. Measuring 7.9 on the Richter scale, Oppenhuis de Jong was standing about fifty miles southwest of its epicenter. While Chingdu experienced only minor damage, devastation and tragedy was in close proximity. Over 80 percent of all buildings collapsed in nearby villages. More than fifty thousand people were killed. Hundreds of thousands more were injured, left homeless, or both.

After the shaking stopped, Oppenhuis de Jong went back inside. The phones were out, but amazingly, the Bookworm's broadband was still connected. He used Skype to contact his parents to let them know he was all right. But they had no reason to worry about him. Several hours would pass before Western media would report that the earthquake had occurred.

He finished his call and started tweeting as reports came in, pausing only to run outside during aftershocks. Oppenhuis de Jong was not trying to become a citizen journalist. He had not come to cover an earthquake, but there he was. He kept tweeting, reporting on what he knew to be true, making it clear when he was only relaying unconfirmed rumors.

A couple of hours later, the BBC, Al Jazeera, and the *Wall Street Journal* were following the Dutch teenager and relaying his reports as well. From there it spread throughout much of the world's most popular media.

This was the first time that the world's traditional media swarmed to a citizen tweeter, treating him as a primary news source of a fast-breaking event. It would not be the last.

> @pzriddle: Newark employee and I sharing a quiet corner at gate C82, me tweeting and he praying to Mecca. Salaam aleikum, friend.

Mumbai Terror: Feet on Bloody Streets

On November 28, 2008, terrorists assaulted multiple sites in Mumbai, India, the world's largest city. Two luxury hotels, a Jewish center, a train station, and a hospital were among the sites seized by ten well-armed terrorists who acted with military precision.

The siege would last three full days. Before it was over, 173 people would be killed and more than 300 wounded. Traditional press in India complied with government requests to stay away from sites under attack. Citizen journalists were another story.

Mumbai is southern Asia's financial center, making it also one of Asia's most connected places. Digital cameras and Internet-enabled cell phones are ubiquitous in affluent sectors.

Despite the warnings, some ventured into close proximity to sites under siege. There were tweeted reports from people on the ground and watching from windows of homes and office buildings. Eyewitness reports were tweeted and retweeted at amazing speed, often exceeding a rate of more than a thousand per hour.

Some were factual accounts. There were numerous inquiries regarding the well-being of loved ones. There was speculation as to who the perpetrators were and why they were doing it as well as expressions of outrage that police were not storming the places being held. Others pointed out the threats such actions posed to live hostages.

Anyone wishing to follow this tweetstream could just go to Twitter Search, type in "#mumbai," and see the surging flood of commentary. Among those using Twitter to find information were the BBC, the *New York Times,* NPR, and CNN.

More than a few false rumors started on Twitter, but more often than not they were squelched minutes later via tweets. The heavy traffic made the usual vetting process more challenging. It was often difficult to determine from where or whom the information was coming.

But the real heroes of citizen journalism, from my perspective, were a handful of amateur photographers who got dangerously close to the violence, then uploaded their photos on Flickr and shared the links via Twitter.

Vinukumar Ranganathan, a nineteen-year-old who happened to live near the Taj Mahal Hotel, photographed armed terrorists holding weapons, images gathered at some risk. He took well over a hundred shots, showing wounded people lying in the street and flames shooting into the air. His work was viewed more than a hundred thousand times on the first day. Many of his shots found their way onto newswires and into newspapers, as well as onto television, often without attribution.

Interestingly, Ranganathan has made his Flickr photo collection private. If you want to use his content, you need to contact him and negotiate a license fee. Two other eyewitnesses, Apoorva Guptay and Soumik Kar (@technoindia), took photos that are free for reuse if you credit them under Creative Commons license.

During the Mumbai events, I found myself talking directly with a tweeter reporting what he saw from his apartment window across the street from the Taj Mahal Hotel as it ignited into flames. People in nine countries joined our conversation over a thirty-minute period.

A great many people on Twitter got a "first-person present" sense of what it was like to be in Mumbai as this story twisted and turned. You could feel the fury and frustration of the Indians. Many Americans said it reminded them of 9/11, except this time they were actually talking to people who were at the scene as it unfolded.

Government officials went on commercial television to explain that they were acting cautiously because there were live hostages. Indians went to Twitter, where they posted immediate and often negative responses. Some Indians began talking about retaliation against Pakistan. It had not yet been established that Pakistan was complicit in the attack.

At that point some Pakistanis joined in the conversation; while most posted from Europe and the United States, a few actually were inside Pakistan. When I suggested that India go slow and find out what happened, I received a series of DMs from one Pakistani, who identified himself as a midlevel government employee.

He confirmed that the terrorists had been trained in camps by Lashkar-e-Taiba (LeT), a fundamentalist Kashmirian independence group. The camps were on Pakistani soil, and the assault had been launched from Pakistan.

Three days later, the *New York Times* ran a story containing nearly identical allegations sourced from "unidentified Pakistani officials." A month later the Pakistani government officially confirmed what I had heard on Twitter.

This was an interesting dynamic. First, Twitter showed it could serve as a forum between people in a real-time, dangerous situation. This, in my view, adds hope that such conversations can dampen more warlike action. Second, quality of information being shared on Twitter proved to be generally accurate. There had been several false rumors, but each had been vetted and squelched on Twitter.

A few weeks later, when Israel retaliated against Hamas rockets by attacking Gaza, voices from both countries were active on Twitter as well. They used the hashtag "#Gaza," so that anyone on Twitter could express viewpoints.

Neither exchange of beliefs would have been possible without Twitter.

A Funny Thing Happened on the Way to New Jersey

From the Continental Airlines skid through the Sezchuan earthquake, through Mumbai and Gaza, the strands of braided journalism were slowly tightening. Less than one month after Mumbai, an event occurred which, in my view, created this new cord that I call braided journalism.

On January 15, 2009, US Airways Flight 1549 took off from LaGuardia Airport in New York headed to North Carolina, where 105 years earlier Orville Wright piloted the first flight ever, staying aloft for 12 seconds and traveling 120 feet.

Flight 1549 didn't do much better. It lasted six minutes and traveled eight miles. Wright's flight ended on a beach at Kitty Hawk. Flight 1549 skidded to a landing in the middle of the Hudson River, which separates Manhattan from New Jersey.

Janis Krums (@JKrums), twenty-three, of Sarasota, Florida, was on a ferry near where the Airbus A320 skidded to a halt.

When the plane came to a stop, Krums whipped out his iPhone and took what would become one of the year's most memorable photos. He used TwitPic, the new Twitter tool that Mike Wilson had used on Continental Airlines in Denver, to quickly integrate a photo with his tweet.

Never intending to become the most famous citizen journalist of modern times, Krums posted, "http://twitpic.com/135xa—There's a plane on the Hudson. I'm on the ferry going to pick up the people. Crazy."

A few minutes later, Krums was among the passengers who assisted the ferry crew in rescuing people from the wing of a sinking aircraft. He loaned his jacket to a passenger. He helped carry a flight attendant who had broken both her legs.

Krums loaned his phone to someone who may have given out his number, because a few minutes later he was surprised to receive a call from MSNBC. While he spoke live on the air, TV viewers saw the photo he had shot and uploaded.

If there is a single moment when braided journalism came together, this was it. With the photo, there could be no question of credibility. Without Krums, Twitter, and Twitpic, Janis Krums would have an interesting story to tell to his friends. Instead the world got to see what he saw, and the press got to see the value of the new breed of citizen journalists and their network of choice.

After he was done with MSNBC, his phone kept ringing late into the night from other traditional media. Then it started again the next morning. During the forty-eight hours immediately following the incident, he spoke to all major TV networks and a great many newspapers around the world.

Krums was on *Good Morning America, The Rachel Maddow Show,* CNN with Rick Sanchez, *20/20,* and two BBC segments. Two months later, he was still getting about two media requests per week.

You have probably seen the photo Krums took by iPhone, and you probably recall it. It may have taken your breath away, as it did mine. Most of the press published it or showed it to viewers. A few compensated Krums. Some gave him a credit but used it without permission or payment. One national newspaper mistakenly credited the photo to the Associated Press. The AP had offered to buy the photo, but Krums turned them down.

This brings us to an emerging issue that is rapidly evolving from braided journalism, one apparently felt also by Vinukumar Ranganathan, the brave young photographer on the streets of Mumbai. When a citizen journalist posts on social media it is assumed the content can be freely shared so long as credit is given. But what happens when professional media pick it up and use it as ad-supported content? How can someone give away content in one venue while charging another? On the other hand, how can traditional media pay a freelance photographer and not compensate someone like Krums?

As the braiding process tightens, it will be interesting to see how this issue evolves.

It does appear, however, that we social media practitioners are becoming the stringers for the world's traditional media, stringers of the Conversational Age.

The media did not intend to change any fundamental structures when they came to social media. But they have.

Braided journalism may be the salvation of traditional media. This benefits everyone, it seems to me. But whether or not traditional media organizations will be willing to compensate the citizen journalists who are assisting in this salvation is an issue that is just now arising and is far from being resolved.

CHAPTER 13

Conversations with Constituents

Wherever you happen to live, chances are you think your government could do a better job. I've had the good fortune to travel frequently in recent years and to talk with people around the world on many issues. Whenever the topic of government comes up, I see eyes roll toward the ceiling. Complaints about government appear to be fairly universal. All over the world, they seem to fall into the same three buckets:

1. **Inefficiency.** Not only do people feel that their government takes too long to perform needed services, but also that its methods are antiquated—technology could get the job done faster and cheaper; tax dollars could be saved.
2. **Apathy.** It's hard to reach a real human being, and when you do, it often turns out to be a bureaucrat who demonstrably could care less about your problem.
3. **Corruption.** The public trust (and the public's money) is constantly abused.

Twitterville has already started to help some government agencies to become more responsive and efficient. Admittedly there is a long way to go, but things have a way of occurring with great speed in Twitterville. Perhaps, solving corruption is just around the corner too, but I wouldn't hold my breath.

In 2008 UK, Netherlands, and U.S. government agencies started coming into Twitterville in significant numbers.

Today there are hundreds of cabinet secretaries, governors, and mayors, as well as lesser federal, state, and local officials, with Twitter accounts, according to BearingPoint, a management and technology consulting firm. As of March 2009 there were also nineteen senators and fifty congressional representatives tweeting, according to Politico, a government technology watch site.

Politicians, including President Barack Obama, have used Twitter to bolster election campaigns; then, as government employees, they sometimes tweet to directly interact with the people they serve.

While Twitter is a free and easy way to address constituents, it seems that politicians and government workers are only just starting to learn that it works best as a two-way platform. Like so many businesses I've mentioned, many elected officials and some government agencies came to talk and learned to listen.

Much of it was ignited by the 2008 presidential campaign.

> @erikschmidt It occurs to me: If you're in your Stormtrooper mask, how do you blow your nose?

Obama in Twitterville

More than any other elected official, Barack Obama has had the greatest impact on Twitter. His campaign's Twitter effort was the first to be a highly visible component of a successful major election.

What seems to have generated the most attention was the numbers. On Election Day, @BarackObama had more than eighty thousand followers, which in November 2008 was enough to make it Twitterville's most popular account.

But did it get votes? That is more than a little difficult to determine. There were no pollsters or research firms tracking such data. The people who signed up to follow the account appeared to be overwhelmingly in the Obama camp to begin with. The account was never used to discuss specific issues. No one attempted to have conversations with constituents, and it was never really clear just who you were talking to when you sent a message to @BarackObama.

In fact, people in the Obama campaign told me that most of their Twitter posts were put up by well-informed volunteers, never someone senior or involved strategically in the campaign.

Yet Twitterville obviously helped the Obama effort in several ways. People found out how and where campaign events were being held. Some involved the candidate. Others were just local rallies and fund-raisers.

The Obama campaign also used Twitter to mobilize volunteers. It announced where help was most needed. In the closing days of the campaign, volunteers were directed to the states and districts where the vote was predicted to be close. They also got information on the least expensive ways to get there.

There was more going on, however, than just the @BarackObama account. Ev Williams said in January 2009 that the presidential election had been the most discussed topic in Twitter's short history. On election night itself, there were more than a million mentions, the most posts that had ever occurred on Twitter.

Not only did the candidate with the greatest Twitter presence win the election, but just about all observers said that Obama had been the most discussed candidate.

This, I figure, sent a signal to other candidates. When I was a reporter, I had been told the reasons that politicians attended the funerals of well-known people. It was because that's where the voters could be found. It was also where the press would notice you and maybe take your picture. Politicians tend to go where voters can be found, and increasingly they can be found in Twitterville.

If more conversations are going to be held on Twitter, and more people are joining those conversations, it would not be a wise move for future candidates to ignore Twitterville so long as that is where the action is.

In its first 125 days in office, the Obama administration has tackled a remarkably complex array of issues and challenges. The Twitter strategy was clearly not a top-level issue. The administration posted less than ten times in the first three months. It also did not bother to update the fact that Mr. Obama and his family moved from Chicago, where it said he lived. Yet his number of followers continued to grow. As of May 10, 2009, the essentially inactive account had nearly 1.2 million followers and grew by several thousand on most days.

Perhaps to make it clearer that the president of the United States is not spending his time on Twitter, a new account opened up. @WhiteHouse had fifty-six thousand followers ten days after it started. While posts are fairly regular, discussing action and events related to the executive branch, it too is far from conversational in tone. Perhaps at some point there will be a White House tweeter, possibly attached to the the press secretary's office.

Until Obama's election, the Internet was a place for politicos to get their candidate's message out and get campaign contributions in. But in 2008 people of all political persuasions learned the power of Twitter-based conversations. It is unlikely that many successful future national campaigns will be able to ignore Twitter as a factor. For that matter, even local campaigns may turn to Twitter as a viable and increasingly interactive venue for organizing and mobilizing supports, as well as for courting undecided voters.

Replacing the "Governator"

California governor Arnold Schwarzenegger used to be an actor. As the Terminator, he uttered his most famous line: "I'll be back."

Well, he won't be. At least, not as governor in 2010, since California has a two-term limit. He has discussed his regret at leaving before he could resolve a deep budget deficit on @Schwarzenegger, where he is fairly conversational and has been at times surprisingly interactive with his ninety-one thousand followers (as of May 2009). Responding a few minutes after a question was asked on May 10, 2009, by @mommiedearest about what he was doing personally to save California money, he wrote: "Cut my staff from 174 to 147 this year and all staff took a 9.3% cut in hours and pay. As for me, I don't accept my salary." He also doesn't charge the state for the expense of operating his car, a controversial Hummer.

If a Democrat replaces him, it is highly likely California will have a second consecutive tweeting governor. In California, San Francisco mayor Gavin Newsom (@GavinNewsom), a likely candidate for governor, announced his candidacy for the office on Twitter, where he has 385,000 followers. If that indicates anything, he has a comfortable lead on Jerry Brown, another declared candidate, who has 149,000 followers. The dark horse in the Democratic side is Los Angeles mayor Antonio Villaraigosa (@Villaraigosa), who is also said to be eying the governor's seat, but trails in Twitterville, where he has only 1,400 followers. (Villaraigosa bowed out of contention in June 2009.)

So far, no Republicans have declared or even made public much interest in the office. But when one or more steps forward, it is highly likely you'll find her or him talking with constituents in Twitterville.

Opposing Voices

In November 2008 Twitterville may have been an Obama town, but it was also a bipartisan place. Many prominent conservatives such as Karl Rove (@KarlRove) use Twitter to voice opposition to the Obama administration and announce speaking gigs.

Of perhaps greater interest is the grassroots right-wing organization Top Conservatives on Twitter (@TCOT), an aggregate of about a thousand members who collectively use the hashtag "#TCOT." Founded by conservative author Michael Patrick Leahy (@Michael-PLeahy), the group has one hundred thousand entries bearing #TCOT, which according to Leahy makes it the most discussed tag in Twitterville.

Perhaps he should have done it a year earlier, but in December 2008 Senator John McCain (@SenJohnMcCain) joined Twitter, where he had amassed about six hundred thousand followers, and he posts about three times each weekday to tell you what he's doing and what President Obama is doing wrong. He says he writes his own tweets, and his posts have an authentic sound. But he never engages anyone else in conversation.

Tweeting International

It's not just in the United States that politicians are finding their way into Twitter. Toronto mayor Sandy Kemsley (@Skemsley) and London's Boris Johnson (@MayorofLondon) both have Twitter accounts. Both are apparently authentic and conversational.

Few people have even called for the actual official to author the Twitter page. They just want to be able to watch or join a conversation with someone authorized to represent the politician, such as the unnamed communications assistant who authors @DowningStreet, the official account of the office of Prime Minister Gordon Brown. Constituent comments usually are promptly answered.

While Twitter generally has been more rapidly adopted by Americans, the British government seems to have gotten on to it earlier than the American government, particularly in day-to-day activities in which Twitter can be helpful in making life a bit easier for constituents. For example, British ferry schedules were first posted on Twitter. Now the Unitied States has followed, with transit authorities all over the country now posting schedules and announcing delays or other problems.

> @pistachio: I can't even begin to explain the scope and magic of the "team" behind Pistachio Consulting. Because in a very real sense you're ALL on it.

Snows to Newcastle

Some British government accounts are on the municipal level and drill down to highly localized issues. To me they show Twitter as a new, viable communications tool that can help everyday people and their governments interact with greater ease.

Take, for example, Alastair Smith, a communications adviser to the City Council, Newcastle, a city of about 275,000 at the mouth of the Tyne River. Among his many duties is to maintain a Twitter account (@alncl), where he can respond to residents when there's fast-breaking municipal news. He had just under six hundred followers in June 2009 and his tweeting is no more central to his job than, say, his telephone, perhaps even less so. But it's a new channel of communications that has its advantages.

For example, when the city was hit by a snowstorm in the winter of 2008, Smith used Twitter to announce school closures. Even parents who did not follow him on Twitter were able to see the announcement. It was a lot easier for Smith to post the information one time in one place, where any parent or pupil could see it.

When the BBC posted the closings incorrectly, Smith tweeted the BBC and got the news corrected in near real time.

Smith told me how he used keywords on Twitter Search. If someone posts the word "Newcastle" on Twitter, he finds it fast. Twitter Search lets him filter out the beer and the Australian town of the same name, in the same manner you would do it on Google.* Mostly he uses the Search feature the same way Richard Binhammer at Dell does. They both look for complaints so that they can respond.

If a Newcastle resident tweets about a problem, Smith sees to it that someone in the municipal government contacts that resident directly. Newcastle, being a relatively small city, actually has few complaints registered on Twitter. But that was once true of the city's Web site and phones.

Over time, however, the Twitter usage is likely to grow. It remains to be seen if municipalities like Newcastle or, for that matter, the U.S. government will be able to keep pace if Twitter adoption rapidly ramps up among constituents.

The same snowstorm that hit Newcastle also hit the London borough of Camden, where an unnamed resident wanted to enjoy a winter stroll. He was disappointed to find his favorite park locked, and tweeted about it. A city council associate saw the tweet and investigated. He discovered that the storm had prevented the park's keeper from getting through with the keys. He used @CamdenTalking, an early-phase municipal tweet account, to explain, and tweeted the next day to announce when the park reopened. The resident saw both tweets and thanked him for it.

@CamdenTalking serves as sort of a community bulletin board, where information is posted and confusions explained. The account

---

* You enter "Newcastle -beer -Aus" using minus signs as indicated. That will filter out any online entries that contain those two words.

was used again to explain changes and reasons for a new recycling program. It had a mere 315 followers in May 2009, but the city believes that if they build it, constituents will come, and those who do come will tell others why it is a good idea to join in.

Three Action Areas

All sorts of government activity is showing up on Twitter. In the United States I have noticed three areas that seem to be growing legs.

1. Transportation: Mobile access makes Twitter an ideal medium for broadcasting time-sensitive transit information. Ferry and train schedules as well as highway delays are being tweeted by at least twenty public agencies in the United States, Canada, the United Kingdom, and Greece. In most cases authorities and passengers use them to discuss delays or hazards and to suggest alternative routes.

@SFBart, a Twitter account supporting the Bay Area Rapid Transit System (BART)—which provides over 100 million rides per year—has started to repost user-generated blog and video content if it connects in any way with the transit system. Some riders have started taking videos and serving them up in hope of being linked to @SFGate and its four thousand followers. The user-driven content seems to be driving still more followers to the site.

The San Diego Metro Transit System (@SDMTS) finds several advantages to using Twitter. Natalie Andrews Wardel, a communications officer who tweets several times daily for SDMTS, walked me through them.

In addition to alerts, SDMTS reduces passenger hostility simply by explaining the cause of problems that previously may have remained mysteries to constituents.

For example, a passenger was at a bus stop, annoyed that the vehicle was ten minutes late. He tweeted about it from his cell phone.

Wardel checked out the situation, tweeting back that the driver had to provide another passenger with wheelchair assistance and would be at the designated stop shortly. This not only demystified the situation, it showed that delays were sometimes caused by acts of kindness rather than negligence.

I asked Wardel why she thought the effort was worthwhile, considering that her Twitter account had just 821 followers as of May 2009, and the system she served provided more than ninety million rides a year.

"We feel that it's worthwhile to reach riders using the communication that they are using," she explained. "We tweet—but we post information to our Web site and place printed material on the buses, trolleys, at bus stops, and where we feel riders will see it.

"We hope to grow on Twitter and other social media sites. It allows us to reach a unique audience that the printed word doesn't because it is so instant. Also, tweets are retweeted, so even now, with a small audience, our word spreads. It is free, and in times of budget crisis and cutbacks, that is a perk."

That last point is relevant to what SDMTS is about on Twitter as well. Being part of government means that—like it or not—politics come into play. Wardel uses Twitter to conduct transparent conversations with transit advocates, people who may not even use the system much but who pay attention to the quality of the service provided. "We get our money from voter-approved ballot measures, and we need more than our riders to get the two-thirds approval," she said. The conversations build trust, understanding, and awareness of the metro service's efforts.

Perhaps most important, Twitter is affordable. Wardel talked with me a few weeks after California recognized a $24 billion deficit, making imminent financial cuts painfully widespread. As Wardel noted, "It's hard to spring for the money for a fancy alert system, but Twitter allows us to inform riders and answer their questions using a resource that many riders are already using."

2. Law Enforcement: The second area where I found widespread yet still nascent activity was on all levels of law enforcement. It seems to be developing fast, however.

When I first did a search in October 2008, I could find no law enforcement agencies using Twitter. By March 2009, a fifteen-minute search produced more than thirty accounts. Here's a sampling:

Homeland Security had gone from zero to two over this five-month period: @HomelandSecurity reports on investigations of possible threats in a police-log fashion, and @DHSJournal still seems to be trying to find its voice and focus. Sometimes it appears to be written in the voice of Homeland Secretary Janet Napolitano, and at other times it's about her. Neither account is conversational. In March 2009 it seemed to be about the secretary's schedule. In May it was mostly updates on the bird and swine flus.

The U.S. Border Patrol, @CBP_update, reports almost exclusively on its seemingly endless stream of drug busts, with occasionally useful warnings. On Mother's Day it warned people to make sure Mom's flower bouquet contained no harmful pests.

I smiled when I discovered a cyber-squatter had claimed @FBI, but it was easy to find @FBIPressOffice. I tweeted an inquiry about rumors that an FBI arrest had been made because of citizen-tweeted information. A self-described FBI "spokestweeter" promptly responded that it was "not yet true" but pointed me to a news item regarding some Pittsburgh Steelers fans who had dragged a couch onto the street and torched it in a pre–Super Bowl celebration. Someone took a photo and posted it on Facebook, where police examined it, managed to ID the culprits, and arrested them, saying the photo would be used as evidence.

Los Angeles (@LAPD) and Boston Police (@Boston_Police) also post arrests and incidents on Twitter accounts, as does the police department in tiny Dalton, Georgia (@DaltonPD). So do the Wyoming State Police and numerous other departments.

To date, there have been no dramatic incidents of police apprehensions through Twitter. Most law-enforcement Twitter accounts are used to post activity logs. The tweeters follow each other and the media. But it opens a new venue where citizens and law enforcement can communicate and perhaps help each other, as well as improve understanding.

But social media finds a way, just like life did in *Jurassic Park*. It starts with a small, one-directional effort that grows and becomes multidirectional. Then it gets copied.

In the last chapter we discussed how social media has shed light on police abuse. It also has the capability to display good law-enforcement activities that protect lives and property. It is only a matter of time before Twitter-based conversations start improving citizen understanding of police efforts that contribute to public safety.

The real Twitter test in this area will probably come during a high-profile incident: an abduction, an act of terror, or a hostage situation when a real-time dialogue between police and other parties can make a difference to lives, property, or both.

3. Disaster Response: Twitter has played a role during many natural and manmade disasters. Earthquakes are routinely reported on Twitter well before traditional media pick it up, as Casper Oppenhuis de Jong demonstrated in the Sezchuan earthquake.

The American Red Cross (@RedCross) used Twitter to report on damage during the Grand Canyon flood in August 2008. They asked other tweeters to give the names and possible locations of people who might be in the canyon. The request was retweeted rapidly and often. From the tweetstream, CNN found out about the Red Cross and its emergency shelter that at one point housed thirty-five people via Twitter, and ran a prominent story on it. @CNNBKN kept relaying everything @RedCross reported.

Businesses also have started tweeting and helping during natural disasters. Both The Home Depot (@TheHomeDepot) and Whole Earth Foods (@WholeEarth) used Twitter to keep residents posted on what to do and where stores would stay open with emergency supplies during the 2008 Gulf Coast hurricanes.

Twitter didn't exist when 9/11 or Hurricane Katrina took place. If it had, the U.S. government would have been able to impart a great deal of information useful to victims and their loved ones; rescue organizations could have been shared. Unprecedented levels of co-ordination could have happened starting at ground zero and working outward.

It was nice to see that Homeland Security used Twitter to report on swine flu occurrences when pandemic fears spread in early May 2009. In June they turned to Twitter again to mitigate fears about severity when the United Nations World Health Organization declared a pandemic. It gives one an optimistic note for the role Twitter may play when inevitably something large and awful happens.

The Los Angeles Fire Department (@LAFD) has been a pioneer in emergency services tweeting. Brian Humphrey, an LAFD information officer, told me that two months after he started the account, he posted real-time reports on a huge fire in Griffith Park, the city's largest open space. In June 2008 @LAFD posted almost nonstop information on the status of a Southern California siege of wildfires. People were alerted to what areas to avoid and the status of loved ones who were being rescued. There is no way for Humphrey to know how many people avoided dangerous areas because of what he posted—what is relevant is that officials have a new way of distributing information in an emergency.

In 2009 Humphrey picked up a tweeted report of a nightclub that was ignoring fire and safety codes. LAFD moved fast to shut the place down. Was a tragedy averted? We don't know, of course. What we do know is that Twitter allowed LAFD to be fast enough to avoid the possibility.

Emoticons from Mars

Without doubt, the most innovative government contributions to Twitterville have come from the National Aeronautics Space Administration (NASA), which has started several accounts, the most popular and groundbreaking one being @MarsPhoenix.

On May 25, 2008, the Phoenix, a robotic spacecraft, landed on Mars, where it began gathering data by taking photos, testing the atmosphere, and gathering soil samples. Shortly after the landing, someone at NASA started a @MarsPhoenix tweet account and assumed the form of a humanized narrative of what the spacecraft was experiencing.

The tweets continued for five months. The robot reported as it bored into the planet's surface, looked for signs of moisture, and measured ambient temperature. It expressed excitement when it discovered snow. At another point @MarsPhoenix talked about the beauty and loneliness of being on Mars.

The account terminated when the successful mission ended, with a message posted in binary computer language: "01010100 01110010 01101001 01110101 01101101 01110000 0110100," which means "Triumph." As a last flourish, a small heart emoticon was added in code.

More than forty thousand people followed the tweets and many of us regularly retweeted what was posted. This was happening at a time when there was much talk of cutting the budget for space exploration, which some called a luxury inappropriate for the times. Encouraging citizen support has previously helped NASA. In early 2005 a petition to save the Hubble Space Telescope was signed by five thousand voters, who were also encouraged to contact elected officials. Legislation to abandon the telescope in space was dropped.

Then, one year after @MarsPhoenix began, NASA outdid itself, in May 2009, as a manned spacecraft departed from Cape Kennedy to the aging Hubble Space Telescope orbiting 350 miles away from Earth. Hubble had already taken over twenty-six million photos of "near outer space," but some of its parts were worn and others needed upgrading.

A three-member crew on the spacecraft *Atlantis* drew alongside the orbiting nineteen-year-old space telescope and performed a series of tasks that NASA called the "most complex and intricate yet performed in space."

Veteran astronaut Mike Massimino, age forty-four, had used Twitter during his training to let other people know what the experience was like. Now he became the first to tweet from outer space.

Checking in as @Astro_Mike, his first report was simple enough: "Launch was awesome!!" He kept updating with reports that he's "feeling great and working hard."

Like @MarsPhoenix, Massimino was using a spacecraft computer to relay his tweets to a NASA space center, where a coworker who was trusted with Massimino's password, posted onto the space repairman's Twitter account.

On Friday, May 15, 2009, he was the first of the three astronauts to step out in space to work on the telescope. Minutes after he returned, he relayed, "My spacewalk was amazing, we had some tough problems, but through them all, the view of our precious planet was beautiful."

> @sarahdopp: The more closets I come out of, the more I realize I'm still in.

A New Channel

Someone recently asked me how Twitter improves communications with government. Why can't people just call or send an e-mail? In my view, Twitter replaces neither of these two channels of communications any more than rock replaced opera. It is a new way to communicate, and it has its own characteristics. I think an increasing number of people over time will prefer tweeting to phoning.

The point is people should have as many options as possible to hear from and talk to their governments.

I worked in the Massachusetts State government many years ago in the department that dealt with housing and urban development issues. My coworkers and I were at first passionate about serving constituents in housing projects and urban areas in need of renewal. We wanted to hear from them and to tell them what we were trying to do and to explain how sometimes our good intentions had unexpected consequences.

The bureaucracy made it difficult for us to talk directly with the people we were paid to serve. There were procedures to follow, constraints on whom we could talk with and what we could say. To this day I am convinced that we could have done our job with less effort and greater results if we just could have maintained an ongoing dialogue with the people we were paid to serve. I left government service in 1976. My views have not changed much, but the tools that make it easy, affordable, and fast to have conversations with constituents certainly have.

Tools like Twitter are now available to a growing number of people. A new president has taken office and has declared e-Government and transparency to be priorities.

The result is that just a few months into the Obama administration's tenure, government activity swelled from near zero to scores, perhaps hundreds of government-related Twitter accounts—with thousands, perhaps tens of thousands of people following.

At this early stage, few of these government tweeters are engaging in actual conversations. But there are lots of reasons to assume they will follow the patterns of business tweeters who so often came to talk and learned the value of listening.

It's human nature. Sooner or later people on Twitter see a conversation and just jump in. They can't resist. And as they increase their participation, Twitter is likely to help government become more responsive and effective. At least we can hope.

In *Naked Conversations* we coined the term "Corpspeak" for the artificial language filled with ambiguity, legal disclaimer, and marketing hyperbole that erodes most substance and humanity from public utterances.

Government also has a language of its own: "Governmentese." I'm sure you've heard it spoken, and it has probably left you as baffled as it has left me.

Because messages must be so short, Twitter filters out adjectives and conditional phrases, leaving posts that are unusually succinct, candid, and clear. On Twitter there is a new hope that government and constituents can find both common ground and common language.

Rise of the Goverati

I told you earlier about Dr. Mark Drapeau, the Department of Defense consultant who tweets as @Cheeky_Geeky. He is among a growing number of professionals inside the Beltway evangelizing the benefits of social media to those in government.

Drapeau calls this emerging group the goverati, a merger of the term "digerati" with "government." They are agents of change, and their numbers are growing. Yet collectively they remain a small flame under a humongous bureaucratic glacier.

"The average government workers are almost completely oblivious to Web 2.0," Drapeau told me. "It's not their fault. There are only so many hours in the day. But government needs to tap into that global brain to solve problems more efficiently, cheaply, and probably better."

> @hotdogsladies Blog Pro Tip: Write headlines that make it fast and easy for commenters to misunderstand what you didn't say in the post they didn't read.

Taking Government to Twitterville Streets

There's one more piece to the story, and that lies in the ability of a government representative or politician to take a case directly to the people without intermediation by the press.

Back in *Naked Conversations*, we wrote about Mark Cuban, the controversial Dallas Mavericks owner. Cuban told us that he started blogging because he was frustrated with how the media handled his side of the story. He told us about a four-hour interview with a *Fortune* magazine editor, who wrote a mere five hundred words that Cuban felt "mischaracterized the conversation."

Cuban started blogging so that he could talk directly with audiences. He maintained that a direct conversation would benefit both him and his followers. The blog remains popular, and I would argue he has made his case.

Bob Lutz, vice president of General Motors, related a similar story. He told me he had started GM FastLane, the automaker's first blog, because the press had given GM a bad rap.

During the Israel-Gaza conflict at the end of 2008, the state of Israel came to the same conclusion. Hamas, a recognized terrorist group that controlled Gaza, responded to Israel's offer to extend the peace by escalating its launch of rockets into southern Israeli residential areas.

Israel responded with a ferocity that stirred both controversy and pro-Gaza sentiment. News organizations, particularly the BBC and Al Jazeera, seemed to many to be relentlessly supporting the Gazan point of view. In their defense, Israel had shut down its border and would not talk with the media during the three-week conflict.

The Twitterville conversation covered every possible angle of the dispute. Comments ranged from summaries of both recent and biblical history to words of brotherly love or neighborly hate. A situation similar to what had happened in Mumbai emerged, where people in Israel, Gaza, and the rest of the world all joined into one massive conversation that could be followed at the "#Gaza" hashtag, which was used nearly twenty thousand times during the brief conflict.

Israel had its Twitter proponents, me among them. But overall it was not winning a great deal of sympathy in Twitterville.

Israel decided to take its case to the people. Its venue of choice was not a news conference. It did not arrange for an exclusive interview between its prime minister and a famous journalist. Nor did it buy airtime on a broadcast network.

Instead, it argued its case in Twitterville.

The Israeli Consulate in New York City held a world news conference on Twitter on December 30, 2008. David Saranga, Israeli consul for media and public affairs, had opened @israelconsulate and at a given time started taking questions from people all over the world. It was like being hit with a fire hose; it was impossible for Saranga to answer them all as they came in.

But the questions were all recorded, then answered in batches over the next several days at the consulate's IsraelPolitik blog.

The Q&A was clearly unscripted. Some questions were overtly hostile toward Israel's bombing of Gaza cities; some commented more than queried. In the end, Saranga answered every message sent to him.

The question, of course, remains: what difference—if any—did the Twitter conference make? "In public diplomacy it's hard to measure results, especially on a single act," he told me. He is certain, however, that the conference allowed Israel to get their side of the story told.

He then pointed me to the media list that had covered the event, which included most of the top-tier American press as well as news organizations in more than a dozen countries and coverage in more than twenty blogs, some of them very prominent.

What is truly relevant here is that an entirely new dynamic took place. A government official, involved in a hostile action, took questions from citizens of the world. The same can happen for a mayor who wishes to hold a virtual town meeting. Twitter can be used to answer questions during an emergency and in ways that cannot yet be imagined.

It may be years away or sooner than we realize, but I'll wager that the next president of the United States has conversations with constituents on Twitter, and perhaps your next governor, mayor, or senator if you happen to live in a place where such titles are used.

CHAPTER 14

Goodwill Fund-raising

In July 2007 Beth Kanter (@Kanter), a well-known nonprofit activist and social media evangelist, was invited to visit Cambodia to deliver a keynote speech at the first-ever Cambodian blogger conference, and then lead a series of fourteen workshops to teach social media to 1,700 Cambodian students.

Kanter had visited the country frequently over the previous fifteen years; she had worked on behalf of several nonprofits, teaching them how online communications tools can help raise awareness and funds. She's shown a particular interest in helping children. In 2000 she adopted two Cambodian children.

"I tend to learn new things, then share them with others," she told me. She has made a business of writing, teaching, and coaching nonprofits on social media. The work is unlikely to make her wealthy, but when you talk with her, it's clear it makes her happy.

While the Cambodian invite was right up her alley, the not being wealthy part caused a snag. The loosely joined blogging organization that had invited her had no money for her trip. So Kanter turned to her global community: the people who followed her blog, wiki, and Twitter account, and shared her interest in goodwill fund-raising.

She asked for their help to raise the $4,000 the trip would require. She may not have been the first to turn to Twitter to raise funds for a cause, but she is the first one who gained a lot of notice doing so, blazing a path that others followed.

On July 30, 2007, Kanter announced her fund-raising effort on her blog and on Twitter. If she were going to make the trip, she would have to book a flight by August 10.

Kanter achieved her goal with time to spare. One week after beginning her campaign, fifty-eight people had contributed $4,162, putting her over the top. All but one of her fifty-seven contributors donated a relatively modest amount, averaging a little more than $35 each.

The fifty-eighth contributor was a new little company called ChipIn, designer of a fund-raising "widget," a little box you can drop into any Web page. The ChipIn Widget allows people to use PayPal, the most popular online small-payment service, to make charitable contributions. Of equal importance, ChipIn gives site visitors an instant visual report on how much money has been raised toward a goal and how many people have contributed.

ChipIn, a free service, agreed to contribute $2,000 to Kanter's trip if she would use the widget and talk about it during her campaign. Smart move. ChipIn became an instant standard for goodwill fund-raising in social media, and has been the overwhelming tool of choice for most causes that have followed Kanter's first effort.

Before she departed, Kanter turned to Twitter again to ask for T-shirt contributions for the Cambodia students, and wound up collecting three hundred. She came back once more to ask for money, this time to raise $1,000 to pay for a Cambodian girl's junior year in college. She met her goal in twenty-four hours, with fifty-three people contributing.

Some of Kanter's tactics have been replicated by others with a cause. But what is essential to note is that her success was achieved in part because she was a known entity. Kanter has been involved in goodwill fund-raising on the Internet since the 1990s. She has been a prominent early adopter of just about every social media platform that has gained prominence. Before that she was involved in online forums—the precursors to social media. In every case, Kanter was espousing the virtues of a grassroots cause. Kanter wasn't some stranger coming to the door with a story of dubious veracity.

Nor was Kanter's work ever associated with a branded charity, many of which have come to be eyed suspiciously, a cumulated result of numerous scandals coupled with citizen group complaints of high administrative costs and budgets that dedicate more investment to fund-raising than they do to research.

Twitter alone probably wouldn't have raised a dime for any cause or person. Kanter used Twitter for what it does better than any other tool—spreading the word with great speed. She used her blog to drill into details. She uploaded to YouTube to give a visual sense and to entertain just a bit while asking people for help. Kanter used different forms of social media in tandem with one another pretty much in the same way a carpenter uses tools to build a house. The blog gave the details, and YouTube allowed her to please audiences and touch their emotions.

But Twitter was her glue. She used it to spread the word, to keep the conversation going and people informed. "It wasn't just 'give me money,'" she told me. "It was also thanking, updating, and being funny."

As I've mentioned, Twitterville seems to be the home to a very large cult of generosity, one that is used by people in more ways than simply fund-raising. For example, when Mary Walters (@MaryWWalters) of Saskatoon, Canada, dropped an heirloom necklace down her bathroom sink drain, three tweeters had her take photos of the pipe and then walked her through uncoupling the U-joint to retrieve it, one tweet at a time.

Peavatars Against Cancer

The Frozen Pea Fund's story doesn't start with a fund-raising effort. It starts with cancer.

Susan Reynolds was diagnosed with breast cancer in December 2007. "There is nothing good about breast cancer," she later told the *Washington Post*. "It helps start a conversation, though."

Reynolds started the conversation at the end of a most unpleasant day, during which she underwent five breast biopsies. They hurt. When she went home she tried getting some relief, but a standard ice pack felt like a brick on her breast. Her husband, Bill, suggested trying a bag of frozen peas. It worked significantly, easing her pain.

Reynolds had friends on Twitter, and she needed the support of people that mattered to her. She also thought that if she could engage in conversations there, it would lessen the emotional burden on her husband and their three grown children.

But just how do you break the news that you may have breast cancer in 140 characters?

Reynolds took a new Twitter photo of herself with a bag of frozen peas tucked modestly under her camisole. The shot added some levity as she broke the news. Word of Reynolds's experience spread rapidly across Twitterville. The response was huge. The conversation moved from one tweetstream to another with great speed. People were supportive and many shared their own experiences. Most just tweeted a few words of support.

Two days later, Reynolds began a blog, Boobs On Ice (susanreyn olds.blogs.com/boobsonice). She made clear that her purpose was to share her experiences with others and help educate people who might have to go through the same ordeal. She started posting with a mix of humor, grit, and calm that inspired and engaged a great many people.

Among them was Cathleen Rittereiser (@CathleenRitt), author

of *Foundation and Endowment Investing*, who tweeted a suggestion that people on Twitter contribute $2.50—the average price of a bag of frozen peas—to fight cancer in Reynolds's honor.

That gave Connie Reece (@ConnieReece), now chief social media officer for New Media Lab in Austin, Texas, an idea. Reece is a dynamo of positive energy and among the best-known social media practitioners in Texas.

To honor Reynolds, Reece followed Reynolds's lead by making her own Twitter avatar a close-up of frosty peas, with one pea replaced by Reece's face.

Reece asked her followers to show their support for Reynolds by changing their avatars to "peavatars" every Friday. Based on Rittereiser's suggestion, she also asked them to donate $5 on these "Frozen Pea Fridays."

As word of mouth spread, those without the Photoshop skills to create their own peavatars were helped by volunteers. The following Friday, about three hundred Reynolds supporters had reposted their photos with peas, lots and lots of peas—in pods, as hats, in hair, as face replacements, as background or foreground—all in a show of support for Reynolds. Soon a group Flickr account was created for visitors to see the diversity of peavatars.

Nothing like this had previously occurred in social media. It could not have happened without Twitter. It would not have taken off if Reynolds and Reece weren't already known and respected in Twitterville, and the campaign probably would not have spread had the contribution request not been so small.

The seriousness of cancer was not forgotten, but the levity lifted spirits, including those of Reynolds herself. People were having fun, but more significant, the peavatars were generating conversations that were spreading the word about cancer and this, of course, raised more money for the fight.

On December 21, 2007, seven days after the first Frozen Pea Friday, two milestones occurred. Susan Reynolds underwent a mastectomy, and Connie Reece launched the Frozen Pea Fund (frozenpeafund.com) in Reynolds's honor.

Reynolds did not need charitable contributions. Instead, Reece said the fund would help cover miscellaneous expenses for cancer patients "who did not have a safety net."

In fifteen hours, 118 people donated $3,500 to the fund. Eventually the Frozen Pea Fund contributed $10,000 to the American Cancer Society earmarked for patients in economic need.

But then ooVoo.com, an online video conferencing start-up, invited twenty-four social media luminaries to create content on ooVoo to connect with their respective communities. They could talk about anything they wished and, for each participant; ooVoo would contribute $1,500 either to the luminary's favorite charity or to the Frozen Pea Fund. This added $30,000 to the Frozen Pea Fund in just twenty-four hours.

Reece and Reynolds had become close, but almost all their interaction took place through social media. In February 2008 the two met for the first time in Austin. It was another example of old friends meeting in the tangible world for the first time.

> @totalcio: Diversity video shown at conference this week: 5 white men and 1 white women. Go figure!

A Sad Sidebar

One of the most ardent supporters of Susan Reynolds and the Frozen Pea Fund was Ashley Spencer, a twenty-nine-year-old mother of two small children living in Baton Rouge, Louisiana. Spencer so admired Reynolds that she changed her Twitter name to @ashPEAmama. She was driving home from a football game in January 2008 when she was killed in a car crash.

The family was neither affluent nor insured. It faced funeral costs of $6,000. Lieutenant Colonel Dan Mosqueda (@DanCMos), a U.S. National Guard reserve officer who had recently returned from Iraq, had never met Ashley, but he learned about what happened on Twitter and was touched by it.

He thought something should be done to help the family. He got ChipIn to provide a blog space for family and friends to raise money. Then he used Twitter to generate traffic to the blog space.

It took two weeks to raise $8,000. Mosqueda drove from Colorado to Louisiana to hand deliver the check to Peter Spencer, Ashley's husband, who worked in a local bottling plant.

Spencer and Mosqueda have stayed in touch. The colonel returned to Baton Rouge in March 2009, spending the weekend with Ashley's family.

I spoke with him shortly after. He told me that the generosity of the Twitter community had touched the family, who had used the extra $2,000 to cut debt. "Ashley's parents hugged me and hugged me," he told me. "They treated me like a member of the family."

Helping Daniela

David Armano (@Armano) at that time was vice president of Experience Design for Chicago-based ad agency Critical Mass (criticalmass.com) and a prominent member of the social media community.

He lives with his wife, Belinda, and their two children in a one-family home in Glenview, Illinois, a suburb just north of Chicago. One day in January 2009, Belinda introduced him to Daniela, a house cleaner, and her three children.

It seemed that Daniela had just walked out on a habitually abusive husband, and she intended to divorce him. She had no money and no place to go. Her youngest child had Down syndrome. The Armanos agreed that she and her kids could stay with them until they could sort out what to do next.

It would be cramped and challenging with three adults and five children in their modest home. All of Daniela's belonging were to be stashed in the garage.

"I really didn't quite know what to do," Armano told me. Like Reynolds and Kanter, Armano was a known and credible entity in Twitterville and, like them, he decided to share his situation with his Twitter friends, as well as ask for help.

He wrote a moving blog post showing a photo of Daniela and her family and then, using the same combination of tools as Kanter and Reynolds, drew attention to the post through Twitter. He asked people to help him raise $5,000 so that Daniela could get her own apartment and buy some basic furniture. He also asked his Twitterville followers to spread the word, installing ChipIn so people could see how the effort was going.

"Twitter was perfect for raising awareness and generating a viral effect, which spilled beyond my network," he told me. "I primed my followers, and they started paying attention quickly. When the word got out, it was retweeted hundreds of times." Armano's blog traffic increased to thirty times its usual rate. In twenty-four hours, he raised more than $12,000. Before he closed the campaign, 545 people had donated $16,880, an average of $30.90 per contributor.

With the Armanos serving as the fund's steward, Daniela found a clean two-bedroom apartment a few miles away in a North Chicago suburb, where she was living as of this writing. She still cleans houses to meet living costs. At her request, Armano is the steward of her fund, which is used to pay rent and make sure the children's needs are met.

After the money was raised, Armano used his blog and Twitter account to keep the community informed. He used TwitPic to show a photo of the family's belongings piled to the ceiling in his garage. He posted an emotional video on his blog thanking people when contributions blew past his $5,000 goal.

"This story just would not have happened without Twitter. The immediacy of the donations would not have been possible had it not been for Twitter," Armano told me. His call for help resulted in hundreds of retweets by his estimate. It was the way conversation spread across Twitter that made it so fast and easy to raise the money.

"Having large networks doesn't give us the right to ask for anything," he said. "Belinda and I found ourselves in a crisis situation and didn't know how else to get help. I was fortunate to have enough people who alerted others on our behalf, just like in any other network."

Armano has since taken a new job and commutes between Chicago and Austin. He and his wife remain close with Daniela.

Epic Change at Shepherds Junior

In a two-day period just prior to Thanksgiving 2006, another Twitterville goodwill project raised $11,000 from 372 people in forty-eight hours. It was called TweetsGiving (tweetsgiving.org), and the money helped build a schoolhouse in Tanzania.

In 2007 Stacey Monk (@StaceyMonk), a former freelance project management consultant, went to Africa for a long, slow journey from Cape Town to Cairo. She was part of a small group; the trip was part adventure vacation and part community service. "We traveled by puddle jumper, safari jeeps, boat, *dala-dalas* (shared taxis), and any other means of transport we could find. You've got to be resourceful," she said.

In Arusha, Tanzania, her volunteer efforts connected her with Mama Lucy Kampton, a local woman who had sold chickens until she raised enough money to build Shepherds Junior, a primary school, on land she rented adjacent to her home and chickens. Monk helped out at Shepherds for a while. She and Mama Lucy became solid friends.

"To say I was impressed with what she'd created would be a vast understatement," she said. "At the time I was there, there were over a hundred children at the school, and most paid tuition. The income covered the costs of other children who could not afford to pay. Teachers were paid, meals were served daily, and, most important, the children were getting a much better education than other local alternatives provided."

After Monk returned home to Satellite Beach, Florida, she kept in touch with Kampton. A few months later Kampton told Monk that a developer had purchased the land where the school had been built, and that the school was going to be demolished.

Monk had earlier created Epic Change to serves as a grassroots fund-raising organization. But she had not yet done much with it. Now she determined it would help people like Mama Lucy raise the capital they need to expand successful community improvement programs like Shepherds Junior.

Twitter was essential to Monk's strategy. But unlike Kanter, Reynolds, Reece, and Armano, Monk wasn't particularly well known in social media circles. If she just started tweeting on her own, she feared that she lacked enough credibility to raise much more than lunch money.

But she knew Sam Lawrence (@SamLawrence), one of the ten thousand top-ranked tweeters. He was also author of Go Big Always (gobigalways.com), a popular blog, and at the time he was CMO at Jive Software, a top-tier community software provider to large-enterprise customers. She asked Lawrence if she could do a guest post so that she could leverage his credibility and reach a larger audience.

"I stayed up all night to get my story right," Monk told me. The resulting post was well received and generated much discussion and retweeting.

By piggybacking on Lawrence's credibility, Monk had established her own. She had already decided that she wanted to stop working with large companies as a project manager so that she could follow her passion of nonprofit contributions to underdeveloped countries. Epic Change was on its way and helping Mama Lucy would be its first project.

Her guest post caught the attention of Avi Kaplan (@meshugavi), a reader of Go Big Always. He was moved by Monk's story of Mama Lucy and her school. He connected with her on Twitter and offered to help by posting about the effort. Kaplan's post inspired her to create TweetsGiving just six days before Thanksgiving. The hope was to use the spirit of the season to raise enough money to save Mama Lucy's school.

She made her goal, of course, and then some. A new school was built on land that Mama Lucy owns. As you walk in, you can see the names of each Tweetsgiving donor on the wall, inscribed by the schoolchildren as a token of their thanks.

Epic Change has gone on to conduct additional peer-to-peer fund-raising projects using Twitter, Facebook, Monk's blog (epicchange .org/blog), and e-mail. As of April 2009 it has raised more than $70,000 in small donations. Epic Change is an all-volunteer organization—including Monk. About 95 percent of all money raised has gone to cause recipients. The remainder mostly goes for the PayPal transaction fees used to collect money online.

> @bbtouring: the neighborhood grocery store, missing my "Don't Hassle Me I'm Local" t-shirt.

Twestival

As of this writing, the largest Twitter-based fund-raising effort has been Twestival (charitywater.org/Twestival), held on February 12, 2009. Events were held in over two hundred cities worldwide to raise money for fresh water in communities inside developing countries, including Ethiopia, Uganda, and India.

On that single day some eighty thousand people donated a total of a quarter of a million dollars. According to charity: water, the organization behind it all, the money raised will be used to drill wells to serve seventeen million people who currently do not have access to clean water. "Water is the most basic human need," said cofounder Scott Harrison. Unclean wells, he said, are the source of 80 percent of the world's disease. He estimated that a baby dies every fifteen seconds because of unclean water.

Twestival happened so spontaneously and rapidly that traditional media barely noted it; there were also very few blog posts about it. But on Twitter, it was the most-discussed topic for the week leading up to Twestival and the days immediately following it. As a result, hundreds of thousands of people learned more about the water problems of developing nations and saw how far small contributions can go.

Most of the organization's leadership was not well known. Nor was charity: water a recognized brand in established nonprofit circles. Twestival worked because the organization trusted volunteers around the world to design events that would succeed in their respective communities. The international organization provided the locals with some basic images and logo material, and set a date. Then they stepped back and the volunteers in more than two hundred communities worldwide took over.

In Los Angeles, the event called for glitz and glamour. Volunteers organized their local Twestival at Club 740, a trendy downtown nightclub, and enlisted *Fear Factor* star Joe Rogan, actress-filmmaker Felicia Day (@FeliciaDay), and a string of other well-known talents. About five hundred people showed up, paying anywhere from $100 down to $5 at the door and raising about $20,000, the second-highest tally of any Twestival event. Cost of producing the event, not counting the time invested by dedicated volunteers: zero.

Giants Join the Party

Whenever there is a groundswell of bottom-up grassroots success that raises money and gets noticed, large, traditional organizations are sure to follow. Some adapt to the new environment, others try to transform the new environment to fit their old ways.

Corporate social responsibility (CSR) is nothing new. Almost every enterprise has a small CSR department, and executives who give lip service to it. Occasionally, though, a company demonstrates its long-term dedication to a social cause.

When Molson Canada, which I discussed earlier, arrived in Twitterville, they already had CSR credentials in Canadian communities. Though the ultimate goal behind their charitable efforts might be to sell more beer, so what? People benefit.

Tyson Foods is another example of a company coming to Twitter with both the right attitude and the right record. Tyson has been active in community-level antihunger and antipoverty campaigns since 2000. It maintains an educational hunger relief Web site and has donated 54 million pounds of food, or 216 million meals, to food banks. So when Tyson showed up at SXSW 2009 asking for community support to deliver a truckload of food for the hungry children of Austin, Texas, it arrived with well-established credentials.

To supplement its real-world credibility in Twitterville, Tyson enlisted Twitter luminaries Beth Kanter and Chris Brogan to serve as cochairs for its Tyson Pledge to End Hunger campaign (pledgetoendhunger.com). Tyson was not looking for money. It was looking for community engagement.

The company's offer was simple: for every person who clicked a Web site button affirming their pledge to end hunger,* Tyson would feed 140 Austin children in need—140 being, of course, the maximum number of characters in a tweet. In all, 140,000 pounds of food were donated.

The results were so positive that Tyson ended up sending four additional trucks to other locations, donating an additional 560,000 pounds of food to hungry children in other states.

The company sold no T-shirts and took in no money. Instead,

---

* You can't install a button on Twitter—you need the flexibility offered by a blog or social networking page.

they engaged a community and demonstrated a remarkable level of generosity built along a demonstrated long-term commitment.

Proctor & Gamble, the world's largest consumer products company, took a very different approach.

It's unlikely that the word "Tide" brings to mind the fight against poverty, or any other worthy causes. Prior to their so-called experiment to fight hunger in Twitterville, no one at P&G had seemed to have gained any noteworthy prominence in goodwill fund-raising campaigns. However, they affiliated with a credible player: Feeding America (feedingamerica.org), the largest antihunger organization in the country. Then they turned to 150 well-known Twitterville players, people with name recognition and lots of followers.

Unfortunately, the tweeters they enlisted were not generally known for promoting causes or for acts of generosity. They were simply prominent marketers, which made the P&G antihunger campaign look very much like a branding campaign.

The deal was that these Twitter-based spokespeople would sell you a Tide T-shirt for $20. An *undisclosed* portion of that money would go to Feeding America. Then you got to wear an ad after having paid for the privilege. More than one tweeter characterized the approach as "gratuitous" or "contrived."

The results were tepid. P&G sold around two thousand T-shirts, an average of thirteen per spokesperson. Quipped Brian Morrissey, writing in *AdWeek*: "I've seen better results at bake sales."

"You can rapidly gain a large number of 'friends' and build a large Twitter following," wrote Tom Foremski in *Silicon Valley Watcher*. "But if you try to sell access to that network to commercial enterprises you will run into trouble."

As this book tries to make clear, a great many companies of all sizes and in many sectors are succeeding remarkably well in diverse ways in Twitterville. There are a great many ways to succeed, depending on what your goals are.

But a few universal traits hold. First, transparency and authenticity work: if you are in Twitterville to sell refurbished computers, that's fine. Just don't claim to sell them to benefit humankind. Second, it is wise to understand that large numbers of followers do not fully translate into credibility in all areas. The words of the most respected and followed social marketers simply may not have much weight when it comes to the fight against hunger.

Traditional Charities

In late 2008, branded charities began arriving in Twitterville. Among them: World Wildlife Foundation, (@WWF_Climate), American Red Cross (@RedCross), Unicef (@Unicef_UK), Save the Children Foundation (@SavetheChildren), American Humane Society (@Humane Society), Greenpeace (@Greenpeace_International), and American Cancer Society (@AmericanCancer).

Few have achieved any noteworthy success in terms of fund-raising. In fact, the types of projects I've described in this chapter are all small projects. All the drives so far have been bottom-up and grass roots. Large charitable organizations try to raise large amounts; their approaches are often top-down, go to management levels of large corporations for pledges, or employ traditional consumer branding techniques.

Many of the traditional charity organizations also do not seem willing to show the transparency the people in this chapter have displayed in showing how the money raised is actually spent. For example charity: water says that over 99 percent of the funds raised goes to water. TweetsGiving claims 95 percent of their funds goes to the people the money is raised for. But Connie Reese, who oversees the Frozen Pea Fund, told me that the American Cancer Society refuses to tell her how much of the money raised by her group's efforts is used to cover administrative costs.

Furthermore, big charities on Twitter are still in the initial phase, where their efforts are mostly dedicated to getting the word out and money in, rather than having conversations. Having your mouth open and your palm up among people who don't know you tend to have the same impact in Twitter as it does on the streets of any large city—very little.

You just don't raise money in Twitterville the same way you sell detergent. The Tide people came looking for marketers with big numbers. They'd have been wise to heed the words of Paula Drum when she was at H&R Block. Twitter doesn't work when you apply mass media techniques. It is far more up close and personal.

The Kanter Model

Beth Kanter's entrepreneurial approach in 2007 seems to have emerged as a set of best practices for goodwill fund-raising in social media. While every case has its own variables, it seems that there are some constants that usually factor into success:

- **Have credibility.** Don't just show up one day and ask for money. People need to trust you—or be able to see that others trust you.
- **Build in urgency.** I could find no successful ongoing fund-raising campaigns. Instead, the ones that worked best seem to be project oriented and launched at the eleventh hour. Most were announced, executed, and completed within a seven-day period.
- **Raise a little from many.** From the projects I looked at, the average individual donation was under $40. Because of the short, urgent nature of Twitter-based goodwill fund-raising, there have been few corporate contributors. Perhaps this will evolve, but as it stands currently, Twitterville is not structured for corporate contributions.
- **Use the ChipIn widget.** This is a fund-raising visual box that you add on to your blog or Facebook account. Using

PayPal, it makes it easy to contribute a small amount of money instantly. But it serves another purpose: it lets your followers keep score.

- **Show recognition and gratitude.** Kanter tweeted thanks to everyone who contributed. The Tweetsgiving kids inscribed Twitter handles on the schoolyard wall.
- **Keep updating.** Two years later, Kanter was still posting updates on what was accomplished by her trip to Cambodia. While the fund-raising may be short-term, the storytelling should continue. This will add to the credibility you may need in the future.
- **Use multiple tools.** Twitter provides headlines that travel faster and farther, but to tell a story fund-raisers need to use other tools, blogs, wikis, photo and video sites. Twitter is the front end to the fund-raising platform.

I've read a few books about the formation of many of the largest traditional charities. It is interesting to me how many of these social media success criteria were once their criteria. Many of today's established charities were born during the Great Depression. Urgency was often connected to a campaign in the form of set financial goals that had to be reached before a deadline. Large visual "thermometers" measured how much money was received and still needed, just like the ChipIn Widget does in social media. The most successful campaigns reached family members in schools, movie theaters, door-to-door campaigns, and workplace pledges. People who were known and trusted were linked to campaigns, such as Franklin D. Roosevelt to the March of Dimes and the comedian Jerry Lewis to the Muscular Dystrophy Association. All of these programs were community-based and respected prior to the era of mass media advertising, when programs became ongoing and celebrity endorsements less effective.

It is in the worst of times that communities seem to become the most generous. As good times are restored, it will be interesting to see if social media goodwill fund-raising will remain as grass roots and credible as it is today.

This chapter has shown how the best in us can emerge in Twitterville. Most people you meet there are trustworthy and transparent. But just like every other community, there are exceptions.

CHAPTER 15

Dark Streets

Even the nicest towns have sleazy neighborhoods, and Twitterville is no exception. We all know this, but we sometimes forget that unsavory characters don't just lurk in the shadows. They come out to prey on unsuspecting people. And they disguise themselves to look trustworthy.

Their presence should come as no surprise. Historically, when a new community flourishes, it attracts bad guys as fast as a new starlet draws paparazzi. When prospectors with pick axes and sifting pans went into the frontier and struck gold, their camps were joined by followers who tried to siphon away the new wealth with gambling, bordellos, and snake oil.

Twitterville is overwhelmingly comprised of honest people and businesses. It strikes me as an uncommonly generous place. But as it grows it suffers from an ongoing assault of a steadily increasing flock of spammers, scammers, stalkers, phishers, and plain old-fashioned flimflam artists.

Twitter and its community leaders have been vigilant in weeding out wrongdoers. But the bad guys are clever and come back in new forms, only to be deterred again. It has become a form of cold war.

A few of the reported abuses could be considered amusing. Most are not. And even the amusing ones often cloak uglier intentions.

Here are some of the unsavory incidents that have happened so far in Twitterville. I offer them not to scare you off, but to make you aware so that you may avoid them.

Spam

Spam is the Internet's most common form of abuse. Much of it is just annoying, but some is worse than that. It is based on the premise that the more people you can approach with an enticing but deceptive offer, the more people will take the bait.

There are a few easy ways to detect spam Twitter accounts. "Lee (@scamtypes) runs Scam Types dot Com, a site dedicated to reporting online deception. I sized up Lee as a suspicious type when he refused to give me his last name during an e-mail exchange.

Lee offers three ways to spot a Twitter Spammer:

1. The profile picture is a young girl (usually blonde) and typically showing a rather generous amount of cleavage.
2. Even though the user is newly registered, he, she, or it follows hundreds of people and has very few followers.
3. The user name is complete gibberish—a weird and random collection of letters and numbers.

If you do follow a spammer, the least that will happen is that you get a lot of unwanted and often unsavory marketing messages. You can also get attempts to corral your Twitter log-in information and whatever information that can be gathered will be shared or resold to other unsavory types as well.

Twitter's defense in the cold war against spammers makes their behavior very dynamic. Twitter watches the ratio of following-to-followers. If an account follows too many followers and has too few following them, Twitter investigates and takes them down.

To circumnavigate this, spammers follow people for forty-eight hours or so. If you don't follow back, most of them just drop you and go for someone else before Twitter can catch up with them. By moving fast and snagging a few, the spammers can then follow larger numbers because the ratio is within limits.

Spammers count on the fact that some tweeters will follow them back. Many luminary tweeters automatically follow anyone back. So do many Twitter newcomers, and spammers are sufficiently sophisticated to go after both of these groups. The luminary followers can give the false impression of credibility. The new-in-Twitterville folk may be statistically easier prey than jaded veterans. When my real-world neighbor Tom Hodges (@HTHodges) started on Twitter, he almost immediately received follows from beckygal22 (@fJPsAB) and Pixie (@zCbxKe). Both sent him links to Web sites that were hawking assorted undesirable goods.

Often spammers pretend to be individuals who stumbled upon a link that provides too-good-to-be-true saving opportunities that they just have to share with strangers. Other times they just pitch you to buy something. It rarely works, but the cost of spamming is low and it's worth the bad guy's time, apparently.

To stave off these intruders, Twitter has created the "@spam" account. When you suspect spam—or another abuse—send a direct message to @spam. Point to the suspect's account, and Twitter usually investigates promptly.

Very often, I take an additional minute to block what I suspect to be a spammer account. Then I announce that I've done so and encourage others to do the same. Twitter seems to notice when an account picks up a lot of blocks and takes appropriate action.

The question often arises, why bother paying any attention at all to the spammers. If you ignore them, they just go away. This, for the most part is true. But they nearly always come back again and again in increasingly larger numbers. They have begun to corrupt the quality of conversations in the eyes of many tweeters. They also can start making people less willing to open conversations with people they don't know.

Twitter seems to understand their need to aggressively combat spam to maintain the general quality of conversations.

While Facebook has been quite successful, direct marketing and spam caused many people—including me—to abandon it and join a smaller, less-spammy community called Twitter.

As vigilant as Twitter is in fighting spam and other abuse, I do not believe they can defeat it alone and will be hard-pressed to even control it. That's why I spend some time on most days weeding, reporting, blocking, and tweeting about spammers I find. It is going to take the entire village to contain the spammers, or so it seems to me.

> @spurdave: Ran into my first really nasty person on Twitter last night. Strange venom. But I guess there's always one.

Bots

The weapon of choice for spammers and other sordid abusers in Twitterville and for most of the interactive Web is the bot, which I mentioned in earlier chapters. Basically, a bot, short for "robot," is Internet software that tirelessly executes redundant tasks at great speed.

There are many legitimate uses for bots. For example, Internet game publishers search for players who have padded their scores. Weather services use bots to find keywords like "earthquake" or "monsoon." Google doesn't disclose exactly how its search technologies work, but experts assume bot technology is involved. While I might prefer that they didn't do it, China's censors use bots to find taboo words like "Tibet" or "free Taiwan" that they don't want discussed.

The bad guys have found all sorts of ways to use bots to their advantage. Hackers use them to keep firing passwords and user-name possibilities to break into accounts. They lurk silently on Internet conversations until a keyword triggers them to send an instant comment, sometimes to market goods, other times to spew hatred.

Bots somehow know a little bit about whom you are when they follow you. They seem to know how many followers you have. The more legitimate followers you have, the more spammers you get. They know that Twitter newcomers, like my neighbor Tom Hodges, are faster to follow back. They also know that if you don't follow them back within forty-eight hours, you probably never will, so they'll stop following you and go hit on someone else.

Hackers have used bots at least twice to break through Twitter security using password bots. Recently, Twitter started defending itself from bot-driven incursions by using their own bots to detect them. Sometimes it takes a bot to catch a bot.

Bots can be at the core of nasty schemes, as was the case with the Hummingbird, a site that offered a free download of mysterious software that promised that if you bought it for $197, it would let you earn $4,000 a week. All you had to do was: (1) retweet the message to others, (2) register by giving the Hummingbird your Twitter account information, and (3) follow the cofounders Kyle Graham (@Kyle Graham) and Ryan Wade (@RyanWade).

By requiring that you follow them, the two founders amassed thousands of followers, giving them both a false appearance of credibility. The retweet requirement got those being fleeced to also serve as an inadvertent sales force for the cheap bot being sold, which incidentally was the tool being used by the Hummingbird site.

Twitter took down the original @TheHummingbird account. The founders then came back, using their own names. Twitter has taken them down as well. One can only speculate on what the next steps may be.

Jim Mitchem (@smashadv), CEO of smashcommunications, a

virtual ad agency, told me one of the ugliest Twitterville bot stories I've heard. Mitchem was tweeting during the Obama inauguration. He commented that he was proud his country had elected a black man. He must have used a keyword spotted by a bot. His post triggered a racist bot that spewed several racially venomous comments at him in very rapid succession.

His attempt to reply apparently triggered a second automated program. "I was inundated with roughly fifty follows by other kinds of malicious bots that raged on hate for race, sexuality, and so on," he recalled.

Mitchem locked down his account and left Twitter for a couple of weeks. He blocked all followers that he could not confirm as real people. He is now quick on the Block button whenever he "smells a bot." He says that by being careful who he follows, he is enjoying his Twitterville conversations more than he did prior to the incident, when he simply followed everyone back.

Ruses of the Phishermen

Phishing is a time-tested online criminal activity. Basically, someone creates a fraudulent site that impersonates an authentic one. Often the phishing site looks like a site you know—counterfeit eBay, Google, PayPal, and bank sites are common.

The bad guys lure you into baited traps. The ruses take two common forms: rewards and alarms. A reward phish promises a worthwhile prize of some kind if you just go to the site and answer a few questions that almost invariably include a request for your login information.

Alarm bait, as it is called, might warn that your bank account is under attack and that you need to verify your user information with the bank to protect your money. Your account is indeed under attack, but the assailant is the fraudster who sent you the message.

You have probably seen these kinds of messages in your e-mail.

They invariably have a link for you to click on that appears legitimate but takes you to a different domain entirely. Now the same tactic has moved into Twitter.

Twitter has a unique attribute that appeals to phishers. Most tweeters use URL-shortening services such as tiny.url or bit.ly to save precious space.

But there is a side effect of shortened URLs: you can't see where you're going until you get there. If your browser is not current, landing on a malicious site can also make you vulnerable to viruses or such malware as spyware that reports where you go and what you look at to someone who should not know. When you land on a site from a truncated URL, always closely examine the address bar to make sure you are where you think you are. Another option: when you get sent to your bank or another site where you might make a transaction, open a new window and type in the long URL that you know is correct.

For a moment, though, let's say you take a phisherman's bait and visit a site that may look like that of Bank of America but in fact belongs to Franco of the Cayman Islands. So you go there thinking you are giving your own bank your account information when in fact you are helping Franco buy an island-hopping yacht. You do this by following instructions to enter your user ID, password, and credit card or bank account information.

Your trouble doesn't end when you shut down your credit card, either. The bad guys now have your user ID and password, which they resell to one another on a regular basis. They also can find other sites where you use the same login information, and they can pretend to be you. On those sites they may buy something by confirming that the credit card on record, ending on those last four digits, is still good.

Phishing has been around for years. In its early days, Twitter seemed fortunate to have avoided it. But as Twitter's popularity grew, the phishers followed the crowd, arriving in Twitterville with a vengeance in early 2009.

One of the first and best-known cases involved a widely distributed tweet. It declared, "I can't believe I got a free laptop," then linked recipients to a shortened URL so you could get one too. "Just give them your Twitter ID," it urged. "And please, tell all your friends."

Many people got this message from what appeared to be someone they followed. In fact, the scheme was self-perpetuating. The phishers were stealing one person's ID, then sending it to all his or her followers. Word kept spreading; the more it did so, the more credible the deal sounded, and the more people submitted user information.

The trouble was, of course, nobody ever got a free laptop. But the bad guys got a lot of people's online login data. And chances are good that they abused it. Twitter has shut this one down, but the offenders have not been apprehended as of this writing.

It is wise to be wary of urgent messages. Large institutions that handle millions of financial transactions rarely send out "yikes" messages. If they did, most people would rethink trusting them with their finances. But phishers know that the faster you are coaxed to move, the less time you have to think through what you're doing.

There are times when it is particularly easy to dupe people— when they want something badly and they're in a hurry. The Michael Jackson London concert of January 2009 was a shining example of this, and it was one of the first successful so-called Twitterphishes.

Concerts by the late Michael Jackson were rare, and British fans were frantic to get seats. Legitimate tickets sold out in less than an hour. The ticket hotline was soon permanently busy, and requesting tickets at the concert Web site simply put you into a virtual queue without telling you how far back in line you were.

Fans searched for tickets everywhere, including Twitterville. Suddenly, people were receiving tweets from unknown parties telling them that the official Twitter blog was offering tickets for sale but you "had to hurry because they were going fast." The tweeted link took you to a site that looked very much like the official Twitter blog; unless you examined the URL you wouldn't realize that you were at a counterfeit site.

That fake blog linked to a fake ticketing site that took your real credit card information in payment for a concert you would not get to see. Most people, of course, have credit card protection. But the credit companies got bilked, people had to replace their cards, and worse, they never got to attend the concert.

The two-step process showed a sophisticated touch. Getting a link from someone you don't know pointing you to Jackson tickets would arouse more suspicion then someone sending you to the trusted Twitter site. Few stopped to think that Twitter had never as a company offered its customers any advice on how to buy anything prior to the incident. The second site looked legitimate too. Because tickets were scarce, fans felt greater urgency. They didn't stop to think, and they paid the price.

> @athletes4acure: "If there were twitter rules" #85—If a follower's resume went from Investment Banker to Social Media Consultant in the last 6 months, block.

A Joke on You

Lee's @Scamsite account and blog are filled with useful warnings about Twitter scams. While the Michael Jackson ticket fraud was in full swing, Lee called attention to another Twitter phishing expedition promising those who clicked the link looking for a "funny blog" were quickly tricked into revealing their Twitter username and password.

When bad guys get your password on Twitter, the first thing they do is change the password. That means you are locked out and they can pretend to be you. They can see who you follow and who follows you, then contact them pretending they are you. They can ask for favors or recommend fraudulent sites. And they do it all using the trust you have built up.

When you discover the problem, all you need to do is notify Twitter. They ask you a confidential question that proves you are who you say you are. You get your account back and the hacker is locked out. But in the short time the bad guy was there, chances are he moved very fast—perhaps with the help of a software bot—to deceive others in your name.

In mid-January 2009, hackers broke into the @BarackObama account, creating the first new post since the election: "What's your opinion of Barack Obama? Take the survey and win $500 in free gas." To the suspicious mind, the president of the United States is not likely to run a sweepstakes on Twitter to poll public opinion. And if he were, I doubt he'd be rewarding participants with free fossil fuel. Still, some took the bait.

In early February an eighteen-year-old East Coast hacker broke into a handful of celebrity Twitter accounts including those of President Obama, Britney Spears, CNN's Rick Sanchez, and Fox News. On the last account, the young miscreant tweeted the unauthorized declaration "Bill O'Reilly is gay."

In an interview on Wired.com, the anonymous hacker described how he used a software bot to run common passwords against a support staffer's user name. He discovered "happiness" was the magic word.

Fortunately, this particular hacker's intentions were relatively benign. He did it simply to demonstrate how easily he could do it. Twitter quickly responded by making future incursions more difficult.

On May 1, 2009, the London *Telegraph* reported that a French person calling himself Hacker Croll claimed to have broken into Twitter's administrative computers and accessed millions of accounts. Biz Stone confirmed a break had occurred and ten sites had been tampered with; they were repaired promptly

The *Telegraph* did not reveal how they learned of Hacker Croll but implied that some of the attacks were designed to generate publicity, and perhaps notoriety, more than damage reputations or steal information.

Porn Names looked comedic at first, but was really devious. In mid-May 2009 it buzzed around Twitterville as a game: go to a Web site (since taken down), give it some trivial information, and #Pornnames would make up a racy Twitter account name for you to either use or just share with followers for a laugh.

But those so-called trivial questions were not so harmless. You were asked the name of the street where you grew up, your mother's maiden name, and the name of your favorite pet. Sound familiar? They're the questions financial companies ask you to file for security purposes. Now, what would a bad guy do with that information? Hundreds, perhaps thousands of people fell for it before the site was taken down and its perpetrators disappeared into cyberspace.

> @chrisvoss: To accomplish great things we must not only act, but also dream. Not only plan, but also believe.

Stalkers, Trolls, and Identity Thieves

Sometimes the bad guys don't want your money. They just want to damage your reputation.

In chapter 8, which explored logo Twitter accounts, I told you about how a MySpace user had usurped Mayo Clinic's brand, changing the logo to a flashing electric chair. Some may call this harmless satire, but chances are its creator had the serious intention of giving you a negative impression of the organization.

There are similar cases of personal and corporate brand theft in Twitter. The owner of @IcelandicAir has tweeted a single message to date: "I'm a lousy airline flying around and burning fossil fuel." You can assume this is neither the company itself nor an airline fan.

This is an example of cyber squatting: an individual taking a company's trademarked identity, registering it, and using it to damage that company's reputation. There is legal recourse, but it is difficult and complex, which may explain why there were 1.72 million cases of it identified on the Internet in 2008, and only about 2,400 companies taking the trouble to file complaints.*

I am of the opinion that Mayo Clinic, Icelandic Airlines, and others have the right to protect their trademarked identities. But others would argue that they are parodying public identities, and thus fair game. And one company official who did not want to be identified said that his company lets a squatted site stand because getting it taken down would draw more attention than ignoring it. Either way, it's a good reason for businesses and people to register their own company names—as well as close misspellings—early and often.

Sometimes there is no question of parody. Sometimes brand theft is downright malicious and intended to seriously damage a person or organization.

Mari Smith (@MariSmith), a social media consultant, found herself being stalked and mocked by a persistent and mean-spirited

---

* This issue—domain squatting—is something new in terms of the law. According to *Naked Law*, an online newsletter, the number of such instances on the Internet rose by 18 percent in 2008, to a "whopping" 1.7 million.

If you are a company wishing to complain, the governing body is WIPO, the World Intellectual Property Organization. In 2008 about 2,400 companies filed complaints, including Nestlé and Google.

Naked Law explains why this is such a difficult route to pursue:

"Normally, brand owners would set their lawyers onto the cyber-squatters, with letters before action being sent threatening litigation unless the cyber-squatter ceases to infringe the brand owner's trademark rights. However, cyber-squatters have become masters of disguise, using identity shields to mask their identities from the WHOIS searcher, which means that it is hard to identify where and to whom letters before action should be sent. This fact, along with the other benefits of resolving a domain name ownership dispute by dispute resolution, explains why brand owners are using the domain name dispute resolution routes such as the UDRP instead of bringing court proceedings against the infringer."

detractor. This is a practice called "trolling" in social media. It began in blogs, spilled over into Facebook, and eventually found its way into Twitterville. The intent is not to fleece money, nor would reasonable people call it parody.

It is more accurately depicted as mean-spirited, with intent to damage a personal or company brand.

Smith had met her troll in 2007 in a Facebook Group, where the two interacted civilly enough. But the troll began to write about a third party in a manner that Smith considered abusive. She said so, and the troll struck back with a vengeance.

He "seemed to exhibit some kind of bipolar disorder or psychosis. He set up a series of fake Twitter accounts displaying my avatar, bio, and a slight variation on the spelling of my name," she told me. Then he started stalking her.

Every time Smith tweeted at her authentic account, the troll retweeted what she wrote from the fake accounts, twisting the words to make the post sound stupid, greedy, or banal. This continued for at least ten months. The fake Smith accounts confused some tweeters who were not yet following her. They stumbled across the counterfeit account MarieSmith or MerriSmith and thought they were reading her tweets.

The troll, apparently enjoying this new tactic, began to do the same to at least four other prominent tweeters, but his central focus remained on Smith.

Smith fought back using multiple tactics. She used the Block option to terminate direct interaction. She frequently visited Twitter Search, checking for misspellings of her name. She checked to see whom the troll was talking to via the false accounts, then direct-messaged those people to make clear that it had been an imposter. She paid attention to the troll's usage patterns; when he went on Twitter, she went off. When he signed off, she signed back on.

Step by step, Smith regained control of her Twitter identity, but the process was exhausting and the troll returns from time to time to take new shots. She is not alone. Many prominent social media participants attract trolls. None would describe the experience as pleasant. No one finds trolls easy to shake.

Smith became too difficult to harass, so the troll, for the most part, moved on.

In chapter 13, I shared the story of the Armano family, who had helped their housekeeper, Daniela, find a new home. As the story gained attention on social media platforms, Smith's troll inserted himself into the conversation with a barrage of derogatory comments about Daniela and the Armanos' motives and credibility. Armano began to fear that the troll might pose a real danger. Yet a simple act seemed to solve the problem. He used Twitter's Block feature and the troll went away, probably in search of someone who was easier to harass.

I cannot speak for trolls, but it seems a good many of them are motivated by getting attention. When their ability to make noise in a public conversation is deterred, very often they just go find someone else to pick on.

Strange and inappropriate proposals also occur in Twitterville. While they are not exactly common, they also cannot be called rare. For instance, one Florida-based user sought out women who had posted about their new babies. He would then send a tweet using the famous slogan "Got Milk?" If he got a response, he requested the new mother send him some of her breast milk.

As its name implies, the @spam was set up for reporting one kind of abuse. But users have found that reporting phishing, stalking, trolling, or other inappropriate behavior to the account often provokes action on the part of Twitter—sometimes quickly.

The cold war is likely to continue.

PART 3

How and Why

CHAPTER 16

Tips, Metrics, and Finer Points

> **@vaspersthegrate: A degree in journalism is a degree in deception.**

t is the nature of most professionals to use a tool for a specific purpose, and to know that purpose from the beginning. Twitter should not be an exception. There are at least as many reasons for professionals to use Twitter as there are to use the telephone. I've discussed quite a few, including: distributing company information, getting closer to customers, joining or building a community or marketplace, providing customer support, generating sales leads, spotting trends, keeping an eye on competitors, and my personal favorite, learning what your customers are thinking and saying about you.

Whichever one of these you choose to get started, Twitter's role is likely to evolve. My research for this book gave me countless examples of companies that came for one reason and found greater value in another.

For that reason, I advise you to start tweeting with an open mind and to be agile enough to accommodate change. Henry Ford Medical Center did not start tweeting with any intention of performing live-tweeted cancer and brain surgery, but they discovered it improved their position. Mayo Clinic only came to Twitterville to protect itself from a domain squatter, but they too have discovered much of greater value there.

Becoming What We Measure

The conventional wisdom is that everything, simply everything in business must be measured. I have no quarrel with that, except you need to think through why you are measuring it. It's not all ROI. Companies like Comcast, for example, see their bottom line being favorably impacted by Twitter, but that isn't what they measure. They measure customer satisfaction. And the more they focus on that, the more effective Twitter is in moving the needle.

"You become what you measure," warns Katie Paine (@KDPaine), CEO of KDPaine & Partners, LLC, who knows more about social media measurement than anyone I know. Her organization conducts measurement and provides strategy for a diverse array of clients that include Raytheon, United Service Organizations, and Georgia Institute of Technology.

Her point is that whatever a company measures becomes a focal point for improving, and companies can go astray by focusing on the wrong measurement issue. For example, many people believe that support departments should measure customer satisfaction rather than the cost of providing it. Dell and Comcast are two companies who have shifted focus that way and the results show measurable reputation improvements.

Dell's Binhammer's social media group measures engagement. He doesn't care how many people follow the 150 Dell tweeters. Instead, he subjectively measures how many conversations people on Twitter have with and about Dell. On the other hand, Dell Outlet measures sales, and once a follower has purchased, the people running the program don't mind if you stop following.

In fact, Guerrero explained how a change in getting started at Twitter has led to @DellOutlet followship numbers becoming downright deceptive. For over a year, the account averaged about 2,500. Most had signed up with the intention of buying a computer, and, Guerrero said, the account had a very high ratio of sales to followers.

But in February 2009 Twitter installed a default page for newcomers called People to Follow. It rotates several commercial account names in and out. Every few days @DellOutlet is included; unless people opt out they automatically follow the account. By May @DellOutlet had a half-million followers because of this factor. Sales did increase, but not accordingly. Guerrero sees little or no value in counting the followers. He also doubts following @DellOutlet has much value to the people who got there by default rather than by searching for a deal on a computer.

Paine sees almost no value in businesses tracking followers.

"All it says is that a bunch of people may or may not see what you have to say, depending on what else they're doing. It's useless unless you've got advertisers paying you to Tweet." Even then, Paine points out that it is not possible to know how many of your followers see any specific tweet at any given time.

Paine says she begins measuring programs by helping clients get clear on the goal.

"Why are you on Twitter in the first place? If you want to end up with a bigger circulation for your newsletter, you're there to drive traffic, so use Google Analytics to determine what impact Twitter is having on your traffic—and, more specifically, on the repeat visitors, subscribers, et cetera."

If Dell wants more people to engage with its brand, Paine advises measuring repeat conversations, time between engagements, and the content of the Tweets. Then they need to compare the results from Twitter to results from other traffic sources like Facebook or LinkedIn.

Suppose the issue is customer service; then she'll track the number and nature of complaints voiced on Twitter.

Paine's group uses Web analytics tools to ensure her clients understand what action is coming from Twitter itself. Some of her tools of choice can be easily found online, including Twazzup to keep tabs on what people are saying, and then Twinfluence or Twitter Analyzer to measure if influence is increasing or falling.

So why use KDPaine & Partners at all?

Because you need a human factor in order to understand what the measurements are telling you. Computer technology is fast, far-reaching, and tireless, but it still lacks common sense.

Says Paine: "You can get a computer to act like a human, but you cannot get one to think like a customer, and that's the essence of what most business measurements are about."

But she urged, "Keep your eye on the ball. All the 'attaboy/girls' are great, but you have to stay focused on what problems Twitter is solving."

> @kevinokeefe: Best time ever to be a Journalism Grad for you get to help invent the future. Dean Peggy Kuhr to Montana School of Journalism Grads.

The Sunlight Approach

One major difference between a telephone and Twitter is that the latter works best in public, where one person speaks and many can respond. Of course, some people use phones for conference calls, which works just fine, and there are many times when a Twitter DM is satisfactory as well.

But some people and businesses use Twitter essentially as a private channel. When they join Twitter, they use an option called Protect Updates, which restricts who can follow them. Protect mode, essentially makes their conversations private.

A woman told me she uses the feature because she is fearful of the sorts of stalkers and trolls I discussed in the "Dark Streets" chapter.

While I'm sympathetic, it seems to me that if you need to be that private, then e-mail is a much better tool. Twitter is best used as a social tool and works best for people who want to communicate publicly.

What is interesting is that organizations with reputations for clinging to privacy seem to be taking highly public approaches on Twitter. In health care we have the Henry Ford Health Service leading a growing number of hospitals who live-tweet delicate surgeries. We have the Mayo Clinic, which only came to Twitterville to preempt a domain squatter and is now a proponent of using Twitter to give out free medical advice.

> @conniereece: RT @whatsnext: I want a 10" notebook. what do you like? ASUS? Acer? Dell? i need geek advice please. where to get best price? (me too!)

Humanizing Your Tweets

With the possible exceptions of Evernote and StockTwits, every Twitterville success story that I've discussed here has involved accounts that integrate a personal factor into a business conversation.

This is one reason that I say Twitter lets us behave online as we do in real life. In my career as a business consultant, I did my best work when I knew something personal about my client. Did they have kids? Did they go to the theater or rock concerts? Did they play golf, exercise, or cook as a hobby?

This social interaction did not take focus off the business at hand; indeed, it often catalyzed it. We humans are social animals, and we do our best collaborating when we know, trust, and understand the people with whom we are doing business.

Twitterville Buddy

If you were to move to a new physical community, chances are you would know someone there in advance. Hopefully that person would show you around, giving you a few tips on where to shop, pointing out the best destinations for entertainment and recreation, as well as which restaurants to frequent or avoid.

If you're a new user, it will be helpful if you can find yourself a Twitterville buddy, someone who will help orient you and introduce you around to some of her followers when appropriate.

And don't worry about being a newbie. Twitterville has been growing so fast for so long that the community has become as accustomed to newcomers as Orlando, Florida, is used to tourists with kids wearing mouse ears.

Most people in Twitterville tend to be friendly, helpful, and forgiving to newcomers who may be confused or make an occasional gaffe.

The Ant Clay Pub Metaphor

I'm obviously fond of the Twitterville small town metaphor, but I also like Ant Clay's analogy comparing Twitter to a British country pub. Clay (@SoulSailor) is a consultant for Trinity Expert Systems (tesl.com) in Rugby, England. "There are lots of conversations going on," Clay explains, "all happening freely and all of them you can hear—that's Twitter's public timeline."

The public timeline lets a user see all the conversations going on in Twitter at that moment. New users tend to go there first to see the entire conversation. Once people are in Twitter for a while, though, they tend to settle in and pay attention to conversations that are more specifically relevant to them.

In the pub, according to Clay, you sit at a table with a bunch of your friends. In Twitterville, those are the people you follow who follow you back. These are conversations you can hear and that you are welcome to join. It's natural to join those conversations, and if you do not behave intrusively, your thoughts are usually welcome.

In the pub, you might want to respond to what your friend at the far end of the table had to say, so you'd call out "Hey, John," and speak while the others listen and watch. You do this in Twitter by using the "@" key, for example, writing "@John."

Other people see the conversation and, again, can join in if they want. It's public.

You may want to find out what people in the pub think of a new movie or restaurant, so you'd go around asking others, or maybe you just hear one mentioned and "your ears prick up," Clay said. In Twitterville you do the same thing with the Twitter Search feature that lets you search for a person or a topic.

Clay also encourages joining the conversation. In the pub, "You may sit in the corner of the bar, just listening. That's okay, for a while, but eventually people will either ignore you or brand you as someone to not bother with. Join in, don't be scared."

> @kyeung808: Attn everyone: due to my camera not speaking to me, no photos will be available for the next few days. :(

My Eight Tips

A while back I posted a blog of tips for getting started on Twitter. To my surprise, it turned out to be among the most popular posts I've ever put up. I have revised and updated it for this book. If you are just getting started, you may find this section useful. If you have been around for a while you may want to skip this section and the next one.

This is generally what I wrote:

If you are new to Twitterville, people will want to know a bit about you in order to decide if they wish to converse with you. This will not happen if you simply start an account, reveal nothing about yourself and your interests, and then go around following people. Some may follow you back, but it will matter very little if you have nothing more in common with them than the shared obsession with aggregating followers.

Begin your Twitterville journey on the right foot.

1. Show Yourself. Scroll through some Twitter pages and see what first catches your eye. Chances are good that it will be the avatar image. Most people like to see who they're talking to; they're more likely to follow someone who uses an authentic photo over another whose avatar is a cartoon or brand icon.

In the small space allotted by Twitter, give some specific info about yourself and your work. Supply links to you blog or Web site. In your bio, say something useful about why you're on Twitter. Say where you live (listing your location with coordinates from your iPhone or, worse, "everywhere," is overused and unhelpful).

2. Read First. Talk Later. When I check out someone new to me, I read his or her most recent tweets. If one interests me, I'll look further. If none do, I'm gone. Start by reading what others have to say. Get a sense of the rhythm of a conversation before you join in. Wait until you have something useful or interesting to add to the conversation.

3. Post Second. Follow Later. After you've read other tweets for a while, it's time to put up a few of your own. When you start, say what you are hoping to talk about. This may start to get you some attention from the neighborhoods that matter the most to you.

4. Friends Over Stars. While Twitterville luminaries may automatically follow you if you back, they are unlikely to join a conversation you start. You may think it impressive that these big names are following you, but since most everyone knows that these stars will follow just about anyone, few Tweeters are impressed. It's wiser to follow people whose conversations matter to you. I'll expand upon this in the next chapter.

Post before you even follow friends you find from the real world, so that when those friends point others to you, there will be something to see. When you join a conversation with people you don't know, they can visit your account and see what you talk about.

5. Avoid Spammer Stats. The worst thing you can do is have stats that show you follow 1,149 people and only 4 people follow you. These are spammer stats. Perhaps no one is following you because you've revealed so little of yourself. You can easily fix this by growing slower. Post more informative tweets, and be more transparent.

6. Have Favorites. There's a little star icon to the right of each tweet. You can use it to make someone's post a "favorite." I often look at what a new follower favors. It tells me a bit about what makes them tick. It shows a sense of humor and passion points—or reveals a lack of them.

7. Take Your Time. Twitterville works like any other neighborhood. People start by chatting about weather, lunch—the day-to-day things. Often the conversation goes nowhere, tapering off into cyberspace. Other times it deepens, evolving into a real friendship or a business opportunity. If you try pushing yourself too aggressively, people may respond to you in the same way they do the loudmouth at the party. They walk away and talk in circles that exclude you.

Use caution in joining in on the middle of a conversation. Two people may have been going back and forth several times. Then one of them says something that grabs your interest and you wish to speak. That's fine, and you will usually be accommodated, but come in slowly and politely, because you change the conversation when you join it. You don't want to be perceived as the latecomer to a party who comes into a room and interferes with other conversations by talking loudly.

8. Think Neighborhood. If you move to a large city, the first things you do are to learn your way around your neighborhood, find the best way to get to work, and where to shop and eat.

Don't think about the tens of millions of people in Twitterville. Meet people one at a time. Focus on those who hang out where you do, talk about things that matter to you such as sports, politics, and business issues, and enjoy the conversations. It's not the numbers. It's the quality of the conversations you have.

Remember the advice of Paula Drum from H&R Block. Do not think of Twitter as a mass media tool, but as a social tool.

> @delwilliams: Well aware of the different types of users on twitter. Observers, engagers, sales, and posters like @oprah

Tom Raftery's Beginner Tips

You may recall Tom Raftery (@TomRaftery), who got his job at Red-Monk (@monkchips) entirely through Twitter-based conversations. Here are a few suggestions from him:

- **Start safely.** Your first few posts should be well inside your comfort level. Talk about your interests, but serve up content that you don't mind anyone knowing.

- **Check out people who follow your friends.** When you find people you know on Twitter, see who follows them. Chances are good you'll find more people you know, as well as new people with whom you share common interests. They, in turn, will show you more people you might consider following.
- **Shortcut.** If you precede someone's username with the letter *d* (e.g., "dshelisrael"), this will send a private direct message, or DM. Make sure not to confuse the private "d" with the public "@"—a common Twitterville gaffe. In short, if you write "dshelisrael," only I will see it. If you write "@shelisrael," others will be able to see what you are saying to me.
- **Be accessible.** Use your Twitter username everywhere—add it to your e-mail signature, put it on your business cards, leave it in blog comments—don't spam; just do it where appropriate.

> @nwjerseyliz: SEO companies are like women in Wonderbras. They want you to be impressed by the rise, but not ask how. :)

Wisdom of the Followers

I have crowd-sourced nearly every *Twitterville* chapter by tweeting about the topics I planned to cover and asking for suggestions. In the end, this is how I learned about more than 70 percent of the cases that I've reported to you.

I asked my followers to share newcomer tips and received more than forty in ten minutes. Many were redundant, but it shows the general inclination of people on Twitter to help.

Joseph Thornley (@thornley), a partner in Thornley Fallis, a Canadian PR and communications agency, provided no less than ten suggestions. Some that I found particularly insightful include:

- You can disagree with someone but do so respectfully. Snarkiness undermines conversation.
- Give generously, and you will receive more than you give.
- Be patient in your conversations. Not everyone tunes in when you do. Never suggest that a conversation is over just because you are leaving it.
- When you start off, try to offer something valuable with every tweet. Once people know you, you can start adding trivia, like what you had for lunch.

A few other suggestions you may find worthwhile include:

- Tamera Kremer (@tamera) advised, "Don't worry about what some people think of as 'rules'—be yourself, be open & honest, be flexible, not everyone will follow you."
- Phillip Che Jacobson (@Infoliberation) suggested Googling people you'd like to follow. Adding the word "twitter" to their names makes them easier to find there than on Twitter Search or the Find Friend feature.
- Donna Tocci @DonnaTocci said, "Listen. Listen. Listen. And relevant, useful content."
- Linda Russell (@lindabeth) offered, "Don't listen to someone telling you what it should/shouldn't be. Use Twitter how YOU want to use it."

Russell is right, of course. So take my advice and the advice of the others I have quoted here—then forge your own course.

And perhaps most important of all: have fun. The business value of fun is often vastly underrated.

Followship Exchanges

There are those who see followship as a transaction. If they follow you, you'd damned well better follow them back or they will drop you. When this happens to me, the only thing I have to say is, "Good-bye." No, I don't like hurting people's feelings. And yes, I would prefer to gain followers than lose them.

But if my followers are really not interested in what I have to say, if they don't engage me in interesting conversations, then what relevance do they have to me? If everyone in Twitterville ignores Katie Paine's sage advice that your followers are the last statistic of business relevance, then Twitterville's entire business district becomes a link exchange rather than a marketplace as Charlene Li described it.

Quite simply, I follow the people who post comments that interest me. I don't care how or where in Twitterville we crossed paths. I care about the quality of the conversation. Sometimes my Twitterville conversations lead directly to business, in terms of speaking engagements, advising companies, or gathering content for this or future books.

Other times I just enjoy having a good chat where I learn something or smile. Twitter makes me smarter. It makes my world larger, and I find that aspect for me to be priceless.

Tweet What You Like

People often ask me what I think they should tweet about. I say, "Anything you like." If you write about what you know and what you care about, people who want to know about those issues will find and follow you. People who don't will probably leave, but so what?

I'm diverse concerning what topics I address, as well as how often I tweet. My interest over the course of a few months may go from cheering for my beloved Boston Red Sox to wanting to understand

how censorship really works in China to my current emerging interest in using social media for better health and e-Government. I'll
write a lot on a topic and people will follow me for a while. Then my
interests change and they'll leave. It's fine with me.

What I do owe my followers is good conversation. I try to bring
new information, thoughts, or ideas to my tweetstreams. Sometimes,
particularly when I'm live-tweeting speakers at industry events, or
when the Red Sox are in a pennant race, I have posted more than a
hundred times in one day. When I do, I post a warning that I am
about to "flood the stream," so that those not interested in the topic
can unfollow me for a while, with the hope they'll come back after
the event concludes. A new program called TwitterSnooze! just
came out that lets you turn off someone you follow for a set time. I'll
probably try that next time.

Sometimes I have very little to say and I don't post for a few days.
Most tweeters take breaks. What's important is what you say, not
how many times a day you post.

If you talk about the issues that interest you most, you will attract
people who care about them most. To my way of thinking, it's not
the quantity of followers but the quality of conversations.

If people do not find what I have to say interesting, they should
stop following me. I am not offended. I do the same when I find
someone I've followed is no longer posting content that interests me.
It simply means our mutual interests have diverged.

> @chrisbrogan: Automated tweets and follows are simply
> a nuisance. They don't add value. They detract.
> Automation = antisocial.

Bigger Is Often Better

Another point to consider is how many people you should follow. I
currently follow nearly two thousand. This number may seem larger

than it actually is, Twitterville isn't all that different from real life. If you think about all the people you interact with, the old friends and current ones, family members, people you work with, former colleagues, your dry cleaner, your neighbors, and so on, chances are good there are well over a thousand.

You speak to some of these folk every day, others only rarely. And you discuss different subjects with the different people. Twitter is like that.

I speak with some of the people I follow quite often, others hardly ever or not at all. It is a constantly changing thing. In fact, because I tend to visit Twitterville at the same time every day, I tend to see the same people each time, except when I travel. Then it's like reading someone else's newspaper.

On my most active Twitter days, I have probably read tweets or or talked with over a hundred people. This is about equal to the most people I've answered by e-mail in one day. But the Twitter interactions go faster, are more fun, and are cumulatively more valuable to me. It's the same in real life: I may see a hundred people I know in one day, but it's a special event when that happens—like a wedding or a birthday party.

I generally think it's best to carefully build a large number of people you follow. It's like it used to be for me when I spent much of my Sundays reading the *New York Times*. The newspaper is filled with writers I had come to know, and guest writers who I wanted to know. The information I received was useful and expanded my world.

And the thicker the paper, the more relevant content there was in it for me. Let the numbers grow, but weed them out regularly, as your interests—and theirs—change. Twitter is better than a newspaper in one important way: I can ask questions and talk back, and conversations are so much better than monologues.

However, when you build up a large number of people to follow, there is one significant trade-off: you lose a certain intimacy.

When I first came to Twitterville, I followed just a few friends and the people they recommended specifically to me. There was a decided informality. We kidded one another a bit, and spoke to one another with the familiarity of close friends.

As the number of follows has grown for me, I find the tone of conversation has evolved into something more businesslike. It has evolved from having the feel of Ant Clay's pub to a professional conference.

Sometimes I miss the ambience of the bar. But I probably learn and benefit more by hanging out at the business conference.

Lose a Few Followers

I've talked a lot about why measuring followers is overrated. I even see benefits in losing a few from time to time.

After a while you discover that certain topics earn you more followers, while others send followers running. For example, when I went to China, I wrote about only China for more than two weeks. I posted more than five hundred times about my experiences there. And I lost several hundred followers as a result. A great many people who followed me because I write about social media turned out to have little or no interest in my visit to the Great Wall.

Should I have stuck to my original subject because that's what my followers preferred? For me, the answer is no. If I wrote only about what interested me yesterday, I would constrain my own growth.

It is easy to assume an obligation to your followers that is not really there. They don't pay you to tweet; they follow you because you give them something.

As a writer, I explore diverse avenues. I experiment with topics and style. I am always trying something a little different on Twitter and learn a fair amount by who chooses to follow or drop me.

Just like the people I follow, my followers shape the conversations I have in Twitter and the quality of my experience. If a follower is consistently unpleasant or generally banal from my perspective, I feel

I benefit if that person elects to just go away. From time to time I have requested someone to do just that and, if they decline, blocked them.

This may not work in your case.

If you tweet for business, your followers may be customers, prospects, recruits, media; you really don't want them to go away.

Take, for example, the case of Howard Lindzon, cofounder of Stocktwits, who I told you about earlier. He's trying to build a community of investors. People follow him because they want insightful information that will influence their stock-trading decisions. They want to make money, as so many of us wish to do.

So if Lindzon, one day, posted a tweet about walking a puppy in a park, investors might live with it. But if he started talking more and more about puppies in parks than whether Apple stock was likely to rise or fall, he would start losing followers, and with the loss, he would suffer in influence.

I would strongly advise Lindzon not to try to lose followers the way I do.

Most business tweeters fall somewhere between Lindzon and me. Their primary reason for tweeting is business related. But if they post all business, all the time, they would likely become redundant or tedious.

Almost all successful tweeters show some humanity in what they post, even Lindzon. This is as it is in business. You know certain personal things about most of the people you work with. It makes the work more enjoyable and perhaps more productive. If you don't insert some of your own humanity, your tweets will probably be about as interesting as your corporate Web site.

Binhammer actually keeps track of how many personal and how many outward-focused tweets he posts. He points his followers to other industry content. He posts about social media. He points you to his professional-level photos on Flickr. About one time in nine he talks about a Dell event.

From time to time he probably tweaks that ratio. When he goes too far in any one direction, he loses a few followers. He then adjusts course and gains some back.

You will need to figure out what the right mix of topics for you and your goals should be. Once you fall into a comfortable track, something will change. It could be in Twitterville, or in your industry, or maybe a plane will land next to your ferry to New Jersey.

The *Twitterville Times*

I could not have written the previous section if I did not follow some pretty smart and generous people. Andrew Lih (@Fuzheado), an American expat and author of *The Wikipedia Revolution,* who I met in China, says that who he follows is more important than who follows him. I completely agree.

I've harped a lot on the ambiguities and deceptions of who follows you. The people I follow are an extremely valuable source of information, insight, and entertainment. In a few ways I think about them collectively the way I used to feel about the Sunday *New York Times*.

In fact, Twitterville has in many ways become my Conversation Age newspaper. By changing who I follow, I can change the topics of news that interest me. I can learn about fast-breaking news like Mumbai and Gaza. I can get recommendations on theater, music, art, and more. I can highly personalize my *Twitterville Times* every day and, best of all, I can talk back to it and be heard.

You can do the same thing to get the information you wish. You can aggregate citizen and traditional journalistic content. And your *Twitterville Times* will look entirely different from mine.

Perhaps Twitterville will be the venue where braided journalism takes seed, grows, and thrives. Perhaps Twitterville will be the newspaper itself, and perhaps someone will figure out a way to monetize such a service. If so, then in the future news services may be superior than what they were at their apex.

Retweet Requests

People who will ask you to retweet for a variety of reasons. Such requests can come from smarmy schemers like the Hummingbird. But at other times they are from proponents of worthy causes such as earthquake relief. A third situation may arise when a friend is proud of something they've posted on Twitter or a blog.

The problem may come after you have been around for a while and you have a good number of followers. There are many worthy causes and you may end up with many proud friends. It does you and your followers no good if you become a retweet factory.

So where do you draw the line? It's easy to offend people you may not wish to offend if you say yes to the first party, then no to the second. There's also the issue of investigating causes before implying an endorsement by retweeting.

The way I've worked it out is not by thinking of the needs of people who approach me but by retweeting only that which I think is useful to my followers. Most of the time, I find something—a tweet, a blog post, or a traditional news item—that they may find useful or interesting. I also retweet sometimes because I find something that I find funny or unusually lame.

If retweeting becomes a way that friends promote their friends, products, or business alliances, then Twitter is in danger of becoming part of marketing rather than a marketplace for interesting conversations. It lessens the value of retweets.

If I retweet and my followers do not see much value in a message, it puts a small chink into my reputation. If I retweet content that is consistently useless, then the chink becomes an entire chasm.

That being said, I think it is more than useful to retweet material for your followers. It is also quite simple to do. When you see a tweet you wish to relay, just copy and paste it into your Update box. In front of it put "RT @source."

If there's enough space, you can even insert your own comment at the end. It's also acceptable to edit the original tweet to create more space. If there are several people who have retweeted, you can eliminate some names, but be sure to keep the original source.

What you retweet is evolving as a way people measure you. Many people feel that the number of retweets is a better measure of influence than the number of followers. There are several sites that measure it, all of which still need some refinement. Retweet.com ranks the most popular retweets at any given moment the way Twitterholic. com ranks the most followers. RetweetRank.com goes further, revealing the actual tweets that are most often repeated.

How you use Twitter is up to you. Just keep in mind that the decisions you make will have a major impact on your personal and business brands.

CHAPTER 17

Global Neighborhoods

Many business books attempt to paint a lofty "big picture" in their concluding chapter. I thought I would use mine to tell you how global neighborhoods can achieve world peace.

To do that, I need to back up a little bit, perhaps a few thousand millennia, to when your ancestors and mine lived in caves.

Chances are our mutual ancestors belonged to different clans. When they encountered one another while foraging for mammoths and berries, we can only imagine what might have ensued.

Perhaps they were neighbors and pretty much understood each other's grunts and gestures. Maybe they had skin and hair the same color, and dressed in similarly fashioned loincloths.

But what if they were not neighbors? What if my ancestors had brown hair and dark skin and lived near the ocean, while yours had blond hair and fair skin and lived up in the mountains?

What if mine used a gesture to say hello that was interpreted by your ancestors to mean, "you are ugly"?

The misinterpreted grunts likely would have led to some serious head bashing. We tend to trust those who are from where we are from, who look like our family members, and when we meet people who appear to be different we sometimes view them suspiciously. And when we don't quite understand their grunts and gestures, the ensuing misunderstanding can lead to hostility and violence.

This has pretty much remained a constant over the millennia of human history. People are perhaps a little taller and stand straighter for the most part, but their behavior has stayed the same. What have changed are our tools. In the case I cited above, our tools have evolved from clubs and stones to guns and bombs.

What's all this got to do with Twitterville?

Let me try another scenario. This time, when our mutual ancestors encounter each other one is hungry and the other is cold. One has food and the other has some nicely cured saber-toothed tiger pelts.

One points at the fur and identifies it with a sound. He gestures toward his food and extends his arms outward. Our ancestors understand one another. A trade takes place.

It seems that we humans contain a variety of qualities. Along with a yen for violence, we also love making deals. I strongly prefer the latter.

> @pistachio: if you do not turn away from the ones and the things that do you harm you are doing that harm to yourself.

Nixon to Mao: "Let's make a deal"

Let's fast-forward. It's the early 1970s. Man has recently walked on the moon. Organizational computers still fill entire rooms, and there is nothing personal about them. The new technology that people care about most is color television. America's most trusted person is a newscaster named Walter Cronkite. Its president is Richard Nixon.

Nixon had a long history of gestures that indicated he preferred war to deals with what was then called Communist China. He was not alone; Asian and Western nations had a long history of mutual misinterpretation and suspicion.

That's why a great many people were stunned when, in 1972, Nixon and his top adviser, Henry Kissinger, announced they would go to China. At that time most Americans were getting their information from newspapers and television. Kissinger started making the media rounds to explain the case for visiting a country that a majority of Americans feared and mistrusted.

I recall seeing him on one of those Sunday morning talk shows. "Countries who do business together," he declared, "don't go to war against each other."

More recently I learned an interesting twist to this historic incident. It turns out that Chairman Mao Tse-tung's motive for meeting and befriending his historic enemy was quite different than Nixon's.

According to Margaret MacMillan in her book *Nixon and Mao,* the chairman had no desire to trade with the United States. And he most certainly had no desire for an endless parade of more than a million Westerners visiting the incredible tourist attractions of China each year, as is now the case.

He probably would have taken a great leap backward from Nixon if he knew that his regime's one week of meetings and banquets with U.S. officials would, forty years later, mean a KFC on nearly every corner of China's major cities, interspersed with Starbucks and a generous splash of Round Table Pizza parlors.

Mao's motivation was manipulation of three powerful clans. For him the meetings were about war games and making sure that the détente between the United States and Russia didn't turn into a two-against-one fight with China being the one, especially at a moment when the mainland was trying to establish its place at the global table, replacing and perhaps assimilating its rival Taiwan-based government.

So, let me tell you why and what this has to do with Twitter.

Conversations Are Peacemakers

I was raised in the United States during the cold war era. I was taught to fear and mistrust Russians, but that the Chinese were even worse. In the 1950s, while I was in elementary school, I was taught a phrase to describe the threat the Chinese allegedly posed.

It was called the "Yellow Peril." It wasn't until years later that I fully understood the political and racial implications of the term. Since that time I have come to know more about China, the Chinese, and the incredible complexities of that country's rapid development.

I did not go to the Beijing 2008 Olympic Games, but I did go to China that year. I met at least a hundred Chinese people and American expats. We talked politics and business, food and travel. Mostly we talked about Web 2.0 and social media, because we shared a common passion for those topics.

I liked a great many of the people I met. Yet many times the barriers of language and the nuances of our gestures, during face-to-face conversations, confused us. I learned that most Chinese found my sense of humor puzzling at best.

But these conversations eventually led to mutual understanding. Over time, we noticed our difference less and our similarities more. We focused on our common interest in Internet technologies and discovered how very much alike we were in so many ways. I came to judge their government and policies less from what I had read and heard about them in the West and more from what people I trusted who lived there had to say.

I may never return to China. But I talk to people there almost every day. I do it on Twitter, where the depth of the relationships I have with people there continuously deepens.

For that matter, I speak with people all over the world every day. Some of us have become quite close. I do not think these ongoing conversations could happen through the telephone, e-mail, or even blogs. But they are easy, free, and open through Twitter.

I believe that people who talk with one another come to understand one another, and people who understand one another almost never go to war against one another.

Twitter is generating conversations between diverse people. These conversations are—for the most part—not being filtered, monitored, or censored. This is true whether government likes it or not. As I mentioned in an earlier chapter, when I asked a Chinese dissident blogger about censors, he quipped: "Too many voices. Too few eyes and ears."

Twitter is letting people talk directly to one another all over the world, often in unlikely situations. Pakistanis and Indians were in the same conversations during the Mumbai terror incident; Arabs and Israelis were doing the same a few weeks later when Gaza broke out.

Yes, the words were hostile and angry, even hateful. When NPR's Andy Carvin (@ACarvin) and I tried to start a movement endorsing a two-state solution in the Middle East, our effort almost immediately fizzled.

But at least people were talking. My experience is that conversations that start with hostility sometimes become more civil as each side realizes the other is listening and has a point of view worth considering. Mao let Nixon come to China as a war gesture against Russia. But millions of Westerners followed and, over time,we came to think more about trade than war. And less than forty years later the Olympics were held there, which demonstrated how very similar the world's people are in some ways. There were protests also regarding Tibet, which demonstrated to me that a delicate balance between understanding and head bashing remains after all this time.

The Power of Personal Communications

Let's return just one more time to my cave-dwelling ancestors. The hunters have taken a huge, wooly mastodon. It will feed the tribe for the winter. There is great celebration in the Big Cave after the feast and the hunt.

Well fed, the tribe members have gathered around the fire. Using grunts and gestures, our hunters are asked to tell how they succeeded to collaborate well enough to take down a fifteen-foot-tall, ten-thousand-pound beast and haul it home to share with the tribe.

Our hunters grunt and gesture to tell their story. To illustrate a point, one uses a stick to draw a sketch on the cave floor. Later, one who tells stories better than he hunts uses blood and berries to describe the story more colorfully on the cave wall.

Just about every aspect of that story describes traits we have in today's society. We collaborate on complex projects. We are social creatures who like reasons to celebrate. We love to tell and hear stories.

And after all these years, most cultures still tell their history in terms of battles and defeating enemies. I will wager more people know that in 1915 the world was at war than know that a young mathematician named Albert Einstein was presenting his general theory of relativity.

There is a straight line from the rock beating on the stump, which cavemen used to signal to the tribe they needed help lugging the mastodon, to the telegraph to Twitter. There is a straight line from feet on the Pleistocene forest floor to a rocket-landing capsule that tweets from Mars.

I like to think that the better our communications tools get, the less likely we will be to use tools of destruction. If so, then Twitter is a great tool for peace.

> @naterkane: I love @chartjes's tagline "Always code as if the person who ends up maintaining your code is a violent psychopath who knows where you live."

Beyond Tangible Neighborhoods

There's one other point to consider: We humans are envelope pushers. We explore. We experiment. We simply must go beyond wherever it is we are. It is in our nature. The cave dwellers lived in a world that rarely went farther than their feet could take them. Their neighborhoods stopped at rivers and cliffs or turf claimed by hostile neighbors.

Their tangible neighborhoods were their entire worlds. With the development of wheels, sails, engines, and eventually spacecraft, we kept shattering historic boundaries that perhaps our own parents deemed insurmountable.

In my parents' day, humans flew from North America to Europe for the first time. In my life, man walked on the moon. In my grandchildren's time, it is possible we will have a colony on Mars, and technology to keep the place free from pollution.

In all these journeys, we continue to investigate the possibility of other life. Perhaps it will be in the form of a tiny bacterium that will defeat a currently terminal disease. Perhaps it will be intelligent and we will learn from it or trade with it. Perhaps we will misinterpret gestures and go to war.

As a species we are curious creatures. We want to know about others, but we seem chronically suspicious of them. It is our nature as a species. That, believe it or not, takes us right back to Twitterville.

The Birth of Personal Communications

We've obviously come a long way in communications since we used the stone to beat signals on the log. Perhaps the most monumental moment happened late in the nineteenth century. Let me take you back just one more time.

It's March 10, 1876. We are in a carriage house in Brantford, Ontario, a very small Canadian town.

Scottish-born Alexander Graham Bell is the twenty-nine-year-old son of two deaf parents. He has been tinkering with sound technology for ten years. To invent a successful device, he is fiercely competitive with others who are working simultaneously toward the same goal.

As the story is often told, Bell spills a small vial of diluted acid and calls out to his assistant in the next room, "Mr. Watson—come here—I need you." Thomas A. Watson hears the summons, not through the wall but through the device that will soon be called a telephone.

The two technically focused entrepreneurs have their breakthrough. They tinker a bit. They try using it over distance with family and friends. When Bell conducts a "long-distance conversation" with relatives ten miles away in Paris, Canada, they think they're good to go.

With anticipation and trepidation, Graham and Watson take their telephone to the World's Fair in Philadelphia, where the public scrutinizes the invention for the first time. It becomes the talk of the show. People go home and tell others about it. A couple of wealthy fair attendees offer to invest.

The telephone starts an important continuum—personal electronic communications. For the first time, people can communicate directly and in real time with each other without intermediation.

To my thinking, Twitter is the most recent and advanced dot on that continuum. And the parallels of the story of Twitter and the telephone are many, despite the fact that they were introduced about 130 years apart.

The way people use Twitter, as Chris Brogan noted, are as diverse as the way they use the telephone. But there's more.

Bell was fascinated with sound transmission. When he was nineteen, he fooled people into thinking his dog could talk by training it to growl, then manipulating its vocal cords with his fingers. When he was a teenager, Jack Dorsey became fascinated with mobile dispatch technology. He didn't manipulate any animals or fool anyone. But both waited many years to see their visions become realities.

Both Bell and Twitter's founders were not alone with what they introduced. Competition was abundant for both of them. But both captured the public's imagination and aggregated critical masses of users much faster than competitors thought possible. Bell and the Twitter guys needed decent technology, but more important, they required a community of support to prevail in their respective markets.

Both had accidental moments of revelation. Bell spilled something and called for help. Ev Williams sent a photo of himself and a glass of Pinot when his partner was sweaty and thirsty.

The Business Model Issue

There was one additional issue. Bell apparently struggled to figure out whether he had a hardware business or a conversational service business. In the end he did both, and both succeeded.

Twitter skeptics have consistently harped on the young company's business model or the apparent lack of one. In writing this book I have been asked more times than I can count why I would write with apparent enthusiasm about a company that has no visible way of monetizing their accelerating popularity.

I am not even slightly concerned about this issue. And just because they have not shared a business model with me or the public does not mean they lack one. It may be a result of my many years of living and working with Silicon Valley start-ups that I believe in the Field of Dreams strategy: "Build it and they will come."

Twitter's challenge has been not to monetize, but to make their platform reliable and scalable. They seem to have done so, despite occasional stumbles. In 2007, when I first met Biz Stone in Spain, he said, "There are just so many ways we can make money. Our investors want us to make the product work right first, then deal with it."

I think that is a wise strategy, and a time-proven one. It's what Google did. Google, you may recall, was the last great Silicon Valley start-up born in the dot-com era. The conventional wisdom of the time was that "search was worthless." No one had ever made a dime off Internet search engines, and the field was crowded.

Later, conventional wisdom maintained the same attitude toward Facebook and other companies. So much for conventional wisdom. Entrepreneurs have been ignoring it for years, and I'm sure they will continue to create and build enduring companies by doing so.

Twitter for Anytime

Several times in this book, I have mentioned how Twitter has been better for business in tough times than traditional marketing or support systems.

Twitter is actually great for business in better times as well. In case after case, I have tried to demonstrate how the platform allows all sorts of businesses to get closer to customers, and to do so with ease and at low cost.

I have also tried to make clear that whatever reason brings an enterprise to Twitter, that enterprise will find additional reasons to stay.

If you are already using Twitter, I hope I have given you some sense of new and better ways to use it. If you are not yet using Twitter, what are you waiting for?

Chances are that right now, there's a conversation going on in Twitterville that can impact what you do for a living.

And while you're at it, see if you can do something for world peace.

Afterword: Getting Started

If you have already spent some time on Twitter, then you should just skip this part. But if you have not been there and wish to join in or just watch what's happening, then the below pointers may be helpful.

(NOTE: You must join Twitter to see how it works. But if you do not like what you see after trying it for a while, you can just click on a box in Settings and close your account.)

1. Go to twitter.com. Click on the Get Started button. On your second screen, fill in the usual username and password information.
2. The third screen is where you will need to make some choices. Twitter asks you to see what friends you have at other Internet locations such as Gmail, Hotmail, AOL, Yahoo!, and MSN. The default is set to do this automatically. If you do not wish to do so, you must click to stop this from happening. If you allow it, then it may make getting started by talking to people you already know easier, so I recommend that you do this. It's your call.

3. On the next screen, Twitter randomly selects some of the most popular tweeters. Again, the default setting is set to do this for you. In that case you will be following accounts that are prominent, and you'll see what a lot of other people see. But you should think a bit about how relevant these tweeters are to you and your profession. If they are not, then you should click on the Skip this Step button at the beginning of this screen.

That's it, you are in Twitterville

The first time you arrive, Twitter has some good suggestions, but I would caution you against their third one of turning on your mobile phone. Twitter's mobile-phone application is not as good as some free or very inexpensive third-party applications (or "apps" for short). If you have a BlackBerry, I recommend you use TwitterBerry. If you have an iPhone, I recommend Tweetie, which cost 99 cents at the iPhone App Store.

Also, make sure you fill in some information about yourself in the Setting section at the top right-hand portion of your screen. I think it helps make connections best if you post a photo of yourself and let people know where you are located.

The remainder of Twitterville is filled with tips and advice on dealing with issues you may encounter after you get started.

> @jeffpulver: Social Media . . . just tastes good.

Twitter Terminology

Not only do people post in at least twenty languages, Twitter itself has its own terminology. The following are some of the most common terms you will see:

Avatar a photo or icon used as a visual ID. It appears on your home page and accompanies each of your tweets.

Block A check-box feature that allows you to stop a person from seeing your tweets. Unfortunately, if that person is persistent, then they can find you through Twitter Search.

Direct Message or DM When two tweeters follow each other, they can exchange private messages. Two methods are used: (1) Click on the Direct Message button on your home page or (2) type the letter d in front of a person's Twitter handle.

Follow a button under each person's home-page avatar. You click to see when that person posts a tweet.

Handle The unique name that identifies you in Twitterville.

Hashtag A short number of letters preceded by the "#" sign, such as #gaza, #TCOT, #SNCR. This allows people interested in an event or topic to use Twitter Search and easily find all tweets on the topic in a single stream.

Retweet The act of reposting someone else's post with attribution, usually as a form of recommendation. Increasingly used as a measure of Twitterville engagement.

Stream a common shortening of tweetstream.

Tweeple People who tweet.

Tweeps Twitter pals.

Tweet (n.) A Twitter post.

Tweet (v.) The act of posting on Twitter.

Tweeter One who tweets.

Tweetosphere (also Twittersphere) The entire Twitterville community.

Tweetstream Any series of Twitter posts. There's a public tweetstream that has a sampling of all Twitter posts, which usually moves too fast for people to watch comfortably for more than a minute. But each tweeter has her public and private personal tweetstreams, as well. Tweetstream also refers to an analogy of tweets that may have been aggregated on a topic.

Tweetup Face-to-face meetings by people who tweet. While it can
be just two people, there are informal gatherings of tweeters
happening all the time; these are also called Tweetups.

Twitterati 1. People passionate about Twitter. 2. Twitterville luminaries.

Unfollow When you start following a tweeter, this replaces the Follow button. Click on it if you ever wish to break off dialogue
with someone.

Acknowledgments

Paula Israel, my editor and inspiration
@adelemcalear Adele McAlear
@algonquincolleg Bob LeDrew
@alncl Alistair Smith
@AmyBlogTalk Amy Domestico
@anniemal Annie Heckenberger
@ariherzog Ari Herzog
@BenitoCastro Benito Castro
@bethharte Beth Harte
@BookofJames James Burgos
@BrianEngland Brian England
@BrianSolis Brian Solis
@Bronwen Bronwen Clune
@BryanPerson Bryan Person
@CathyWebSavvypr Cathy Larkin
@chronotope Aram Zucker-Scharff
@clutterdiet Lorie Marrero
@cmegroup Allan Schoenberg
@DalydeGagne Dayle de Gagne
@DanHowarth Dan Howarth
@DavidBoleyRN David Boley
@distanlo Jeff DiStanlo
@djwhelao David J. Whelan
@Ed Ed Shahzade
@Edw3rd Edward O'Meara
@EisoKant Eiso Kant
@EricaOgrady Erica O'Grady
@EricBeato Eric Beato

@ernieattorney Ernest Svenson
@flid2 Amir Lehrer
@Franswaa Frank Barry
@Geechee_Girl Leslie Poston
@GinaKay Gina Kay
@GobiernoUSA B. Leilani Martinez
@Hjortur Hjortur Smarason
@HRheingold Howard Rheingold
@HT Hodges Tom Hodges
@infoliberation Phillip Che Jacobson
@IowaDirtLawyer Pat Burk
@jacasman André Luiz
@jamunfer Juan Andres Muñoz
@JFortheMoney Jana Byington Smith
@JohnAByrne John A. Byrne
@johnburg John Burg
@JohnCass John Cass
@jojeda Julio Ojeda-Zapata
@kamichat Kami Huyse
@KevinOkeefe Kevin O'Keefe
@lebrun Marcel LeBrun
@LifeofJenn Jenn Castro
@LoVince Vincent Lo
@LParsons Luke Parsons
@LuisRull Luis Rull
@Marc_Meyer Marc Meyer
@marilink Marilín Gonzalo
@martinxo Martin Black

@mattblock Matthew Block
@MelWebster Mel Webster
@Merredith Merredith Brancscombe
@merubin Michael E Rubin
@mexiwi Arturo Pelayo
@Michael_hoffman Michael Hoffman
@michaeljbarber Michael J. Barber
@Mikescott8 Mike Scott
@missrogue Tara Hunt
@Natallini Natalie Koeplinger
@netzoo Andy Sternberg
@Nitchblog Andrew Lane
@pambaggett Pam Baggett
@Poneal Pam Oneal
@rahafharfoush Rahaf Harfoush
@roblagatta Rob la Gatta
@RoPrice Rowan Price
@Ruchitgarg Ruchit Garg
@ryankuder Ryan Kuder
@sconsult G. Saunders

@scottszur Scott Szur
@sdeclomesnil Sacha de Clomesnil
@SheilaS Sheila Scarborough
@shonali Shonali Burke
@Simon_Baptist Simon Baptist
@SoloPocono Elaine Gardner
@SteveAmes Steve Ames
@Tamera Tamera Kremer
@thornley Joseph Thornley
@TheKenYeung Ken Yeung
@Thorpus Justin Thorpe
@TimBursch Tim Bursch
@Tommaso Tommaso Sorchiotti
@tstitt Tom Stitt
@WallaceWilson Wallace Wilson
@WalterAkana Walter Akana
@WebConsigliere Joseph Zuccaro
@WhatsNext B. L. Ochman
@YarinHochman Yarin Hochman

Index